Books by Joseph E. Persico

THE IMPERIAL

ROCKEFELLER

*A Biography of
Nelson A. Rockefeller*

Joseph E. Persico

SIMON AND SCHUSTER

NEW YORK

Published by Simon and Schuster
A Division of Gulf & Western Corporation
Simon & Schuster Building
Rockefeller Center
1230 Avenue of the Americas
New York, New York 10020

SIMON AND SCHUSTER and colophon are trademarks of Simon & Schuster
Designed by Eve Kirch
Photo editor: Vincent Virga
Manufactured in the United States of America

1   3   5   7   9   10   8   6   4   2

Library of Congress Cataloging in Publication Data

Persico, Joseph E.
The imperial Rockefeller.

Includes index.
1. Rockefeller, Nelson A. (Nelson Aldrich), 1908–
1979.   2. United States—Politics and government—
1974–1977.   3. New York (State)—Politics and
government—1951–   .   4. Vice-Presidents—United
States—Biography.   5. New York (State)—Governors
—Biography. I. Title.
E748.R673P44   974.7'043'0924   [B]   81-16754
AACR2
ISBN 0-671-25418-9

ACKNOWLEDGMENTS

THOUGH THIS WORK is essentially a personal memoir, many people helped me bring it into being. Principal among these are my former colleagues on Nelson Rockefeller's staff, who were generous with their time and memories. At the Library of Congress, Margrit Krewson and David McGee were of inestimable value to my research, as was Mildred Ledden of the New York State Education Department Library. I particularly appreciate the assistance of George Humphreys, Secretary to the Minority Leader, New York State Assembly, and his aides. Charles Dumas, Director of Communications for the New York State Senate, and his staff were indispensably helpful, and State Senate officials Gerald McLaughlin and Richard Roth were unfailingly cooperative. Others to whom I am grateful are Herbert E. Alexander, University of Southern California; James Rentschler, National Security Council; Victor Glider, New York State Department of Environmental Conservation; and Walter Pforzheimer, CIA, retired. James Lehrer reviewed the manuscript, much to my profit. I am indebted to my editor, Michael Korda, for his perceptive and creative judgments throughout, and to my literary agent, Morton

ACKNOWLEDGMENTS

Janklow, for his support for the project from the outset. I benefited from the talents of Deborah McPherson, Jean B. Gentry, and my daughters, Vanya and Andrea, in the preparation of the manuscript. Finally, I thank my wife, Sylvia, for her unwavering commitment.

To a New York adventure

CONTENTS

CONTENTS

PREFACE

DURING THE CHRISTMAS HOLIDAY in 1969, back-to-back storms left upstate New York buried under four feet of snow. Roads were impassable, airports were closed, the State Thruway had shut down— and I was calling the State Police to get me to the railroad, the only remaining link between Albany and New York City. I left my wife, my mother and two small children snowbound in a house in the country, miles from Albany, with the family car long since vanished under soft white drifts, and was driven in a chain-equipped patrol car to the railroad station. There, by luck, a train, already six hours late, had just arrived from the west and was headed for New York City. In a refugee scene reminiscent of World War II, people pushed and shoved their way aboard coaches already jammed to overflowing, and harried conductors shouted that no one else could board. I pleaded with one of them, argued, finally slipped through the clot of riders jamming a stairwell when his back was turned. I stood between cars, shivering for five hours, until we arrived at Grand Central Station.

The object of this zeal was to get to the Governor's offices in New York City to work on speeches with Nelson Rockefeller. And I knew that whatever obstacles they may have encountered, the rest of the staff would be there too. For Nelson Rockefeller had a powerful hold over virtually everyone closely associated with him. To tie one's fate to the Rockefellers, particularly this Rockefeller, was to gain entry to a world of enlarged possibilities, the chance not only to realize one's potential but to lift that potential considerably by the booster rocket of the Rockefeller connection.

When Nelson died, somehow untimely even at age seventy, I remembered something that Richard Reeves, the political journalist, had written. After Nelson Rockefeller's nearly twenty years in politics, his associates had produced "no books, no memoirs, no nothing. Think about it," Reeves said. "It's unique." I do not know why other associates of Nelson, or of his brothers for that matter, have thus far chosen not to write of the experience. There were never any overt pressures not to do so, no stipulations of employment, no agreement to be signed pledging eternal silence. It may simply be that the advantages of continued good relations with so pervasively powerful a family have outweighed, among potential memoirists, the risks of possibly offending. I have chosen to record my experience precisely because it may help to fill a missing perspective. Tax laws being what they are today, it is doubtful that another family like the Rockefellers will emerge again in the United States. And Nelson was the dominant Rockefeller of his generation. Thus, my story may help readers to understand the premier American example of the intriguing phenomenon when great private wealth is wedded to great public ambitions.

This work is a personal memoir based largely on the eleven years from 1966 to 1977 during which I worked for Nelson Rockefeller as his principal speech writer. The period embraces his final two terms as governor of New York, his one serious hope for the Presidency in 1968, and his final frustration in the Vice-Presidency, that strange coda to a career aimed at the political pinnacle. During these years, I saw much of the man; others on the staff saw more, and others less. I recount essentially what I knew and was part of. I have refreshed my recollections with the help of colleagues who were closest to him and who have been most generous to me with their time, but this book remains entirely my responsibility.

Chapter I

AT COURT

THE BLADES WHIPPED THE SNOWFLAKES into fine, blinding swirls as the helicopter settled to earth. The pilot cut the engine, the rotor slowed and, as we stepped out, the air cleared, unveiling a setting of wintry enchantment. Faint rises in the snow suggested the outlines of a garden. All around us half-covered statues stood in white anonymity. Later I would discover what the snow concealed, Calders, Giacomettis, Noguchis, an Aphrodite once thought to be the work of Praxiteles.

We had landed alongside one of the formal gardens surrounding Nelson Rockefeller's home at Pocantico, the family estate, twenty-eight miles north of midtown Manhattan. Though I had by then been with him for three years, this was my first visit to the dynastic seat. It was a Saturday morning, and the Governor, minimizing the amount of time he had to spend in Albany, had chosen to work at home. Thus a half dozen of us from the staff had flown down from the state capital. We made our uncertain way up the icy stone stairway, trading the stilted repartee by which people try to put themselves at ease in the presence of extraordinary wealth.

Kykuit,* Nelson's house at Pocantico, struck me at first sight not as a home. There was a gray institutionality about the place, suggesting the official residence of a Middle European chief of state. As we stamped the snow from our feet, a black-suited servant opened the door and wordlessly motioned us in. Kykuit had the ambiance of a museum after hours. A bust of John D. Rockefeller, with lemon-puckered mien, watched as we passed through a sitting room. A primly benevolent portrait of his son, John D., Jr., dominated another room. The static formality was shattered by a plastic dinosaur in green and yellow snaking along a mantel from which emptied stockings hung. The richly carpeted floors were treacherous with abandoned toy trucks and windup gadgets. It was just after Christmas, and the place looked as though a suburban family had spent the holiday frolicking at an historic site.

That unmistakable honking voice suddenly greeted us from above. Nelson, wrapped in a robe, waved cheerily from the railing outside his bedroom. He told us to make ourselves at home in the main living room, to which the silent servant led us. The beauty of the room was almost too carefully, too painstakingly wrought in the choice and placement of every object of furniture and art, as though the shift of a chair would destroy the balance. The high ceiling was bordered in a deeply carved frieze and the mantelpiece was a gilded marble. George Washington gazed down from a Gilbert Stuart original, and in an arched window stood a full-sized male nude, the *Age of Bronze*, Rodin's first major work. One half expected to see red ropes across the chairs to ward off actual use. Only the flotsam of Christmas toys and decorations managed to break the stiff perfection.

Minutes later, Nelson strode in with the casual force that marked all his entrances. He exuded an exuberant self-assurance so unshakable that it must have been instilled from birth. Not a social arrogance, but rather an almost child-like openness which he assumed before anyone or anything. The servant took drink orders, Nelson addressing him in French, and we quickly settled into reviewing the latest draft of a budget message from the Governor to be delivered to the state legislature. T. Norman Hurd, then state budget director

*Kykuit is Dutch, meaning "lookout."

and a leading authority on public finance, was explaining a passage when a towheaded child bounded into the room. Dr. Hurd stopped as Nelson swept three-year-old Mark, his youngest son, onto his knee. As Dr. Hurd started to speak again, Mark began talking. Nelson stopped to listen, not to Dr. Hurd but to Mark. Hurd stopped too, with a frozen smile. Thus we plodded on, halting whenever Mark had something to say. "Yes, that's right, Marky. That's a two. And that number is a nine. See, we're on page twenty-nine," Nelson patiently instructed his son. Everyone grinned on cue.

I thought of how I was raising my own children. I did not like them to interrupt when I was talking to friends, and I did not enjoy having other people's howling Indians intrude on good conversation. But, little Mark went on happily having his say, while his father responded and we waited. Nelson Rockefeller was passing along an unspoken lesson absorbed from his own father—"These people work for us. Never mind their age, their position, they defer to you." Thus are young princes bred. I was doing it all wrong.

Nelson Rockefeller and Joseph Persico may as well have come from different planets. I was born into a working-class family in the upstate town of Gloversville, New York, just as the country slipped into the Depression. My parents, Blanche and Tom Persico, were the children of Italian immigrants, and both of them worked in the town's glove industry. They were ardent Roosevelt Democrats, understandably for working people of that time and place. Republicans were the people who owned and ran my hometown. The newspaper that I grew up on was the *Leader Republican*. My mother sewed gloves at home, and the pungent smell of leather and the hum of a Singer machine will always summon memories of my childhood. One day, while my father was out looking for work, an agent of the Niagara Mohawk Gas & Electric Company came to disconnect the power because the bill was unpaid. After he left, my mother fought back the tears and vowed that she would just have to work harder. She marched to the corner of the kitchen where the sewing machine stood and resolutely seated herself. Of course, the machine now could not run.

My mother was widowed in 1948 at age thirty-seven. I was then seventeen; my brother, Richard, was fourteen and my sister, Anna-belle, was twelve. After my father died, we received an insurance-policy payment of $900, our total capital. A few days later, the funeral director came to the house and took the check.

After my father died, I felt an instant maturation, even an odd pride that I was now the man of the house. I began to smoke and willingly tended the furnace, throwing in the coal and hauling out the ashes, chores that my father had gone through hell to get me to do just days before. I also mentally canceled my earlier intention to go to college.

Both of my parents had an obsession with education, hardly a universal passion among Italian-Americans of that era. Both had been forced to leave school early to go to work, a reverse that they believed had slammed the door of opportunity in their faces permanently. Their children were not to suffer this fate. When I told my mother that I was not going on to school, but staying home to help her, she punctured my proletarian romanticism with one swift jab. "Isn't it bad enough that I lost my husband? Do I have to lose all our hopes too?" Thereafter, I returned to my original objective. When I was in the ninth grade, I had won an essay contest and had determined to become a writer. Twenty years were to pass before I began to write seriously. In the meantime, I had gone to what was then the New York State College for Teachers and graduated with what turned out to be a felicitous twin major, political science and English. During summers and after class, I was building up those author credits so appropriate to book-jacket biographies, railroad track hand, radio an-nouncer, beer-truck driver.

When I first met Nelson Rockefeller in 1959, he had just been elected governor of New York and I was on the staff of the defeated and departing administration of Averell Harriman. I had become part of that one-term performance after applying for a Public Administra-tion Internship in state government. I had been interviewed and hired by a gangling fellow with a pasted forelock and the elegantly offhand manner that I associated with British intellectuals. Daniel Patrick Moynihan was then not long out of the London School of Economics and served as assistant secretary to Governor Harriman.

On New Year's Day 1959 I went to an inaugural reception for the incoming governor. Planted at the doorway of the Red Room of the State Capitol was a man who suggested a block of pure energy, square shoulders, square torso, a square, handsome head. Nelson Rockefeller thrust a strong, square hand into mine, fixed me with an only-you look and said in a voice that seemed to emanate entirely from his nose, "So nice to see you!" I thereafter went off to work in Latin America with the U.S. Information Agency and did not see him again for seven years. As someone who had by now been seasoned in politics, I resisted seduction by a single handshake. Still, throughout those years, Nelson Rockefeller persisted in my memory as an attractive compound of casualness and force. I was half right.

In 1964 I was back in New York State writing speeches for the state commissioner of health and growing restless at it. My boss, Dr. Hollis Ingraham, was a distinguished public-health administrator and a speech writer's dream. He had a magnificent presence and scant interest in rewriting what I submitted to him. Having studied elocution long ago at Harvard, he delivered the speeches with great flair. One day in 1965 I received a call from Hugh Morrow, who was then chief of what I assumed must be a stable of speech writers on Governor Rockefeller's staff. "The Governor's making a major speech on the environment next week," he told me. "Could you give us a hand? Some facts. Some language maybe."

Dr. Ingraham got short shrift as I worked almost nonstop for forty-eight hours, completed the draft, sent it to the Governor's office, and collapsed. The day the speech was to be delivered, Morrow called again and asked, "Who are you?" I recapped my background. "The Governor wants you to know that he loves the speech," Morrow said. "Sometime when you're free stop by the office." For the next eight months I was tapped by Rockefeller for his speeches on health issues. Then, in May 1966, Morrow called once more. It was time to staff the Governor's re-election campaign. Rockefeller had asked Morrow to recruit me as a speech writer.

My hiring was prototypical in one sense. It illustrated Nelson Rockefeller's complete indifference to the blood-loyalty view of politics. His disregard for patronage could make a Republican county chairman cry. No one asked me what party I belonged to. Had anybody done so, I would have said that my only previous enrollment had been as a Democrat while working for Governor Harriman. I had, in fact, served as executive secretary of the New York State Young Democrats during the campaign in which Rockefeller defeated Harriman.

Out of respect for my future employer's affiliation, I did some reading in the current literature of the Republican Party before reporting to the campaign staff. This was a brief task in the mid-sixties. One of the few books I came across by a Republican of any stature was *The Challenge of Change*, by Edward Brooke, elected Senator that year, a call for the party to champion civil rights and other social causes. Brooke was hardly representative of traditional Republicanism—but then neither was Nelson Rockefeller.

I had a mental image of what a Rockefeller's office must be. Yet I passed right by Nelson's New York City office the first time. "Twenty-two West Fifty-fifth Street," Hugh Morrow had directed me. I backed up and rechecked the numbers. Fifty-fifth Street between Fifth Avenue and the Avenue of the Americas is a quiet block with several fine restaurants and boutiques. No sign or plaque marked the Manhattan seat of state government. The blue-green front door bore only the brass numerals "22." I rang a buzzer and a red-veined face peered out. Security at the Governor's New York office consisted then of one paunchy ex-cop at a desk in a hallway.

I had arrived during the week of July Fourth while Nelson Rockefeller was vacationing in Europe and most of the staff were also away. Thus I had the opportunity to examine my new surroundings at leisure. I was astounded that so powerful a state as New York, governed by a Rockefeller, was run from this bureaucratic tenement. Twenty-two West 55th was actually two adjoining town houses at slightly different floor levels, so that in crossing from one side to the other one was forever dipping down one stairway and up another. While the building on the right was in slightly better condition, the overall impact of both town houses was unremitting seediness. Not shabby gentility, seediness. The floors were covered in indoor-outdoor carpeting that looked as though it had been picked up at a sale for slow-moving colors, in this case bile green. The walls appeared to be done in shades of gray. Once handsome moldings around windows, doorways and staircases had been painted and repainted. The places where the paint had chipped away revealed several incarnations of color and the original mahogany beneath.

Offices were wedged into and carved out of the original living quarters. Thus my office on the fifth floor had once been a bedroom and my secretary occupied an adjoining closet. The stenotypists who transcribed the Governor's speeches worked in an ex-bathroom. Removal of the commode had allowed room for a desk, and a plywood panel over the bathtub provided shelf space for piles of old speeches. The bathrooms still serving their original function had scarred and tarnished *fin-de-siècle* fixtures. The elevator in the newer building was postwar, but the one serving the older building, where Nelson Rockefeller's personal office was located, rose and descended with bitterly complaining clanks and whines.

The resolute drabness of 22 West 55th Street extended to the Governor's own quarters on the second floor. Little distinguished it from the others, although the rug in the office above his was of double thickness because footsteps overhead disturbed him. On the walls hung a proclamation presented to him by the New York City Uniformed Sanitationmen's Association, a hand-lettered scroll from the mayor of San Juan, Puerto Rico, and two undistinguished watercolors of eighteenth-century Rio de Janeiro. None of his great art.

He had only one family photograph in the office, a picture on his desk of his late son, Michael, lost in 1961 in the waters off New Guinea. From time to time, the desk also displayed painted rock paperweights and lumpy plaster casts of undefinable identity, the sort of objects familiar to every parent of school-age children.

The Governor's steady stream of callers had worn a hole through the rug next to the desk of Mrs. Whitman, his executive assistant. Having stumbled over the bald spot on a previous visit, A. Linwood Holton, then governor of Virginia, brought a handsome red rug as a present for her. As Nelson came out of his office, a smiling Holton held up the new rug. The smile was not returned, and the rug was never used. Nelson liked his office the way it was.

Twenty-two West 55th Street suggested a fly-by-night mail-order operation a step ahead of the postal-fraud unit. Why, with his resources, did Nelson Rockefeller choose such a place from which to govern New York State, for he spent most of his time here and as little as necessary at the state capital. Mrs. Whitman had asked him, but never got a satisfactory answer. There was one possible explanation. The building was connected back-to-back with another town house, which he also owned, facing on West 54th Street, thus affording Nelson the privacy so coveted by and rarely available to public men. It was in the connecting 54th Street town house that Nelson Rockefeller was to die in 1979.

Chapter II

⌘

THE EARLY YEARS

WHEN I WENT TO WORK for Nelson Rockefeller in 1966, he was fifty-eight years old. His arrival in the world, on July 8, 1908, had been reported on the front page of *The New York Times*. He was born on the birthday of then the richest man on earth, his grandfather, John D. Rockefeller. John D. was worth roughly $900 million, in an age when no one paid income taxes and when each dollar had the buying power of at least eight today. The latest Rockefeller was christened Nelson Aldrich, after his maternal grandfather, a Rhode Island farm boy who had risen to become the ironfisted ruler of the U.S. Senate and an unabashed champion of big business in government. At the time of Nelson's birth, the family had not yet undergone that metamorpho-sis-by-giving through which the Rockefeller name acquired its later philanthropic luster. That year John D.'s Standard Oil Company was mired in legal struggles as the government sought, with eventual success, to dismember his corporate octopus. "The greatest criminal of the age," Senator Robert La Follette called John D. "Malefactors of great wealth" was Theodore Roosevelt's verdict on the family.

Nelson was the third of the six children of Abby and John D. Rockefeller, Jr., the only son of the Standard Oil founder. The first child, Abby, was named for her mother, and was called Babs. In a family where males were regarded as heirs in a royal line, the eldest Rockefeller child soon virtually disappeared from public awareness. John D., III, born three years after her, was the first male, followed by Nelson, Laurance,* Winthrop and David.

The children grew up behind the formidable facades of several Rockefeller homes, the town house in New York City, the country estate at Pocantico Hills, the summer place in Maine.** Their home in town at 10 West 54th Street was magnificent enough, though, by the conspicuous consumption of that era, hardly overwhelming: nine stories embracing a private playground, squash court and family infirmary. Persian rugs in silver and gold thread, Gobelin tapestries and a treasure of art graced the rooms. Classic works, favored by John D., Jr., contrasted with abstract paintings, for Abby Rockefeller was an early exponent of modern art. Both parents were such avid collectors that only one recourse remained: buy the town house next door to accommodate the overflow.

The children's upbringing, unlike the hermetically sealed childhood of their father, combined common and uncommon touches. They played with other children in Central Park, just blocks from the town house. Yet governesses, always French, lurked at a discreet distance. They attended a school so far uptown that years later Nelson Rockefeller could tell black voters that he had gone to school in Harlem. The children walked or roller-skated to the Lincoln School, at 123rd Street and Amsterdam Avenue, until they became tired, when a family limousine, creeping alongside, picked them up to finish the journey. In the ultraprogressive milieu of Lincoln, they mixed with children of every class and race, but with a notable distinction. Their family's money had built the school. Lincoln was the product of Abraham Flexner's unorthodox education theories, implemented by Columbia University Teachers College and financed with $3 million from the Rockefellers.

Nelson often disappeared from the line of march en route to

*The odd spelling is a result of the family's intention to name the next child Laura, if a girl, after John D., Jr.'s, mother, Laura Spelman Rockefeller.

**Nelson was born in Bar Harbor, Maine, while the family was vacationing there. Shortly thereafter, his father, John D. Rockefeller, Jr., moved his growing family from 13 West 54th Street to number 10. Grandfather lived at 4 West 54th Street.

school, unnerving the family bodyguards. One morning they found him in a sewer. He had crawled through an open manhole "to find out what goes on down there." Nelson, while neither the oldest nor biggest of the brothers, became the indisputable leader. John III, the eldest, born encased in an impenetrable shyness, withered before the force of Nelson's personality. Laurance, who followed Nelson, grew up in affectionate admiration of his older brother, a feeling that Nelson reciprocated. They became inseparable, which left the next in line, the outsized and awkward Winthrop, isolated, while David enjoyed the perquisites of the baby of the family.

Nelson was of the all-boy genus that alternately has parents beaming or at wits' end. He was engaging, outgoing and undisciplined, dominating more than domineering. He was forever clasping people, squeezing, clapping them on the back, a tactile form of communication lightly employed by most Rockefellers, but highly useful where he was headed. John D., Jr., sensed in his thirdborn the qualities of energy and character that augured success in life. Yet, puzzlingly, Nelson was a dismal student. He had great difficulty reading; he confused words and transposed numbers, particularly disastrous in mathematics. Unknown to his parents, or teachers, the student was afflicted with dyslexia, a condition that would not be diagnosed yet for another generation. He nearly failed the ninth grade and was mired in the bottom third of his high-school class. He could not meet the requirements of Princeton University, where he had been expected to follow his brother John. But his scholarly deficiency did not daunt him. Nelson remained forever ebullient and confident to a point that skirted cockiness. Finally awakened to the likelihood that he might not be accepted by a good college, he demonstrated a discipline that throughout life would serve him in lieu of brilliance. He uncomplainingly did remedial work with tutors, broke off with a girl friend who distracted him from his studies, and was accepted at Dartmouth.

Whatever inadequacies he may have exhibited in French or math, Nelson Rockefeller absorbed early a sense of station. Before leaving for Dartmouth, he asked his father, "Do you think it would be all right if I call on Dr. Hopkins when I get to Hanover?" Thus virtually the first person Nelson went to see on campus was the college president. Rockefellers like to deal with the head man.

By the time he left home, young Nelson's relations with his parents were fixed and his place at the forefront of the brothers was established. The parents had contributed vastly different influences in shaping their offspring. Abby poured in wine and John D., Jr., provided mineral water. The father, known throughout the Rockefeller family offices as Junior, though not to his face, was an austere figure who viewed his children as students in a classroom, to be inculcated with the family ethic. The young Rockefellers saw Junior most often at breakfast, where he led them in prayer and delivered short homilies. His constant refrain was duty, responsibility, the purposeful existence. Nelson, though the most self-willed, went through much of his life as his brothers did—ever seeking the approval of this remote arbiter of worth.

Abby was a healthy counterforce to the Olympian rectitude of her husband. Where Junior was priggish, she was vivacious. Where the father preached sobriety and purpose, the mother talked of music and art. Junior was measured and cautious; Abby, warm and spontaneous. The father sermonized. The mother conversed, joked and gossiped with her children. It was Junior who offered to pay each of his offspring $2,500 if they reached twenty-one without smoking. It was Abby who rescinded his Baptist ban on Sunday dancing and games.

Toward his mother, Nelson displayed unabashed adoration. At the age of twenty, he wrote to her from Dartmouth of his fear that he would never find a girl to love. "Mum, if only you were a girl, that would solve the problem. But then, of course, I'd be without the best mother in the world." Much later, Nelson observed, "My father's life was guided by a great sense of ethics, purpose, responsibility. My mother was much more cosmopolitan. She gave us a love of art and beauty. We benefited from the crosscurrents of both." Indeed, both forces were evident in the mature Nelson. The outer man reflected the effusive humanity of the mother, the inner man forever retained the measured detachment of John D. Rockefeller, Jr. In an early letter from Dartmouth he wrote: "I met some awfully nice fellows already. But I'm sort of going slowly so as not to make any mistakes." Junior no doubt approved.

Nelson lived his Dartmouth years with characteristic exuberance.

He delighted most of his fellow students with an unaffected extroversion and put the more skeptical on guard by his too easy familiarity. John D., Jr., gave him $1,500 a year, out of which he had to pay his own tuition and board. Hardly a princely stipend, but certainly adequate considering that most American families at the time lived on incomes under $2,000. Still, he occasionally had to borrow from the other boys, transactions certain to flatter less affluent creditors.

The college years were characterized by a copybook wholesomeness. Nelson pleased his father by teaching a Sunday-school class for grade-school girls at the White Church in Hanover. Before graduation he wrote home, "I shall miss my little girls very much." He signed the letter, as he always did, "Nell." At Dartmouth, he neither drank nor smoked.

Only rarely did the fact of his family's celebrity intrude on a normal student's life. When Nelson ducked out of a group photograph of the Dartmouth soccer team, he explained to a friend, "If we get our picture in the paper, Father cuts our allowance." His performance on the team typified his lifelong experience in sports. Though rugged and certainly looking the part, Nelson Rockefeller was no athlete. He once confided to a political crony that he had scored one goal at Dartmouth, and that for the other side. His modest prowess may have been the fault of his father. Nelson was born left-handed at a time when this condition was viewed as a correctable misfortune. Whenever the boy reached for his fork with his left hand, his father yanked on a string attached to a rubber band around Nelson's wrist. Thus was Nelson conditioned to eat, write and play sports with other than his natural handedness. By the time Winthrop and David came along, Junior had evidently absorbed a more modern psychology and let the two younger boys favor their left hands.

Curiously, neither Nelson nor any of the other Rockefeller boys played baseball, which may reflect the semi-insulation in which they were raised. Sandlot baseball is a game of the streets, of kids coming together spontaneously to choose up sides, hardly the childhood environment of the Rockefellers.

If Junior was a cool and not entirely approachable parent to his children, their grandfather, John D. Rockefeller, was a distant star.

When in their company he would regale the children with funny but endlessly repeated stories enlivened by a gift for mimicry. But John D. was a rare visitor, remote from them in both distance and years. Indeed, when Nelson started college, his grandfather was eighty-seven years old. Thus Nelson was introduced to the public view of John D. Rockefeller by his history and economics professors. This combative youth rebelled at their description of his grandfather as a malefactor and robber baron. He confessed his outrage to his father and delighted Junior with his decision to write the true story of the origins of Grandfather's Standard Oil as his thesis in Economics II.

Nelson asked Junior if he might sit down with his grandfather to get a horse's mouth history of the company, but old John D. declined. Instead, Junior sent his son material on Standard Oil prepared by company employees. One in-house history enraptured Nelson. He wrote his father, "It was thrilling! For the first time I felt that I really knew grandfather a little—got a glimpse into the power and grandeur of his life . . . I wanted to write Grandfather and tell him what I had never realized before. But after several weak attempts at expressing my feelings, I gave it up. For the first time, I realized the significance of his life and its influence for good on this earth, and I was speechless."

Thus inspired, he wrote a forty-five-page paper on Standard Oil and the methods that had nurtured the colossus. Rejected outright were the muckraker contentions that the company had crushed its rivals by unscrupulous competition. Young Nelson's Standard Oil emerged as a benign and simply more efficient monopoly. His defense of the company's vast profits had a novel ring—"If things had developed without the Standard monopoly, prices would probably have been somewhat lower, but the profits would have been proportionately much lower and the industry most likely would not have developed nearly as fast. The Standard took in profits that would have otherwise gone to waste . . ." He received an A on his thesis, and in the course of writing it, conducted his own rite of initiation into the family ethos.

Nelson acquitted himself creditably at Dartmouth, disciplining a solid, if unspectacular, intelligence into membership in Phi Beta Kappa and graduating *cum laude* in 1930. Also, before college was over, he had fallen in love. It was family custom to summer at Seal Harbor, Maine, where young Rockefellers consorted with the heirs of the Fords, of Charles W. Eliot, Harvard's president, and other American *prominenti*. For years, Nelson had been driving his gadget-decked Ford touring car over to Northeast Harbor to visit the six Clark brothers. The Clark estate in Philadelphia had been granted to their ancestors by George III, and their maternal grandfather, George B. Roberts, had been president of the Pennsylvania Railroad. Thus the Clarks, by that purifying process through which money, like wine, improves with age, enjoyed a higher social standing than the Rockefellers.

There was also a Clark sister, Mary Todhunter Clark, known as Tod, and it was to her that Nelson found himself drawn. To describe her background is to trace an American prototype of a time and place: born into the Philadelphia Main Line; skilled in the respectable exertions, riding, tennis, and golf; educated at the Foxcroft School in Virginia; and finished with a year in Paris. Tod was lanky, no great beauty, and a year older than Nelson, but she had a quality that would appeal to Nelson Rockefeller all his life, whether in a man or a woman, bedrock self-possession. In Tod's case, this inner certitude was enlivened by intelligence and wit. She had a gift for incisive observation, amusingly expressed without diminishing a dignity that clung to her like an expensive fabric. She provided, at first, the perfect counterweight to Nelson's indiscriminate enthusiasm.

The choice pleased Nelson's parents. John D. Rockefeller, Jr., understood, accepted, and played the game of good connections, although high society per se did not interest him. He was fathering a dynasty committed to elevated purpose and good works, a dynasty that was to extend his own life's objective, the apotheosis of his father's ruthlessly won fortune into an honorable force for the betterment of mankind. Suitable heirs for advancing that goal would not likely result from his sons' association with the idle rich. The Philadelphia Clarks, fortunately, were not of the sybarite class.

Yet so strong is the idea of class embedded that even a young Nelson Rockefeller, who could have bought and sold any companion, once confessed: "The only time I ever felt shy or uncomfortable was at certain society affairs when I didn't know the boys who were from the better prep schools. I didn't fit into their group." Still, he was never much for flaunting pedigree, though when the occasion suited, he would cite his descent, on his mother's side, from Elder William Brewster, who came over on the *Mayflower*. But his assertion that his father's people were French Huguenots, driven from France to Germany, where they changed their name from Roquefeuille to Rockefeller, was disputed by genealogists who traced that side of the family to German peasantry.

In 1930 Nelson and Tod were married in the fashionable Philadelphia suburb of Bala-Cynwyd, immediately after his graduation. Nelson made what was to become his patented entrance: arriving at the last minute, bounding from an automobile and on up the church steps, tossing his top hat into the hands of the startled sexton and clapping the man on the shoulders. The bride's lean, patrician face had a radiance approaching beauty on her wedding day. Beneath her gown she wore flat slippers out of consideration for her shorter husband. After the reception, they boarded a ship for an around-the-world honeymoon that lasted nine months.

Grandfather Rockefeller had consulted with Junior about an appropriate present for the newlyweds, and they had decided on something with which the Rockefellers were comfortable, money, in this instance $20,000, which was rather like a baker giving his children pastries as a gift. Junior's present to the newlyweds was the global trip. While certainly a comfortable heir at this point, Nelson was yet to come into a great personal fortune. The first installment, however, arrived in 1934 when John D., Jr., created trust funds for Nelson and his other children estimated at $40 million each.

The honeymoon took on a character that would later become familiar to Nelson's aides. The family office set up a crowded schedule of appointments with overseas representatives of the Chase Bank, Standard Oil, the Rockefeller Foundation and foreign government leaders at every port of call. The newlyweds boned up on such unlikely honeymoon manuals as the *Growth and Development of China*. In Honolulu they balanced attendance at a command performance of hula dancers with a tour of a leper colony. In Japan they talked to university professors and geishas.

The most incongruous pairing occurred in India where Nelson

Rockefeller squatted beside Mahatma Gandhi, then briefly out of jail in the course of his struggle for India's independence. The man's nut-brown bald head, shriveled legs and white dhoti gave him the aspect of a starving child as he sipped from a bottle of milk. But not a word was exchanged. After looking at each other across a thousand un-shared values, Gandhi passed Nelson a note: "Come back tomorrow. I'll talk to you." As Nelson gamely explained later, "Mr. Gandhi was having his day of silence. But he doesn't mind seeing people." The next day, Rockefeller and Gandhi did have a fifteen-minute conver-sation, and Nelson came away impressed. "He's a remarkable man," he wrote, "and terribly nice, too."

In April 1931, the young Rockefellers were back in New York City, and the time had come for Nelson to decide what he wanted to do with his life. In his senior year at college he had fired a warning shot across the bow of his father's expectations. He had written home, "Just to work my way up in a business that another man has built, stepping into the shoes of another, making a few minor changes here and there and then finally, perhaps at the age of sixty, getting to the top where I would have real control for a few years. No, that isn't my idea of living a real life."

But that is precisely what he did. He went to work in the family office, then located at 26 Broadway, where he was as bored and hamstrung by entrenched family retainers as he had feared. After executing a few high-grade errands for his father, Nelson began root-ing about, still under the Rockefeller tent, for space of his own. He applied for a real-estate broker's license and in 1933 plunged into finding tenants for the newly rising Rockefeller Center, then the world's largest office complex. Renting office space during the depths of the Depression was a hotly competitive affair, and Nelson went at it with the zeal of a hot-shot sales trainee. He raided other office buildings by offering to take over unexpired leases if tenants would move into Rockefeller Center. He lured prospective clients with tempting introductory offers at below-market rents. Some found his methods too clever by half. He was sued for $10 million by outraged competitors, but the suit was later dropped before coming to trial. His aggressive ingenuity suggested that the methods which had built Standard Oil may have been genetic in origin. His father was sufficiently pleased with his performance that he conferred *de facto* supremacy upon Nelson among the five brothers by naming him, in 1938, president of Rockefeller Center.

But it was an investment Lilliputian in size alongside Rockefeller Center that changed his life. Standard Oil of New Jersey had a Venezuelan subsidiary, the Creole Petroleum Company. In 1935, Nelson made an investment in Creole and became a member of the board of directors. In the budding Nelsonian style, he immediately gathered about him a coterie of oil and other experts for a firsthand look at his new holding. He conducted his own fact-finding mission to Latin America, and he fell in love with a continent.

In July 1940, two Hudson River gentlemen, separated by a generation and differing political loyalties, faced each other across the President's desk in the White House. Nelson Rockefeller, then thirty-two, had come to give President Franklin Roosevelt an answer. Several months before, Nelson had returned from a second journey through Latin America much disturbed by what he had witnessed. Upon his return, he had persuaded Roosevelt that the fall of Western Europe to the Nazis that summer was having a devastating effect on the economies of Latin America. The Western Hemisphere had become fair game for Axis propaganda, even military penetration, which would ultimately threaten the United States unless we helped to buoy these nations economically and win their allegiance. After considering Nelson's report, Roosevelt had offered Nelson his first job outside the orbit of the Rockefeller universe. The President wanted him to form a wholly new organization defined with typical Rooseveltian vagueness, but with a clear purpose: to prevent what Nelson feared was happening in Latin America.

Washington was then a magnet to young men of ambition and idealism like Nelson. Still, he played it safe. After hearing FDR's offer, he had made a reservation under the name "Mr. Franklin" and flew to Salt Lake City for a confidential meeting with Wendell Willkie, the Republican nominee for President that year. As Nelson described the dilemma of a Rockefeller Republican being enticed into the Roosevelt Administration, Willkie cut him off. "If I were President in a time of international crisis, and if I asked someone to come to Washington to help me in foreign affairs, and if that man turned me down—well, I don't need to tell you what I would think of him."

Nelson had now returned to the Oval Office to give the President his answer. There, facing the seductive aura of FDR, he registered his reservations lamely. "Are you sure you want me for this job? There's my family's connection with oil companies in Latin America. And I'm a Republican." Roosevelt dismissed the objections with a wave of his cigarette holder. "I'm not worried." Nor was he dismayed at the prospect of bagging an ultra-Establishment Republican for the Roosevelt Administration in an election year. Further, like him, this young Rockefeller was a princely paradox—the highborn manner wedded to a genuine social conscience. Nelson Rockefeller went to work for the U.S. government at a salary of one dollar a year and brought his growing family to a twenty-six-acre estate in the fashionable Foxhall Road area of Washington. He became, in one observer's view, "the eager beaver to end all eager beavers." He feuded with old bureaucracies, like the State Department, and new rivals, like the Office of Strategic Services, the fledgling American intelligence service under General William "Wild Bill" Donovan. He stumbled and blundered, but righted himself. Within little more than a year, his Office of the Coordinator of Inter-American Affairs became one of the glamour agencies to work for in wartime Washington. He made the cover of *Life* and achieved a celebrity that even Rockefeller money alone could not buy.

Still his status made him vaguely uncomfortable. He was a healthy young man. All his brothers were in uniform, Laurance and John in the Navy, Winthrop and David in the Army. All were commissioned except the maverick Win, who had enlisted as an infantry private a year before the war began. What about Nelson? He never doubted the value of his contribution to the war effort, but there were appearances to consider, his and the Administration's. In August 1942, in his second year as Coordinator of Inter-American Affairs, he told Roosevelt, "You're my Commander in Chief. Any time you want me in the Army, I'm ready to go." Again Roosevelt must have been reminded of his younger self. When America entered World War I, he had been thirty-five, a tall, dashing figure of extraordinary vigor who was serving as a civilian assistant secretary of the Navy. Roosevelt had gone to President Wilson in precisely the same quandary, and he now gave Nelson the answer he had received twenty-five years before. "I'll let you know when I want you in the military and that would be only if there were some special job for which you're especially qualified."

By the fall of 1944, Nelson had outgrown the agency of his own creation and Roosevelt named him assistant secretary of state for Latin America. He played a shrewd power game to have Argentina, under the fascist Juan Perón, admitted to the new United Nations. He maneuvered to have the U.N. Charter drafted to recognize regional spheres of influence, to preserve America's Monroe Doctrine. He won battles but lost his career. His protector, President Roosevelt, died in April 1945, and under pressure from the liberal foreign-policy community, President Harry Truman gave Nelson Rockefeller the sack in August 1945. Thus, at age thirty-seven, Nelson Rockefeller, for the first time in his life, tasted defeat.

The marriage of Nelson and Tod underwent a deep if common enough metamorphosis during the war. Nelson had gone from college boy to husband to father of five by age twenty-nine. Thus he had largely bypassed that period when a man knows both maturity and personal freedom. By the time the couple moved to Washington, Tod's role, as the mother of a large young family, was established. Nelson, conversely, as he gave more time to his work, had less time for the family. He plunged deeply into the heady currents of wartime Washington. Rugged good looks and wealth were now joined to power and ambition. He was and remained throughout life a vigorous and virile man. In his later years, he enjoyed pointing out that he was the first and also the last of his Dartmouth class to become a father. He was attractive to and attracted by women. He began to display that paradox of a certain breed of man, a fanatical obsession with work that seemed only to generate excess energy to be exhausted elsewhere. Few of his women companions were idle socialites; most, like himself, had been drawn to Washington to work in the war effort. When a relationship cooled, Nelson evidently set down his female friends gently and with lingering mutual respect and affection. Those

34

of us who worked for him later found the various Rockefeller enterprises dotted with women from his past, most of them impressively capable people. The effect of his private behavior on his relationship with Tod was not immediately fatal, but it marked the beginning of a protracted death of the marriage.

Back in New York, Nelson resumed old responsibilities in the family's enterprises. He took over Rockefeller Center again and led his brothers in a civilized revolt. Three fortresses still remained under Junior's control—the family's professional staff, the Rockefeller Center complex, and the Pocantico estate. Nelson led the new centurions home from the war in a genteel power struggle with Junior's palace guards. When he had finished, the next generation controlled all three enclaves, and Nelson ruled as the undisputed prince regent. The old man's reaction was a confusion of pride at having reared sons capable of supplanting him and a muted sadness that power had at last slipped from his hands.

Still, those enterprises that "another man had built" could not satisfy Nelson. He yearned to experience again the global role of his Washington years. And so, he launched a Marshall Plan of his own design for Latin America, the American International Association. AIA was to help modernize the region's educational, health, and agricultural infrastructure. AIA was nonprofit and philanthropic. Its commercial counterpoise was IBEC, the International Basic Economy Corporation, Nelson's chosen instrument to deliver to Latin America the blessings of Yankee enterprise, the supermarket, mass distribution and low retail prices, all at a fair profit.

He launched IBEC on a typically Nelsonian scale and, initially, failed grandly. The firm financed a modernized tuna fleet, which the fishermen then diverted to more profitable smuggling operations. Huge, heavy pieces of American-made farm equipment sank in Latin marshlands. Small retailers fought his plan of lower prices because they feared lower profits. In IBEC's first decade, Nelson Rockefeller absorbed losses that would have sunk a lesser vessel, $7 million of his personal fortune. He retreated, consolidated, lowered his sights, and kept the operation afloat. The failures were not necessarily those of an entrepreneur with more money than brains. He was trying to go beyond the bottom line and to wed the profit motive to social change in foreign and often resistant cultures.

In 1949, four years back in private life, he sensed an opportunity to return to the international arena. President Truman had announced his Point Four program to bring technology to underdeveloped countries. Nelson wrote Truman flattering letters praising Point Four, which indeed had been patterned after his own AIA, elevated to worldwide scale. Nelson's lobbying produced no more than the chairmanship of a committee that Truman created to advise on the implementation of Point Four. Nelson did not get the big job that this committee conveniently recommended, a U.S. development czar for the world. Such authority hewed too closely to the turf that Averell Harriman, then heading the Marshall Plan, had staked out for himself.

When his own party recaptured the White House in 1952, after twenty years in the wilderness, Nelson again tried his favorite approach. He wrote to President-elect Eisenhower suggesting it was high time for the federal government to reorganize. He offered the names of three people capable of doing the job, tactfully omitting his own. Eisenhower got the point and named Nelson, along with Arthur Flemming, an administrative expert, and the President's brother Milton, to study an overhaul of the bureaucracy.

Out of this effort, the Department of Health, Education and Welfare was born, and in June 1953 Nelson became the agency's first under secretary. But he soon found something more to his taste. In 1954, he persuaded Eisenhower to name him special assistant to the President for foreign affairs. Through the prism of latter-day experience, the title suggests a powerful post, like that held by Henry Kissinger or Zbigniew Brzezinski. It was not. Nelson became essentially a player in the psychological games of the Cold War. His most conspicuous success was to persuade Eisenhower to deliver a speech at the 1955 Geneva Summit Conference proposing that the United States and the Soviet Union open their territories to aerial inspection to reduce the risk of surprise attack. This plan was called "Open Skies" and had been proposed to Nelson by a young Harvard professor of government, Henry Kissinger, whom he had recruited as a consultant.

Just before he moved to the White House, Nelson suffered a small but instructive defeat. While still at HEW, he proposed that the United States recognize the eightieth birthday of Winston Churchill by striking a medal in honor of the British lion. Eisenhower approved. Indeed, the President made available a portrait he had painted of Churchill as the model for the medal. After protracted bureaucratic buck-passing by the U.S. Mint, the Treasury and Justice departments, a medal was at last struck and presented to Churchill with suitable pomp.

The question then arose as to who was to pay for this noble gesture. The White House ducked the bill. Treasury Secretary George Humphrey, who had never thought much of Rockefeller and his schemes that had to be underwritten by taxpayers, disclaimed all responsibility. A frustrated Nelson paid the $2,000 cost out of his own pocket. The matter was trivial, but symptomatic of what lay ahead as he joined the White House staff.

The secretary of state, John Foster Dulles, did not like Nelson or the place he had carved for himself in the White House. Dulles resented any threat to his virtual sole ownership of Eisenhower foreign policy. As Nelson described it, as soon as Eisenhower picked up the phone and said, "Foster, I've got Nelson here and he's suggested . . . ," he knew that his proposal was dead.

Nelson, however, did win one admirer. In the course of reorganizing the Department of Defense, he found a patron in Secretary Charles Wilson. Later, as Wilson prepared to resign, he wanted to install Nelson as his deputy secretary and heir apparent at Defense. Nelson hungered for the job, but Humphrey, a fiscal watchdog who lived in fear of "hair curling" recessions, reached the President first. The last thing the Administration needed, he persuaded Eisenhower, was a "spender" at Defense.

In December 1955, a frustrated Nelson Rockefeller told Eisenhower that family enterprises demanded his presence back in New York. He resigned and left Washington for the second time. The death of a thousand cuts in the capital had made one fact inescapable: appointive office, however elevated, was the proxy of someone else's power. He told a colleague, "You can't have a real voice in your party until you've proved you know how to get the votes." He savored a phrase that he had picked up in Latin America which described the route to real power. He had to become *"un auténtico representante del pueblo,"* an authentic representative of the people.

Letting this idea ferment, Nelson meanwhile resumed his family business affairs. Then he began to act on his ambition. He invited Thomas E. Dewey, the former three-time governor of New York, to lunch with him in the executive dining room at Radio City Music Hall. Nelson explained that he wanted to run for governor. Dewey was blunt: "I think that's a poor idea, Nelson. You're not well known enough." Then, after a frowning pause, Dewey's eyes brightened. "You know, I think I could arrange to have you appointed postmaster of New York City!" Nelson politely declined, and said, "I think I'll try for Albany anyway."

Less than two years later, he stood with his hand on his great-grandmother's Bible to be sworn in as New York's governor. The inaugural guests included a sweetly aging little man in stiff white collar and high-button shoes buffed to a high gloss. The presence of John D., Jr., that day spoke more than a shelf of historic monographs. He and his son symbolized the completed rehabilitation of the Rockefeller name in America in the half century since Nelson's birth. From malefactors to benefactors. From accumulators of wealth to sharers of it. From a grandfather called "the greatest criminal of the age" to a grandson now addressed as "Governor." From intensely private princes to an authentic representative of the people.

When Nelson was elected governor in 1958, he became the brightest new star in the GOP firmament. In that year of recession, Republicans all over the country had suffered defeat. Yet Nelson Rockefeller had unhorsed the workmanlike Administration of Averell Harriman to be elected governor of the country's then most populous and powerful state. Rockefeller saddled Harriman with blame for the weak economy, ran a brilliantly researched, well-financed race, campaigned as though he actually enjoyed it and flattened Harriman by more than half a million votes.

New Yorkers had just finished with one rich governor, but no accounts of Harriman extravagance had ever titillated the plainer citizens. Virtually the only suggestion during those four years that a man of substance occupied the state house was an exit on the New York State Thruway marked "Harriman." The road passed near the baronial estate that had been built by the Governor's father, E. H. Harriman, a railroad tycoon of consequence, but hardly in John D. Rockefeller's league. New Yorkers soon knew that they had elected a multimillionaire of a different stripe. For his inaugural celebration, Nelson imported the New York City Ballet to Albany to perform at the inaugural ball in a state armory. As he prepared to journey to the capital to assume his prize, he bought a sleek Lincoln limousine. He ordered the license plate number 1 installed on it. His chauffeur returned from the State Department of Motor Vehicles, the crestfallen bearer of bad tidings. "Governor, Motor Vehicles says no privately owned car can have number 1." Nelson saw no problem. He donated the Lincoln to the state, the bureaucrats promptly placed plate number 1 on it and assigned the car to the Governor.

He was governor of New York for barely six months when he began to run for the Presidency. It was no modest toe-dipping, but an effort of typical Nelsonian style and scale. Seventy people went to work researching issues and testing his chances of winning the 1960 Republican nomination. Their answer stunned him—he had not a prayer of overcoming Richard Nixon's lead. In December 1959, he publicly withdrew from the competition.

His surprise at his poor prospects is explained by a truth about American politics that Nelson Rockefeller could not or would not accept until it was too late. The route to the Presidency runs on two tracks, the Popular Track and the Party Track. The Popular Track is visible, dramatic, intellectually stimulating, fun to follow. Issues and personalities dominate here, and indeed, much of the theater of the Popular Track concerns who stands where on what. Operating most visibly on this track are the news media that determine candidate coverage and, by so doing, become arbiters, indeed creators, of the significant. They are our guides along the Popular Track, educating us politically in seven-hundred-word columns and sixty-second takes. The Popular Track is reported speeches, major bills passed or defeated in Congress. The Popular Track is syndicated opinion polls telling us whom we like, whom we trust, whom we cannot remember. It is the dimension of political life that the public sees, hears and talks about. But, the Popular Track delivers no convention delegates.

The Party Track, on the other hand, is a low-profile road traveled by a breed who love a game called politics. These are the congenital joiners, team-minded sorts with an us-against-them, game-oriented outlook on life which they apply to politics. What happens on the Party Track is either not visible to the public or too dull to hold its attention. Those of an intellectual bent often find the mechanics of the Party Track a grubby bore.

The political professionals and regulars on the Party Track are astonishingly similar in their approach to the game, whatever their party allegiance. The differences in them are often superficial, little more than sartorial. Republican gatherings resemble a country-club dance attended by local lawyers, the fuel dealer, insurance broker and funeral director. Do not look for writers, artists or professors. The homogeneity, from Seattle to Miami, is astonishing. Only the accents change. People at Democratic Party functions lack such outward cohesion. But the professionals, Democratic and Republican, all savor the game and its unwritten rules. They live by loyalty, regularity, favors done and repaid, disloyalty remembered and punished. They relish struggles for power, where factions rally around a figure for the joy of winning rather than around issues for the purpose of changing the world. Issues are often more important as weapons chosen to club the opposition in the public arena. Party Track followers hope to back the right horse and hitch a ride to glory. They are a loyal brotherhood of precinct captains, county chairmen, state committeemen. In their temperament and their pleasures, the professional players of the game, whether Republican or Democrat, are virtually interchangeable.

The fact that thirty-eight states now hold presidential primaries has only partly reduced the influence of the Party Track. The significant difference between it and the Popular Track, however, remains: the Party Track delivers presidential delegates.

In 1960, an unseasoned and unbloodied Nelson Rockefeller found it hard to accept that a presidential candidate to lead the Western World would be chosen on the strength of who had attended the most

Lincoln Day dinners, who had been most solicitous about the Yates County chairman's hernia operation, or whose agents had captured control of an obscure town committee. How could this minutiae matter when measured against a grand new vision and fresh answers to the nation's problems? How could a bright new political star fail to triumph over party wheelhorses? The answer was simple. Those who cannot understand how a major party could nominate so narrow a man as Barry Goldwater in 1964, resurrect a seeming political corpse like Richard Nixon in 1968, and nominate an initially unlikely Ronald Reagan in 1980 see only the Popular Track and do not understand what goes on along the Party Track of American politics. Nelson Rockefeller was long numbered among them, as his behavior in 1960 proved.

After ostensibly taking himself out of the race, Nelson later issued a nine-point program for saving America, which came out looking like a stinging indictment of his own party's national Administration. "We cannot, as a nation or a party," his manifesto proclaimed, "proceed to march to meet the future with a banner aloft whose only emblem is a question mark." This colorfully out-of-character prose had been written for Nelson by Emmet Hughes, a former journalist and onetime Eisenhower speech writer who had later outraged Eisenhower by writing a book on his White House experiences. Nelson had taken on Hughes as his chief ideologue. The tenor and substance of the statement deeply offended Eisenhower. Thus Nelson had turned a popular and beloved leader into a tacit but unforgiving opponent of his own presidential ambitions.

Rockefeller next appeared to humble Richard Nixon publicly by what came to be called the Compact of Fifth Avenue. Nixon went to Rockefeller's apartment and swallowed the price of Nelson's support: agreement to what had now grown to fourteen points to be included in the Republican Party platform. While this meeting seemed to demean Nixon, it actually revealed his adroit timing in shifting from the Party Track to the Popular Track, and Nelson's obliviousness to both. By dogged cultivation of delegates, Nixon had tied up the nomination. His "compact" with Nelson bought off the remaining liberal Republican opposition. Now, he was only too willing to run for President on Nelson Rockefeller's lofty planks.

In 1962, Nelson ran for re-election as governor against Robert Morgenthau, an opponent whose political personality made the good, gray Averell Harriman look iridescent. Rockefeller beat Morgenthau by a comfortable half a million votes. Thus, by 1964, Nelson was again ready to run for the Presidency, but in the years since the 1960 national campaign, death and love had altered his life.

Until 1961, Nelson Rockefeller had played by the rules of social convention. He had remained faithful to the forms of marriage if not the oaths. He and Tod lived a conjugal truce, a common enough condition among Americans of their age and class. But, even before running for governor in 1958, Nelson was living a secret life. He had fallen deeply in love with a woman eighteen years his junior, married and the mother of young children. She was Margaretta "Happy" Murphy, the wife of Dr. James "Robin" Murphy, a microbiologist at the Rockefeller Institute for Medical Research. The couples had begun as family friends, and Happy had subsequently been drawn into the orbit of Nelson's political career, first as a volunteer, then as a regular member of his staff.

Temperament and appearance apart, Tod Rockefeller and Happy Murphy came out of the same mold. Happy too was from old-line Philadelphia stock. She had been born in Bryn Mawr and ended her formal education at Shipley, a fashionable finishing school. Among her ancestors was the first president of Princeton. The victor of Gettysburg, General George Gordon Meade, was her great-great-grandfather, and a great-grandfather had been mayor of Philadelphia.

An associate, Carl Spad, offers a glimpse of Nelson in love. During the early sixties, few people worked more closely with Nelson than Spad. He had entered Rockefeller's service from Young Republican ranks before the first gubernatorial campaign, and he served as companion, adviser and political factotum. Spad, like most of those around Nelson, was aware of the fact but not the intensity of the relationship with Happy. Early in 1961, while the two men sat alone in Nelson's plane, Nelson blurted it all out. He was going to divorce Tod and marry Happy. Spad calmly began to inventory the political damage of this decision. "I'm telling you, Carl," Nelson said coolly, "not asking you."

In November 1961 Nelson officially announced his legal separation from Tod. Disaster followed with a swiftness calculated to make one believe in a vengeful God. On the day after his statement was reported, Nelson received word that his son Michael was missing on an anthropological expedition in New Guinea. Of his five children, Michael was considered the most promising and was thought to be Nelson's favorite. The tragedy postponed but did not alter Nelson's timetable. His marriage was dead; his romance with Happy remained at white heat.

The party line that the staff played for the press had it that the Rockefeller marriage went aground over Nelson's political career. According to this thesis, Tod was as temperamentally unsuited for the political life as Nelson was born to it. She responded with frosty disdain to the inanities that reporters reserve for political wives. Shortly after Nelson was first elected governor she was asked if she had ever been to Albany; she replied, "No, I haven't. Have you?" in a tone suggesting the reporter had questioned her sanity. Another reporter asked what she did with her hair. "The gray is natural," she answered without an ingratiating smile. Tod was said to be cerebral and Nelson adrenal. She was intellectual and he visceral. Her taste in art was informed, his intuitive. He loved being governor. She hated being the governor's wife. On it went. They were unmade for each other.

"Nonsense," recalled a staff member from that period. "Tod loved politics, like another Eleanor Roosevelt. It's true, she didn't much care for the Ladies Republican Tea and the boring receptions. Who in their right mind would? But she was informed, interested and committed to the same serious issues Nelson cared about as governor. But he didn't love her anymore. He loved Happy. And he was determined to marry her."

The divorce and remarriage hit the family as though a quake had shaken the foundations of Rockefeller Center. The behavior of the brothers on Nelson and Happy's wedding day in May 1963 offered a paradigm of their relationships to Nelson. John III not only did not attend but had Tod as his houseguest that day. David, who was devastated by the decision of the prince regent, also boycotted the ceremony. Laurance came through when Nelson needed him most, and it was in his living room that the pastor of the Union Church of Pocantico united the fifty-four-year-old groom and his thirty-six-year-old bride.

Winthrop reacted rather out of character. The one brother who had himself undergone a divorce, and the family's odd man out, was then living in Arkansas. He had flown to New York to try to talk Nelson out of the remarriage, relieved perhaps to see Nelson in the black-sheep role for a change, and eager for the rare opportunity to play pillar of conventional respectability. Winthrop also did not attend the wedding.

To the world, Happy looked like a woman who had given up four young children to indulge a self-centered romanticism. This impression was abetted by the ugliness of her divorce from Robin Murphy. Murphy was damned if he was going to lose his wife *and* his children to Nelson Rockefeller. He held out for legal custody of the children, then aged from three to twelve. But secrecy was part of the agreement, and what they secretly agreed to was an arrangement whereby the mother had the children for more than half of the time.

During the divorce and remarriage, Nelson displayed a royal hauteur. He forged ahead in simultaneous pursuit of his personal and political happiness, but he had overlooked one point. Hereditary princes do not have to run for their offices. Romantics might read his attitude as an Edward VIII placement of the heart above ambition, but to do so would be to misread the character of Nelson Rockefeller. He believed he could have it all. He always had.

Thus, in 1964, he resumed his presidential quest. He won his first primary in Oregon. Next came a crucial test against Barry Goldwater in California. As election day approached, the polls showed him strong. Yet when the votes were counted, Nelson Rockefeller had suffered a narrow defeat. Some analysts concluded that he may have lost by a margin of one. Three days before the primary, Happy gave birth to Nelson Rockefeller, Jr. Nelson flew back to New York to be at her side. But instead of lending the new couple the aura of sanctioned domesticity, the child's arrival appeared to remind some voters, all over again, that Nelson Rockefeller had flouted the rules by which American politicians were then expected to live.

Later that summer, in a speech before the Republican Convention, he attacked the rabid right of his party and, for this, was branded a spoiler, an egoist who would see Goldwater lose if he himself could not win. For Nelson Rockefeller 1964 had been a bitter year.

Chapter III

FRIENDS AND BROTHERS

THEIR REACTION TO HIS REMARRIAGE illustrated the various distances between Nelson and his brothers. As for friends—not allies, associates, or acquaintances—but authentic friends, he had astonishingly few to whom he could turn. His relationships can be seen as a series of concentric circles. The innermost orbit was occupied by one person, his brother Laurance. They were two years apart, inseparable as children and close throughout life. The Rockefeller brothers, as children, were expected to keep to their own bedrooms, but Nelson and Laurance doubled up, raising hell late into the night, to the consternation of the servants. From boyhood, they called each other "Bill," because "Nelson" and "Laurance," they thought, were not manly enough. Their chemistry was that of gang leader and young member, the leader impressing by the daring of his proposals and the follower urging the leader on by his eager complicity.

During a college summer, the two boys talked themselves onto the crew of Sir Wilfred T. Grenfell's sailing ship, as the noted missionary made for the Arctic. On the homeward-bound voyage, after Dr. Grenfell had left the vessel, Laurance was stricken with appendicitis. They were fogbound off the Bay of Islands near Maine. Nelson wanted to get Laurance off the ship and into a hospital, and he pleaded with the ship's captain to chance a run through the fog along the rockbound coast. The man refused. "Look," Nelson insisted, "this is an emergency. Bounce your foghorn off the cliffs out there. That way we can judge the safe distances by the echo and make the harbor."

"I'll take no responsibility for doing that," the captain demurred.

"Then I will," Nelson informed him. The captain buckled to the forceful twenty-year-old, and Nelson got his beloved brother into port.

They were close, but vastly different in their expectations of life and in the faces they turned toward it. Paradoxically, it was Nelson, projecting the soul of a pitchman by his enthusiasms, who had little patience with business for profit's sake alone. Yet the more philosophical, reflective Laurance was drawn to the romance of enterprise, particularly the satisfaction of seeing a new seed flourish through his involvement and money. Not for him Nelson's AIA and IBEC to remake the world according to some free-enterprise vision of the common good. To Laurance, the deal could be the thing.

Nevertheless, Nelson's social convictions and Laurance's business interests were usually compatible. Throughout his life, for example, Nelson Rockefeller remained an advocate of virtually unhampered defense outlays. Once during a lull on a plane ride to Washington, I asked him what he considered mankind's greatest need. He responded without hesitation, "For the United States to overtake the Soviet Union's military advantage." Laurance, for his part, began investing in industries supplying the American defense arsenal almost before he was out of Navy uniform. Immediately after the Second World War, he invested over $400,000 in McDonnell Aircraft Corporation, which merged with Douglas and became one of the country's top three defense contractors. Laurance put the Piasecki helicopter company on its feet, became a major backer of companies making liquid rocket fuels, ramjets, and airborne instruments, and was an early investor in Itek, the company that made cameras for the U-2 spy plane. Laurance had become hooked on aviation during his boyhood, and, while still in his twenties, he had given a lifesaving transfusion of funds to the young Eastern Airlines. (The venture was not to his father's taste. John D., Jr., did not trust airplanes, and at his death, in 1960, he had never flown.)

Laurance later won a more pacific reputation as "Mr. Conservation," just as Nelson was compiling a creditable environmental record as governor. Neither brother, however, was a conservationist of the purist stripe. Both initially favored the plan of Consolidated Edison, the New York utility, to hollow out Storm King Mountain, a scenic massif on the Hudson River, for a hydroelectric pumping station. After a ten-year struggle, the environmentalists killed Con Ed's Storm King plans, despite the Governor's and Laurance's steadfast support. Nelson, further, had no patience with anti-nuclear obstructionists of his state electrical power plans, and Laurance was instrumental in the creation of United Nuclear, the nation's largest private nuclear-fuel enterprise.

However close personally, the two men wore their wealth differently. No Rockefeller flaunted the fortune, but Nelson traveled in overtly grand style. Laurance managed at least to create a fleeting impression of plainness, if one did not look too closely. Dressed in nondescript gray, he would, when rushed, pop into a midtown Manhattan deli for a quick sandwich. But he had cruised to work that morning down the Hudson River in his own converted PT boat. Or, if he had driven, it was usually in a silver Bentley, a car promoted by the manufacturers "For those too diffident to own a Rolls-Royce."

Laurance was successful in developing what is probably the most elegant resort chain in the world. From the Caneel Bay Plantation in the Virgin Islands to the Mauna Key Beach on Hawaii, his "Rock-resorts" were stunning efforts to harmonize the desires of his conservationist heart and businessman's mind. Or was it the other way around?

Public issues could turn on the love between the two brothers. In 1967, Laurance suffered a defeat in his role as Mr. Conservation after recommending that New York's wildly beautiful Adirondack Mountain area be made a national park. Wealthy owners of secluded summer homes and ski lodges were outraged by this traitorous act against his class. Humbler year-round residents of the Adirondacks saw their lives and lands falling into the clutches of federal bureaucrats. The scheme was publicly pummeled to death.

But older brother Bill looked out for younger brother Bill. Nelson may have lacked the authority to realize Laurance's ambition for a national park in the Adirondacks, but from the moment of his brother's setback, Nelson began to engineer the creation of a state Adirondack Park Agency. By 1972, he had succeeded, and by the following year, he had slogged through fierce local opposition to have this new agency equipped with power to decide the future use of every plot of privately held land in the six-million-acre Adirondack Park, unprecedented zoning authority for a state government. Laurance had taken a drubbing in his drive for a national Adirondack Park. Nelson saw to it that the area became a state park. Hundreds of years from now, Americans may still be enjoying the last great wilderness in the Northeast because of Nelson's love for and loyalty to Laurance.

Nelson gave Laurance a wilderness. Laurance could perhaps not repay on the same scale as the governor of the state. But they always exchanged generous presents. One year it was a maroon Mercedes from Laurance to Nelson, the second Mercedes that Bill had given to Bill.

Nelson had no comparable bond with his other three brothers. For the eldest, John III, having Nelson for a little brother must have been similar to the fate of a plodding college senior who is allowed to start the ball games but is always yanked in favor of a more aggressive sophomore. John stuck exclusively to philanthropy and good causes, following in his father's footsteps, leaving, however, a far lighter footprint. He eschewed the rough-and-tumble of Nelson's political world, the risk-taking of Laurance's venture capitalism, David's stewardship of a huge bank, and Winthrop's intemperance and flawed independence.

When the Rockefeller Brothers Fund met to consider new philanthropic proposals, the staff listened respectfully to John. But they jumped at Nelson's ideas like gamblers rushing to put their bets on a sure thing. John had early become convinced that population control was the key to solving many of mankind's ills. In 1952, he tried to have the Fund create a population council, but he ran aground on a competing priority. Birth control was anathema to the Catholic establishment, and the Catholic vote was crucial to any prospective northeastern political candidate. Key members of the staff were already more concerned about Nelson's political future than the evils of over-population. The Fund tabled John's project.

Hugh Morrow was present one day in 1974 when John showed Nelson a copy of his recently published book, *The Second American Revolution*. The work was a call for greater humanism in American values and had been well received. Nelson sat down, scanned the table of contents and dipped into a few pages. "Johnny, this is terrific," Nelson exulted. "But you don't say anything about the brotherhood of man under the fatherhood of God."

"But, Nell, that's not my kind of statement. Though I appreciate it's one of yours."

"And I don't see anything about labor, either."

"But, Nell, I don't know anything about labor."

"Hughie, come here." Nelson gestured for Hugh Morrow to join them. "Johnny, I want you to meet the greatest editor in the country. Hughie, I want you to take a look at Johnny's book. See where we can fit those things in." Edit his already published, widely praised book? John's response was his customary hurt silence before Nelson's overpowering effrontery.

Close friendship with Winthrop was too late. The scars from Nelson's childhood bullying had left Win resentful and Nelson feeling guilty. Nelson's boyhood ragging of Winthrop could take on a mean edge. When Win came down with a kidney disease that had killed a Rockefeller cousin, also named Winthrop, Nelson taunted his younger brother with the similarities, then asked, "And how are *you* feeling today, Wissy?" He had coined the nickname, one guaranteed to enrage. On a rare occasion when Win was able to crack the exclusive circle of Nelson and Laurance for a game of cowboys and Indians, they had tied him to a tree and left him. One has an image of a big, docile kid, uncomprehendingly absorbing abuse and ridicule, slow to anger, then driven too far, lashing out wildly at his older brother.

Winthrop Rockefeller emerges as the poor little rich boy. If he had to be born rich, then better to a family with a less rigid ethic and expectations. He was reasonably intelligent, physically powerful and handsome, six feet three inches, 225 pounds, with a capacity for manly camaraderie and unabashed pleasure in the company of women. But intellectually and emotionally he was ill equipped for the disciplined striving that his father expected of a Rockefeller. Junior managed to have the unscholarly Winthrop accepted by Yale, where he acquitted himself wretchedly. He dropped out and later summed up the fruits of his abbreviated college education. "All I learned was to smoke and drink."

After leaving Yale, Win entered a more congenial classroom. He went to work in the Texas fields of a Standard Oil subsidiary to learn the business from the bottom up. He proved himself among oil-field roustabouts and roughnecks by his work and, he hinted, by his fists. These were, he later reminisced, the happiest three years of his life. His father ultimately yanked him back to New York, but the war saved Win from the agony of an office job with Socony-Vacuum. He enlisted as a private in the infantry a year before Pearl Harbor. Home after the war, he became that Rockefeller anomaly, an authentic play-boy. Winthrop worked El Morocco, Toots Shor's, the Copacabana and the Stork Club, and he palled around with comedian Joe E. Brown and the movies' favorite butler, Arthur Treacher. He dated Mary Martin, Ginger Rogers, Joan Blondell, and scores of other women who did not have Pocantico written all over them. He went through a financially ruinous divorce after a one-year marriage to Bobo Sears, who already had one socialite marriage under her belt. Something of the proletarian in Win must have been drawn to her origins. The bride, much to the columnists' joy, was an ex-show girl and former Miss Lithuania; she had been born Jievute Paulekiute, the daughter of a onetime coal miner, and was raised near the Chicago stockyards.

After the failed marriage, Winthrop pulled out of the hopeless competition with his brothers for his father's approval. He moved to Arkansas and hooked up with an old army buddy. As he set out for this less exacting league, he suggested a flattering distinction between himself and his brothers. "I've always been the one interested in people. I worked three years in the oil fields. I served six years in the infantry. I was perfectly comfortable. Even Nelson doesn't enjoy people the way I do."

Between Nelson and David there existed the distance born of

vastly different temperaments, most visible in David's bankerly diffidence and Nelson's raw ambition. David reacted to people cautiously, from a distance. Nelson plunged in, pushy, rambunctious, physical. The gulf between them is typified by David's hobby. No one associated with Nelson Rockefeller could imagine him crouched for hours over a magnifying glass and shivering inwardly at the discovery of a new species of beetle. Yet entomology was David's passion. His pleasure in identifying, organizing, classifying, seeking to find an essential order and thus a predictability in things was wholly at odds with Nelson's freewheeling improvisations.

I was struck by the differences between the two men during a visit to the Chase Manhattan Bank headquarters. I had gone there after being approached about shifting allegiance to David, who needed a speech writer. After the interviews, the Chase vice-president for public relations showed me through the bank's newly completed home at One Chase Manhattan Plaza on Wall Street. "You'd have a fine office," he promised. "You'd be able to decorate it yourself. Down in the basement we've got the bank's approved art collection you could select from." No other works were to hang on Chase executive office walls. No such conformity was enforced in Nelson Rockefeller operations, where I decided to remain.

David too had once felt the lure of politics. In 1940, he went to work for New York City's Mayor La Guardia as a troubleshooter, expecting eventually to run for office, but he quickly perceived what elective politics meant—indiscriminate elbow rubbing and a loss of privacy. The experience turned David Rockefeller off. It turned Nelson Rockefeller on.

David went to Chase Manhattan as soon as he was mustered out of the Army, and he never looked back. There is a brief news account of him as a young man winning a polka contest in the Rainbow Room atop Rockefeller Center, but little levity is reported in David's life thereafter. At the bank, personality and métier meshed beautifully. He was content to spend the next fifteen years learning the banking business before he assumed his birthright at age forty-five, the presidency of Chase Manhattan. He was, by then, totally aware of the unique power he wielded. He enjoyed an access to world leaders perhaps unrivaled by any other private citizen, and the fleeting glories of high national office did not tempt him. He was asked to be secretary of the treasury by Kennedy, Johnson, and Nixon, and declined each time. He also turned down Nixon's offers of the posts of secretary of defense and ambassador to Moscow. Why suffer a demotion?

It was David's dream to rebuild the Wall Street area as a site worthy of its place as the symbolic heart of free enterprise. Thus he marshaled the street's financial institutions into a Downtown Lower Manhattan Association. The daring centerpiece of DLMA's plan was to be two 110-story towers, then the tallest on earth, the World Trade Center. Soon after the twin towers were completed, colleagues of mine in state government began complaining of being uprooted from familiar midtown offices and transplanted to the World Trade Center at the tip of Manhattan. Behind their gripes lay another tale of fraternal fidelity. As the World Trade Center neared completion, its vacancy rate was troublingly high. Then a remarkable piece of luck brightened the Center's fortunes—it found a wonderful tenant, the state of New York. Sixty floors in one of the new towers were rented to the state under a forty-year lease, $10.3 million in assured annual rents. Brotherly loyalty had helped save the World Trade Center.

In the early 1970s, the family's public relations staff had the Gallup organization poll American attitudes toward the Rockefeller brothers. John, it turned out, was not the only one eclipsed by Nelson. Of the five brothers, the survey revealed, only Nelson had a distinct public image. People confused the other brothers with each other or with their father.

The distance from his best friend, Laurance, to Nelson's next circle of friendship was vast. The fortune interposed a formidable barrier. Who, outside the family, wanted nothing from him but friendship? Who admired and liked him for himself alone? And how could he ever know? His grandfather had once explained his few golfing partners, saying: "I have made experiments, and nearly always the result is the same. Along about the ninth hole comes some proposition charitable or financial."

During the 1964 campaign, flying late at night from New Hampshire, Nelson drifted into reminiscence with Carl Spad, his political aide. Spad had a lame leg, the result of a childhood attack of polio. Reluctantly, he described the handicaps he had faced and overcome.

"Carl," Nelson said quietly, "if you think that's a handicap, you ought to try living with my name. At least you know who your friends are."

His father's early influences had made the unguarded giving of himself to another almost impossible. "Never get too close to the line," John D., Jr., had preached. "Never show more surface than necessary." Nelson liked to quote these caveats to the staff.

Other friends illustrated Nelson's penchant for mental stimulation over simple companionship: Henry Kissinger, for a shared vision of American power; lawyer Oscar Reubhausen, for a liberal Democrat point of view; George Woods, former president of the World Bank, for his mastery of international finance. One exception was Nelson's osteopath, Dr. Kenneth Riland, who, pretending no great worldly expertise, came closest to the simple status of pal. Nelson liked to have Riland around too because the man kept him from tying himself into emotional as well as muscular knots. If frequency of contact were the measure, Kissinger was his closest friend after Laurance. He lunched, dined and met with him most often.

The next circle contained those few longtime associates who occupied an ambiguous way station somewhere between confidant, employee and friend: John Lockwood, the longtime family lawyer; Wallace Harrison, the architect; William J. Ronan, of the gubernatorial staff. He befriended Robert R. Douglass, counsel to the Governor, much as a favored son. He maintained something resembling friendship with CBS's founder, Bill Paley. They lunched together occasionally, but it was always at Paley's invitation.

One man who considered himself a good friend might have been surprised at Nelson's lack of familiarity with him. We once sat working with Nelson while he took a call from Happy. He scribbled on a yellow pad "Dinner 8. Bennett Surf." When he hung up, Bobby Douglass pointed out, "It's C-e-r-f." "You understood it, didn't you?" Nelson retorted.

For the most part, his relationships turned on its head the cliché that "it's not what you know, but who you know." He was likely to choose as a luncheon companion someone who could enlighten him on Ch'ien Lung porcelains. He loved having Mr. Weinberg bring over *objets* from his shop on 57th Street to the office at lunchtime. What people knew interested him more than who they were. He could afford that purity of association.

Chapter IV

⚜

RE-ELECTION AND REBIRTH

In 1966, the year I went to work for him, Nelson Rockefeller considered himself finished politically. As Nelson made his bid for a third term, the polls showed his undistinguished opponent, Frank O'Connor, the former Queens County district attorney, ahead by a margin of two to one. Ten days before the election, a weary and resigned Rockefeller rode the campaign bus upstate. Seated next to him was the counsel to the Governor, Robert Douglass, a fellow Dartmouth alumnus, then in his early thirties, with the blond, boyish good looks that one knew would stubbornly defy the aging process. Bobby Douglass exemplified what Nelson prized in his staff. In appearance and manner, Douglass had the deceptively casual charm and wit of a Fitzgerald hero; but in his work, he applied considerable intelligence to a single zealously pursued objective—the interests of Nelson Rockefeller. As the bus rambled through the night, Nelson confided to Douglass, "Bobby, I've talked to Happy. Psychologically we're ready for the worst."

His pessimism was unfeigned, and he was thinking ahead with cold clarity. He had begun a massive expansion of the State University and instructed Douglass, "I want all proposals for the university under contract before we leave office. Same for the South Mall." The latter was the grandiose government complex then under construction in Albany. "And we've got to buy all the art for the South Mall before we go, too." Rockefeller was selecting, virtually single-handed, the sculpture and paintings to embellish the project. His new Athens was not to be aborted by any Philistine pols supplanting him in office. Rockefeller's orders to Douglass were, in short, to ensure completion of the monuments to his leadership before he left office.

On election night, he gathered a small party of family and staff at his triplex apartment at 812 Fifth Avenue in Manhattan for dinner and to wait out the incoming returns. He appeared calm, still insisting that he was "psychologically prepared," but Joe Boyd, then his chief advance man, remembered that "his hands trembled every time he greeted a new guest." Nelson tried to enliven the evening by recalling the random path that had led him to the Governor's Mansion in the first place. "The party gave me the nomination against Averell Harriman," Rockefeller said, smiling wryly, "because they figured I was the only one who could pick up the tab. No Republican was supposed to win in '58 anyway."

As a newcomer to the staff I was unaware of his underlying defeatism. Indeed, when I reported to campaign headquarters, I had the sensation of boarding the U.S.S. *Missouri* as it prepared to engage a rowboat. Rockefeller had taken over two floors of the New York Hilton, then the city's newest luxury hotel, as his headquarters. None of the disorganization, the scraping for money endemic to political campaigns, was anywhere evident. What we needed, we had. As a new speech writer, I was paid more than double my state salary, plus living expenses, including a room in the Hilton. The internecine rivalries and clash of egos common to political operations had been muted to near silence in this campaign.

The campaign's master strategist was Dr. William J. Ronan, a man of supreme confidence, some might even say arrogance. Ronan had been Dean of the School of Public Administration at New York University when discovered by Rockefeller early in Nelson's political career. Ronan had remained with him ever since, and as secretary to the Governor, he had become, in effect, the state's general manager. Tall and well proportioned, Ronan nevertheless had a softness around the middle from too many years deskbound. His authority lay in the cocky angle of his head, the utter assurance of his speech. He peered out at the world with a face a shade too scholarly to be handsome and with eyes expressing a genial disdain for lesser mortals.

My first exposure to Bill Ronan came while clearing a speech draft. I had tried a fresh gambit, one that had Rockefeller explain why, after eight years on the job, he still wanted to be governor. Ronan leaned back, legs crossed. He took his pen and slashed at my opening passages with lightning strokes. He regarded me with a bemused tolerance. "Nobody gives a goddamn why Nelson Rockefeller wants to be governor!" He went on quickly editing the rest of the speech and tossed it back. I had witnessed, in summary form, the secret of Ronan's hold over Nelson Rockefeller: swift, absolute certitude encased in a shatterproof ego. "He has Nelson buffaloed," one of the staff observed. "Nelson thinks Bill may actually be smarter than he is. And that's not something he likes to concede about another human being."

Managing the campaign was William L. Pfeiffer, a man for whom the word "crusty" had been invented. I received an instructive introduction to Pfeiffer. Frank O'Connor, the Democratic candidate, had charged that Rockefeller was spending $21 million to buy the election, and the media had started to run with this issue. Pfeiffer called me into his office, where, with devilish glee, he said, "I want you to shoot down that goddamned canard." His merriment was understandable. The Rockefeller campaign was indeed spending in a torrent, roughly twice as much as the Governor had pumped out to be re-elected four years before.

We accused O'Connor, with no particular originality, of the Big Lie. We countered with the Big Truth, in which the shock effect of utter candor blunts any further or deeper questioning. "These Democratic charges belong in the Olympics of campaign exaggeration," we retorted. In fact, the Rockefeller expenditures did not begin to approach $21 million; we were spending actually only $5.3 million. Outside of a national presidential election, however, Nelson Rockefeller's 1966 gubernatorial race was, at the time, the most expensive campaign in American political history. For every dollar available to O'Connor, Rockefeller spent ten. The Governor's stepmother, Martha Baird Rockefeller, alone contributed more to Nelson's effort than the entire cost of the O'Connor campaign.*

No matter what he was spending, Nelson Rockefeller still saw himself in a losing struggle. The New York *Daily News* straw poll, right on every gubernatorial election but one for the previous thirty-eight years, continued to show O'Connor with a decisive edge. Now, on election night, as Nelson gamely entertained his guests, he continued to reminisce. "I really loved architecture. I would have been pretty good, too. But the family didn't approve. So I went into father's business. After a while, I got bored there. Banking was David's thing. Laurance had conservation. Johnny took up the philanthropies. But there was no way he could top what Father did. My other real love was always international relations. The run for governor in '58 was supposed to be a detour." He shook his head. The detour had lasted eight years. Then the early returns trickled in. He took a slight lead, which held and grew. In the end, he won by a respectable 392,263 votes.

From that night on, Nelson Rockefeller saw himself differently. If he had offended with his private life, he had evidently been forgiven. If he had taxed heavily, people apparently understood why. If he had alienated the Republican right, he had solidly captured the electoral middle. He had proved what he had always needed to believe. Nelson Rockefeller, apart from the money and privilege, was one hell of a guy. Thereafter, one could almost see him throwing aside the crutches of excessive reliance on men like William J. Ronan. They would still be at his side, not to catch him if he started to stumble, but now, rather, to follow him into the future. Nelson Rockefeller, on this election night, felt himself reborn.

It is a comment on the machined precision of this re-election campaign that during it I wrote more than one hundred speeches for a man I scarcely saw. Not until after the campaign did I come to work closely with Nelson Rockefeller. During the campaign, three men

---

*Nelson's mother, Abby, died in 1948. Three years later, John D. Rockefeller, Jr., at age seventy-seven, had married Martha Baird Allen, the widow of a Brown University schoolmate. A pianist, she had left her mark on American politics by composing the 1940 campaign song "Win with Willkie." Upon his death, Junior had left her $72 million.

had produced the speeches, myself and Frank Gervasi, working under Hugh Morrow. After the campaign, as Hugh Morrow moved up, eventually becoming Nelson's director of communications, I found to my astonishment that in peacetime Nelson Rockefeller maintained a speech-writing staff of one, now me.

The first time he directed me to sit next to him on the plane to go over a text, I found my attention riveted on the man rather than the words before us. Famous faces, first known through the filters of cameras and electronic imagery, have a special fascination seen close as flesh and blood. The first time I ever saw John F. Kennedy, what came through, which had not before, was the burnished quality, the ruddy complexion, an almost electric copper glinting in the hair, an overall fieryness.

Nelson Rockefeller's skin was the color of a sidewalk. Pale-pink patches mottled the overall gray. He had "Aldrich skin," as he called it, inherited from his mother's side of the family. "It makes you look as if you just crawled out from under a stone," he lamented. The patched quality, however, merged as one moved away, just as the thousand daubs of a Monet, seen from a distance, blend into uniform planes.

The square jaw, the pivot of his rugged good looks, loomed larger at close range. And the angle of its protrusion, I was to learn, was the measure of his mood. When displeased, he tended to purse his lips into a tight, freeze-dried smile, a mannerism that would have appeared priggish in a less strong-featured face. His hair had remained full and he combed it in a style preserved since his Dartmouth days. During the tonsorial revolution of the sixties, his sideburns never lengthened a fraction of an inch. His hands, square and thick, were those of a carpenter, retired long enough for the calluses to have faded, not at all the hands of a patrician. The broad backs bore a light down and were flecked with age spots.

His most memorable and least attractive feature was his eyes. There was no warmth in their color, a shifting slate blue, and there was something veiled and remote in their gaze, as though he was always watching you from a distance. As he listened, particularly to what he did not want to hear, the corners tightened and the lids formed small triangles around the deeply recessed eyes. In that otherwise open face, the eyes acted like sentries cautioning, "Watch out. Don't get too close."

He usually struck people as taller than his five feet ten inches, in part because of his solid physique and large, handsome head. But the impression of size had as much to do with the aura of power. Up close, he exuded a calculatedly dispensed charm rather than spontaneous warmth, and one felt a pent-up force behind the casual facade.

My first mistake. I came to the job with a prejudice about those born rich. People weaned on comfort and ease surely grew up comfortable and easy. Toughness, I believed, was acquired in the annealing fire of struggle in a hard world. Wrong. Nelson Rockefeller was as tough a man as I have ever known. He combined the supreme assurance of the wellborn with the tenacity and cunning of a self-made man. He could bite clean through the silver spoon in his mouth. His treatment of the staff was cleverly conceived to wring optimum performance from us. We were motivated, flattered, yet never entirely secure. He kept people committed to him, but never complacent about his favor, rewarded but rarely relaxed.

When the legislature was in session he flew up from Pocantico to the state capital on Monday mornings, often in his favorite aircraft, a Grumman Gulfstream II. Happy thought the plane suited him admirably—it had enormous drive. As his arrival neared, the second floor of the State Capitol, where the Executive Chamber was located, fairly crackled. His arrival was invariably heralded by the voice, that unmistakable, insistent honking. It began when he stepped from the limousine, giving out instructions or exulting over great works to be accomplished that day. It filtered up through the shaft of the elevator as he ascended to the second floor and then it invaded the corridors. He never arrived alone, but in a flying wedge, Nelson striding ahead with easy purposefulness at the point of the angle, while aides trotted at each flank. The honking never faded until he disappeared inside his private office. Despite his ordinary stature, Mrs. Whitman felt, when he arrived, that "he loomed in the doorway."

I was pleased and then astonished at my first Rockefeller staff meeting; pleased by the sherry that was served before we got down to work, a civilized touch unknown to one who had come out of the bureaucracy; astonished to see who emerged as the climate-control engineer and headwaiter. Nelson was no sooner seated than he bounded up to change the setting on the thermostat. Then it was to the window to adjust the blinds, actions he repeated endlessly throughout the meeting. A woman in a waitress's uniform came in with coffee, and he began to instruct her with a pinched smile. "No, not like that. You see. You put the saucers down first, then you take the cups. Here, let me show you." The woman retreated with a dazed smile.

"When I see Nelson Rockefeller," Joe Boyd, his then chief advance man, remembered, "we're arriving in some motel on the campaign trail, and before he's got his coat off, he's rearranging the furniture." He once appeared five minutes before a party for four hundred guests at the Executive Mansion and cheerily announced that he wanted the bar on the opposite side of the room. While the barmen struggled to right the wrong, he made his contribution. He moved an ashtray from one coffee table to another.

Rockefeller fidgeted impatiently whenever one of his cabinet or staff made a presentation. He frequently broke in to explain what the person meant to say or had failed to say. "When he entered a room, he sucked up all the authority," recalled George Humphreys, who ran the state's Environmental Facilities Corporation. The people Nelson gathered around him were forceful figures in their own spheres, but something went out of them in his presence. Plunging fullbacks became sinuous broken-field runners in order to register the mildest dissent. Never in eleven years did I witness a staff member take him head on. No one ever said flatly, "I disagree." "That's wrong, Governor." "That's a bad idea."

His departures from the Capitol were as electric as his arrivals. Warning telephone calls sounded up and down the second floor. The Governor would be departing in five minutes. Aides traveling with him back to New York City threw on their coats and, with briefcases in hand, waited edgily in doorways until he burst out of his office, into the corridor and down in the elevator, creating a kind of suction that pulled people into his wake. All the while, he would be honking, "Louie, Hughie, you sit with me. You too, Al." The seating in *his* car, *his* plane, was never left to chance.

Jim Cannon, long a close aide, described a Rockefeller departure. "The jets are screeching full throttle in a near-vertical takeoff. Coffee cups are flying all over the place and he's banging somebody's ear over the roar of the engines about some new subsidy for the arts."

Chapter V

RUNNING FOR PRESIDENT

LATE IN 1967, I went into the Governor's office to clear a speech. I had also brought with me a batch of clippings. When we finished our immediate business, I flashed the clippings in front of him, columns by Walter Lippmann, James Reston, and other sages with the same message—for the Republicans in 1968, Rockefeller was the only man.

It was a nasty thing to do. His presidential virus was then in remission. Not only was he sitting this election out, he was actively backing George Romney, then governor of Michigan, for the Republican nomination. He had briefly loaned Hugh Morrow to help Romney organize his speech and press operations, and he had sent Carl Spad to help in the Michigan tundra. I was writing speeches for Rockefeller to deliver wherever and whenever Romney asked for Nelson's support. And here I was waving a bottle of political hooch in front of a man who had recently kicked the candidacy habit. In the wistful tone of one who could almost taste the heady spirits, he scanned the clippings and asked, "Is there much of this?"

"Yes," I answered, which did not visibly displease him. But this time he was not going to be swayed by ambitious staffers and political savants who believed that only Nelson Rockefeller could stop Richard

Nixon's nomination. The bruises were barely healed from his last two presidential disasters. By 1968, he had been governor for nearly ten years, and the office now fit him like his skin. He was in that rare position for an elected official of knowing more about his job than his staff did. At home, he had two young sons by Happy, Nelson, Jr., and Mark, who were enjoying much more of their father's attention than he had ever given the children of his first marriage. Happy, too, had no desire to undergo again the shellfire of public criticism and vilification which she had known in 1964.

Thus, in 1968, the fever was quiescent, if not extinguished, as Nelson Rockefeller went about singing the praises of Romney, the man who had saved American Motors and who wanted now to save America. Then Romney erred on the side of candor when a reporter asked why he was questioning the country's involvement in Vietnam when, after an earlier trip to the war zone, he had approved of our role. With fatal naïveté Romney answered that he had been "brainwashed" by the American generals in Vietnam.

At the 55th Street office we discussed whether he would now drop out of the presidential race.

"Is it that serious?" Nelson asked.

"People see it that way," Les Slote, then his press secretary, answered. "He's cut his own throat. He's bleeding to death."

Rockefeller shook his head. I tried to read a meaning in his remote expression. Disappointment that his rider had stumbled? Understanding for a man who had faltered as badly as he himself had on the same trail? Or was it that Romney's mortal wound now forced him to a decision that he dreaded yet desired. Romney finally dropped out nearly two weeks before the New Hampshire primary, and the middle of the Republican road was now empty.

While 1964 may have been a defeat for Nelson Rockefeller within the party, it had, quite unexpectedly, given him his finest moment before the country. On the second night of the Republican Convention at the Cow Palace in San Francisco, he had been allotted five minutes to deliver a minority report to counter the harsh Goldwater platform plank condoning political extremism. Television had impressed indelibly on the public the image of a firm-jawed man who for sixteen minutes took the abuse of the jackals of the far right and who refused to be driven from the speaker's platform. Nelson left San Francisco a Party Track loser but a Popular Track winner.

Rockefeller's defiance of his jeering opponents had as much to do with a natural pugnacity as it did with political conviction. As he reflected on it, "If I am forced into a fight, I have to say that I can enjoy it because I am highly competitive. I can enjoy the competitive aspect of a confrontation. . . . It provides your mental system with something stimulating." He had been promised five minutes and he would have them. He would have stood just as rooted had he been heckled by leftist radicals as by Republican right-wingers. Nelson was unaccustomed to being pushed. His stand in San Francisco was still serving him well four years later as Popular Track opinion makers now urged him into the '68 race. Even more heartening, governors and senators in the Republican center, and five former Republican national chairmen, pledged to back him if he would run again. Among his enthusiastic supporters was the new governor of Maryland, Spiro Agnew, a man, strange as it now seems, who then typified a new breed of Republican moderate.

At this time, Nelson's regard for Richard Nixon was a bare notch above contempt. The former Vice-President provoked one of the few petty comments that I ever heard Rockefeller make. In December 1967, Lieutenant Governor Malcolm Wilson came into a staff meeting waving a Christmas card showing the Nixon family posed before a Christmas tree. Wilson teased, "I'll bet you didn't get one of these, Nelson."

Rockefeller eyed the card with wry amusement and, pointing to one of the women, said, "That one looks like she's wearing falsies." Usually, the strongest sarcasm that he mustered against anyone was an ironic "Isn't he something?" This restraint grew out of no innate sweetness of disposition. Nelson had learned to discipline a naturally waspish tongue, which, he recognized, was particularly unacceptable in a rich man with political ambitions.

With George Romney out of the race, with the shopworn Nixon now the leading contender, with Republican moderates urging him on, Nelson began to move toward declaring himself a candidate. What happened to his presidential prospects in 1968 is intriguing even now. That year was his only serious hope for the office. Had he succeeded in taking the nomination, he likely would have been elected President. Had Rockefeller, rather than Nixon, been inaugurated in January 1969, one wonders what the course of American history might have been minus the Nixon years and Watergate.

His behavior in 1968 reveals, under magnification, the fine cracks in the armor of arrogance in which Nelson Rockefeller encased himself. On Sunday, March 10, he had breakfast in his Fifth Avenue apartment with a delegation representing an Oregon Rockefeller for President movement. The same people had helped him win his only presidential primary victory in 1964. He liked these young, vigorous, progressive people, they were his kind of Republicans. They liked Nelson too and wanted him to enter the 1968 Oregon primary, whose filing deadline was fast approaching.

Hearing the siren song of the Oregonians, Nelson took George Hinman, Republican national committeeman from New York and Rockefeller's liaison with the party, into an adjoining bedroom. He looked at Hinman with an unmistakable glow. "George, what do you think?"

"I think you'd better do it," Hinman said. Rockefeller did not respond directly, but there was no doubt in Hinman's mind that Nelson intended to make another try for the presidential nomination.

That evening Rockefeller flew to Washington to confer with Republican leaders, principally Rogers Morton, who was expected to support him, perhaps direct his campaign. Ann Whitman, the Governor's executive assistant, went with him. She recalled the trip. "There was an excitement on that plane. I recognized it. You can't miss the smell of a candidate. When we got to the Governor's house on Foxhall Road, the place was swarming with reporters. They smelled it too." The press reported that Nelson Rockefeller would formally announce before the week was out.

But soon after Nelson's return from Washington, George Hinman received a call from a shaken Rockefeller. "George, I had a bad experience down there. They're all for me running. But"—his voice took on a bitter edge—"I get the impression they think it would help Nixon, kind of warm him up. I'd be a pacer. I've talked to Happy. She's not so sure I should go."

On the following day, a three-hour strategy meeting was held at Nelson's West 54th Street town house, the building that connected to his 55th Street office. Present were George Hinman, Emmet Hughes and Theodore W. Braun. Ted Braun was another of several mystery satellites in Nelson Rockefeller's galaxy, an influence who suddenly appeared, wielding unassailable authority, and who then disappeared. Braun was a public-relations consultant with cabin-class clients—R. J. Reynolds Tobacco, North American Rockwell, Atlantic Richfield, Transamerica, U. S. Plywood and Champion Papers. He had also enjoyed high-level entrée to the Eisenhower White House.

Braun was tall, impeccably tailored and formidable in manner. With his deep-bronze color and Indian-penny profile, he suggested an Iroquois chief with a Savile Row tailor. Braun also possessed that quality which Nelson Rockefeller worshiped—"a manner of unambiguous certainty," as Mrs. Whitman put it. Joe Boyd had once sat in on a Braun-Rockefeller meeting and was stunned. "Braun was the only person I ever heard lay into Nelson Rockefeller. And the Governor took it."

Another aide described the Braun consulting technique. "He'd set up an appointment with the Governor. That morning he'd stop by and pick the brains of all the key staff. Then he'd repackage the ideas and sell them to Nelson over lunch. He didn't provide anything original." Braun's method was not so exploitive as it appears. He knew his client, and he knew that Rockefeller suffered from a hearing defect common among powerful figures—to Nelson, new ideas always sounded better coming from someone outside his employ.

During the town-house meeting, Braun told Nelson that he was ill prepared for the primaries. His best, indeed his only hope, Braun and the other advisers agreed, was that the party's leaders would ultimately abandon their sentimental favorite, the "loser" Nixon, and move to the one Republican who could win the White House, Nelson Rockefeller.

The next morning the cameras of the national television networks and journalists from all the major media in the country gathered in the grand ballroom of the New York Hilton expecting to hear Nelson Rockefeller announce his candidacy. He stood before a forest of microphones and said, instead, "I am not and will not be a candidate for the Presidency."

Before departing for the hotel to drop this modest bombshell, Nelson had faced the unpleasant issue of alerting his key supporters around the country of his change of heart. High on the list of those he considered calling was Spiro Agnew. But Nelson was finally persuaded by Braun that should he get on the phone, his backers would only try to persuade him to enter the race. As for Agnew, Braun specifically advised no call. He was "a sieve," he said, and would have word of the withdrawal out before Nelson did. Thus, in the end, Nelson called no one, and his staunchest advocates learned that they had lost their champion at the same time as the man in the street. The embarrassed Agnew immediately threw his support to Richard Nixon, a move much publicized and followed by a fair-sized stampede of other former Rockefeller supporters.

Three tumultuous weeks ensued. On March 31, Lyndon Johnson, recognizing that Vietnam had defeated him, took himself out of the presidential campaign. Four days later, on April 4, Dr. Martin Luther King, Jr., was assassinated and the ghettos of America's great cities erupted in fire and rage.

On April 11, I was summoned with a dozen others to a secret meeting in the 55th Street conference room, the purpose of which was to maneuver Rockefeller back into the race. Instead of urging him to stay out, several Republican leaders were now pleading with him to get in to stop Nixon. This was a novel experience, and much to his taste.

Any such gathering of Rockefeller hands had a high ego quotient. They conversed, in the lull before the Governor's arrival, in a breezy repartee designed to convey total self-assurance while revealing nothing of possible value to their competitors for Rockefeller's attention. The meeting was my first exposure to Emmet Hughes and Henry Kissinger. Hughes sat sleek and satisfied, as though savoring a delicious secret. Kissinger, though known then only within the foreign-policy community, was already a legend in Rockefeller circles. As we waited, the conversation drifted to Vietnam. I remarked that the effect of the war was so pervasive that it influenced the most unexpected facets of American life. A major Rockefeller objective, for example, had been to end water pollution in New York State. But Vietnam had squeezed environmental concerns out of the defense budget. Thus two army facilities that were dumping wastes into the Hudson had scrapped their plans to build sewage-treatment systems. My example failed to move Professor Kissinger, who observed, "We don't shape national defense policy with sewage."

Someone asked Henry how much time he would be able to give to a presidential campaign. Kissinger, then still on the Harvard faculty, replied, "Not as much as Nelson will want." I suggested that Zbigniew Brzezinski, then at Columbia University, might be willing to serve as a foreign-affairs consultant. Kissinger shot me a forbidding look. "The wrong outlook. Not at all the required depth." I gathered that Dr. Kissinger had more time for a Rockefeller campaign than he was admitting.

When the Governor came in, he looked determined, almost grim, and spoke firmly, as though trying to shed the skin of indecision produced by his earlier vacillations. "I believe our problems are soluble," he began. "They're man-made. There is nothing basically wrong with our institutions. We just have to give people a sense of hope. We've now got major state business out of the way. So we've got to figure out what our national road map is. What are we trying to accomplish? I want to present an image of confidence, creativity and stability. I don't want that awful feeling of going into something unprepared. Our executive committee will be George Hinman, Ted Braun and Emmet Hughes. Emmet will be in overall command."

George Hinman, as New York's Republican national committeeman, had to sell Nelson to party chieftains across the country, and he remembered all too vividly their unhappiness with Hughes's prominence in Rockefeller's failed 1960 presidential effort. He later remarked, "I had learned of his choice just hours earlier. Nelson went into a lunch with Hughes and Emmet must have hypnotized him, because he came out with the job. I found it unbelievable."

But now the good soldier Hinman was silent as Nelson went on. "I saw all the candidates when I went to Martin Luther King's funeral. I thought Bobby Kennedy looked like he needed psychiatric treatment. I guess emotionally he never got over his brother's death.

Nixon just looks completely out of it. Gene McCarthy was impressive. He's a fine-looking man." He recapped what he expected of us, then turned the meeting over to Hughes and left. Emmet explained that Rockefeller was now to be an "available but not active" candidate.

Nelson stayed this ambiguous course for two weeks, but the ground did not swell. Thus, on Tuesday, April 30, in the Victorian opulence of the Red Room in the State Capitol, Nelson Rockefeller formally announced his third bid for the Republican presidential nomination. He explained his latest reversal by "the unprecedented events of the past weeks"—Johnson's withdrawal and the King assassination.

His late start ruled out entering state primaries. Consequently a substitute strategy was adopted. He would stage his own national primary. Nelson would campaign intensively, make speeches, issue position papers. His bold solutions and personal attractiveness would pull him ahead of Nixon in the polls, and the poll results would be used to persuade Republican leaders and potential convention delegates to latch on to a winner.

We stole a leaf from the Kennedys, anticipating vulnerabilities and attempting to deflect them with humor. "In 1960, they said I dropped out too soon. In 1964, they said I hung in too long. So this year I played it safe. I did both." Nelson was to repeat the line in virtually every stump speech he made in 1968.

His latest presidential campaign was the antithesis of the gubernatorial juggernaut of two years before. When Emmet Hughes proved no political manager, he was moved over to become campaign theoretician, and Nelson named Bobby Douglass, then thirty-six, as campaign manager. The campaign staff reflected the national divisions over Vietnam, the chief protagonists being Henry Kissinger, a hard-liner, and Emmet Hughes, a self-professed "screaming dove."

Prior to the campaign, Nelson had handled press questions about the war like poison ivy. Thus:

REPORTER: "Governor, would you please outline for us your views on Vietnam?"

ROCKEFELLER: "Surely. My position on Vietnam is very simple. I think that our concepts as a nation and our actions have not kept pace with the changing conditions, and therefore our actions are not completely relevant today to the realities of the magnitude and complexity of the problems that we face in this conflict."

REPORTER: "What does that mean?"

ROCKEFELLER: "Just what I said."

But Nelson's inner convictions were unambiguous—he was a hawk in full feather. He approached Vietnam with simplistic certainty. American democracy had provided the soil for the rise of the Rockefellers, who in turn had enriched their country, he believed, almost as much as America had enriched them. Communism was a mortal threat to the system that had blessed his family and his country. The Vietnam war was being fought to stop Communism and to maintain America's world primacy; therefore, it was a just war. It was not much more complicated than that. But this was hardly an utterable public position for a politician who wanted to pull together a country bitterly riven by the war.

In mid-June, he was to address the Los Angeles Town Hall, and I was asked to edit a lengthy speech originally drafted by Kissinger. Two things impressed me—the brilliance of his concepts and the thickset style, for Kissinger was then much more the wordy academic than the lucid public communicator he later became. In this text, he presented an integrated world vision, but in a lumbering gait. I cut the text substantially, not without trepidation, since Kissinger's rages were legendary. Once, when a speech of his had been reworked by other Rockefeller staffers, he had thundered, "When Nelson buys a Picasso, he doesn't hire four house painters to improve it!"

I saw my editing as an opportunity to slip into the text some personal convictions on Vietnam, since a speech is something of a blank check on which the speech writer can write what he dares. Once the ideas are committed to paper, it remains for others to catch them and accept them or throw them out. My wife, then a student at the State University in Albany, had shown me a phrase from her political science reading: "Vietnam is a commitment looking for a reason." In all the torrent of debate, I had never heard the issue stated more trenchantly than in those eight words. Their author was Paul Goodman, the liberal social critic. I paraphrased his thought and added it to the Kissinger draft: "In Vietnam we must not find ourselves with a commitment looking for a justification." I completed the editing and turned in the text. The next day I heard a deep grumbling over my shoulder. "Who rewrote my speech?" I turned to see a frowning Kissinger.

"I did."

He stared, then at last smiled coolly. "Good job. I can't remember what you took out." With that, he turned and strode off. It was a Kissinger mini-performance, calculated for effect, and effective.

Rockefeller delivered the speech, and when he hit the line on Vietnam, I wondered who would be more surprised at their unwitting collaboration, the establishment Rockefeller or the counter-cultural Goodman?

During this campaign, I saw intimations of the unlikely reputation that Kissinger later enjoyed in his early Nixon years as a lady-killer. Some said it was a shrewd stratagem that he used to gain publicity. Perhaps. But I remembered an occasion in 1968 when I had been introduced to an exotic Eurasian beauty, a Phi Beta Kappa as well, with a doctorate in international relations. I went to Kissinger's office and told him that I had a candidate for the campaign staff who combined brains and beauty. "Get your priorities straight," he lectured. "What does she look like?" He had sounded quite sincere.

Our delegate-hunting unit enlisted Kissinger in its operation to woo wavering women delegates to Nelson's side. Henry dutifully charmed them at teas and over dinner. But after the first several encounters, he protested to Tanya Melich of our delegate operation. He had had it, he said, "with that blue-haired set. Don't you ever have any prospects under sixty and worth looking at?"

Near midnight on June 4, 1968, I left our campaign headquarters on Manhattan's West 44th Street for the Hotel Royalton, where I was told that they had given up my room. I had forgotten to renew my reservation. Too tired to look elsewhere, I wandered up to our 55th Street offices and stretched out on a couch. At daybreak, I was shaken by the janitor, babbling, "Bobby Kennedy! Bobby Kennedy! Been shot!" Awakened in this strange setting, the tortured face shouting at me, with images of Jack Kennedy and Dr. King spinning through my mind, I thought I was having a nightmare. I dressed and went to

campaign headquarters where I was to go over a speech that Rockefeller was to deliver that evening at the Waldorf Astoria, though I
assumed that the event would be canceled as Robert Kennedy hov-
ered near death. I found the mood at our headquarters disturbing.
The shock and fear over what was happening to the country were
genuine, but the desensitizing effect of repeated assassinations was
also beginning to tell. Political speculation followed with unseemly
haste on the heels of grief and horror. Another piece had been plucked
from the political chessboard, and conversation too quickly drifted to
how this change would affect Nelson Rockefeller's game.

On the evening that Senator Kennedy's body was brought to St.
Patrick's Cathedral on Fifth Avenue, I joined the crowd behind police
barricades on the opposite side of the street. The hearse arrived, and
members of the family quickly followed in automobiles. Jackie Kennedy stepped out, unexpectedly tall, almost fleshless, her face a resolutely composed mask. The rest of the Kennedy family filed into the
church, erect and expressionless. Absent from the crowd where I
stood were the unifying grief, the sense of personal loss that had been
produced by the assassination of the first Kennedy. Most people
seemed simply curious. The country, I thought, was becoming inured to madness.

Nelson Rockefeller had already called Ethel Kennedy and had
made available to her one of his staff who, he said, might be useful at
this time. Joe Canzeri was then a Rockefeller advance man recruited
originally from the hotel business. A dark-haired, compact dynamo
in his mid-thirties, Canzeri had quickly stamped his personal style on
our operations. On the road, he displayed the sledgehammer authority of a sergeant in an army of occupation, demanding and getting the
best for the Rockefeller party from hotel, restaurant, and convention-
hall managers and police chiefs. He could also adopt the slickness of
a maître d', anticipating the wants of everyone from Nelson Rockefeller to the newest journalist on the press bus. Canzeri did it all with a
side-of-the-mouth irreverence that saved him from appearing the
bully in one role or a sycophant in the other. His style was to state
the outrageous, ethnically or sexually, and, with a Groucho Marx
raising of his eyebrows, get away with it. Shining through the clown-
ing and cheerful impudence was an unsurpassed competence in the

thing that he did. Call it advancing, staging, or producing, Canzeri had the capacity to see grand spectacles in their thousand mosaic pieces and a genius for putting the pieces together. He was later to become a high-level figure in the Reagan White House.

When Martin Luther King, Jr., was assassinated, Rockefeller had sent Canzeri to Atlanta to help arrange the funeral. He had proved invaluable to the stunned survivors of the King crusade and took over the bulk of the planning. His capacity to open the Rockefeller coffers for expenses had not hindered his authority. Now Canzeri had been detailed to the Kennedys with strict instructions from Rockefeller to keep his involvement a secret from the press.

I made my way to the 50th Street side of St. Patrick's Cathedral and convinced the police that I had to see Mr. Canzeri. Joe appeared in the doorway and waved me through the barricade. At this point, virtually the only people in the cathedral were the family, dwarfed in its vaulted interior. Teddy Kennedy stood alone by the casket, his face eerily illuminated by candles at each end of the bier, his head slightly bowed. If one could read any meaning in his expression, it was a hurt disbelief. I had intruded on a moment of intensely private grief and quickly left.

After Robert Kennedy's death, Rockefeller sensed a void in the political center. Nixon was regarded as a man of the right, and the only other semi-viable GOP candidate, besides Rockefeller, was an even more conservative Ronald Reagan. "I think the people who supported Bobby Kennedy are going to come to me now," Nelson confided to the campaign staff. This conviction signaled a shift to the left in our campaign strategy. It also underscored a certain obtusity in our candidate. No Kennedy supporters were going to be delegates to the Republican Convention.

Rockefeller was the first candidate to resume campaigning after a decent interval of national mourning. And the first indication of the shift in the campaign's center of gravity was the addition of the Los Angeles black ghetto of Watts to a West Coast swing. Nelson wanted all speeches on this trip to begin with a tribute to Senator Kennedy, but the draft I wrote made him furious. Within five years, the text pointed out, a President, his senator brother, and the leader of the nation's blacks had been murdered. The country was wracked by divisions over Vietnam, by racial tensions and by the void between the generations. Campuses and inner cities seethed. Bombings had become a commonplace. Bobby Kennedy, I argued, had battled against this illness of the American spirit and had lost his life in the struggle. The most fitting tribute to him would be for Americans to achieve now the healing unity that he had sought.

"I don't want any of that sick society stuff," Nelson muttered darkly. "A few nuts don't reflect the state of the country." Bemoaning tragedy, he said, was "looking backward." Reflecting on what had gone wrong in America was "negative thinking," and not in keeping with the unquestioning optimism that he preached and expected of those around him. Thus the Kennedy tribute was rewritten—his death was a great tragedy, but it was an isolated event, not a symptom of a national malaise.

His attitude toward the Kennedy tribute reflected one of Nelson Rockefeller's deepest convictions. He was able, he was sure, to transcend economic barriers and know what the common people believed and what they wanted to hear. Yet he was often astonishingly detached from the everyday world. In the wake of the latest assassination, Secret Service agents had been assigned to protect presidential candidates. On our flight to the West Coast, Nelson moved down the aisle of our chartered 727 greeting many of the reporters by name, some correctly. One of them kidded him about "traveling now like James Bond."

"Who?" Rockefeller asked blankly.

"You know, James Bond. Double-oh-seven. Sean Connery."

Rockefeller grinned blankly. "How many delegates has he got?"

Occupying the office next to me at our Manhattan campaign headquarters was another speech writer named David Nevin, a low-keyed, idealistic Texan who previously had written for *Life*. Nevin had recently interviewed Rockefeller and had come away infected by the man's irrepressible positivism and receptiveness to new ideas. Rockefeller had also warmed to Nevin and made the reporter feel that if they combined their talents, Rockefeller's capacity to lead and Nevin's gift to articulate, they could deliver America to a brave new future. The journalist returned to his office and immediately asked *Life* for a leave of absence to join Rockefeller's mission. Three weeks later, I had lunch with a confused and dejected Nevin. He had not seen, much less worked with, Rockefeller from the day he had joined the staff. I regarded him sympathetically but offered little encouragement. I had by then seen Nelson operate. I had observed his instant enthusiasms for people, his impatient insistence on having them *now*, and, like a spoiled child, his casting aside of one toy the moment a newer one took his fancy.

"Dave," I said, "you thought you'd entered on a crusade. Instead you're one girl in the harem. That's the way he is." Within a week, Nevin returned to *Life* magazine.

While Nelson Rockefeller was running for President, Alton G. Marshall became, in effect, governor of New York. Marshall's life illustrates the maximizing effect of the Rockefeller connection. Until he met Nelson, Al Marshall had been a career civil servant in the government of New York State. Marshall was an ex-Marine, a handsome bear of a man, shrewd and possessed of a strapping ego. In his capacity for instant, flesh-pressing friendship, Marshall reminded one of Lyndon Johnson, if Johnson had had looks, charm and credibility. His talents had come to Rockefeller's attention while Marshall was serving in the elite state Division of the Budget. Marshall succeeded Bill Ronan as secretary to the Governor late in 1966 as Ronan went on to run New York metropolitan mass transportation. After Rockefeller became a presidential candidate in 1968, he temporarily turned over management of the state government to Marshall.

On May 25, Marshall had gone to bed at five o'clock in the morning, after promoting Rockefeller programs up to the last minute as the state legislature raced to adjournment. By 8:00 A.M., Rockefeller was already on the phone calling from New York. "I need you down here." Marshall protested that he had just gone to sleep. "Get a state plane and come down." By noon, Marshall was alone with Nelson in the 55th Street office. There were no softening amenities. Rockefeller, frowning, told Marshall, "The campaign's not going right. The advance works, but nothing else. Emmet is brilliant. But he's not geared to this game. He can't handle the substance side. And he and Henry Kissinger don't get along. Bobby Douglass is fine, but I need him on the road with me. I want you to take over."

Marshall had never managed so much as a campaign for coroner, but Rockefeller was willing to put this new burden on his back precisely because he had demonstrated a capacity to gain control over power structures and change their direction. Marshall, however, was already overseeing the state government and was well aware that Rockefeller could pile on responsibilities until a man broke and then blithely turn to a strong new oak.

"How can I handle both jobs?" Marshall wanted to know.

"Just go down to campaign headquarters. Look it over. Tell me what you think of the organization, the staffing."

Marshall protested, "But I've got my family in Albany. Where would I live?"

"That's no problem," Rockefeller said, waving aside the objection. "You'll stay at my place on Fifth Avenue."

The next day, outside a recording studio, waiting to tape television spots, Rockefeller announced to an unprepared Hughes, Douglass and Hinman, "Al is coming down. He's going to be my guy running the campaign."

Marshall spent his days and evenings managing the campaign and his nights working on welfare policies and water pollution. He returned to Rockefeller's apartment long after midnight, "exhausted and usually starving to death." Rockefeller was on the road campaigning most of the time, and his family was spending the summer at Pocantico. Marshall had the Fifth Avenue triplex and six servants to himself.

"They'd all be asleep by the time I'd get there, and I'd want to raid the fridge. There was plenty of food. But do you think it's like your place or mine where you open the door and there's three slices of shriveled baloney in a plastic bag, a bunch of limp carrots, some apple butter left over for six months? Do you think they've got one of those cookie jars on the counter shaped like a pig where you can stick your hand in? First, I had a hell of a time just finding the kitchen. Then, when I found it, there's this row of stainless-steel lockers, like a hospital. Everything's wrapped and marked. I couldn't throw a damned sandwich together!"

Still, there were compensations. Marshall left his shoes outside his bedroom at night, and in the morning they were shined. Without a word, his clothes were picked up and laundered. He was awakened by a tapping on the door in the morning, and a maid rolled in a tray with his breakfast and the newspapers. She threw back the curtain to let the sun stream in and wished Mr. Marshall a cheery good morning. Al Marshall, from Fenton, Michigan, wondered, "What the hell am I doing here?"

Nelson's problems in 1968 lay in an inherent contradiction. What he was saying to woo the larger public and thus raise himself in the polls—his late-blooming criticism of the war, his oblique attacks on Nixon, his play for college youth, his attention to the Kennedy constituencies of the poor and the black—was endangering the second stage of his strategy, winning prospective Republican delegates. Days before the Republican Convention opened, his campaign suffered a staggering blow. Nelson's plane was en route to New York when one of the staff brought him the results of the latest Gallup Poll. The poll, prematurely released to the Miami *Herald*, showed Nixon beating either Hubert Humphrey or Eugene McCarthy for the Presidency, with Nelson able to do no better than a tie with the two Democrats. His strategy had blown up in his face. Rockefeller slouched low in his seat, his mouth compressed in bitter contemplation. "Nixon or John Mitchell must have gotten to Gallup." He believed until the day he died that this devastating survey had been rigged and deliberately leaked to destroy him on the eve of the convention.

Still, his advisers thought that all was not lost. Two candidates, Nixon and Reagan, were fighting for the conservative mass of Republican delegates. If they split this block, a moderate Rockefeller might still slip between them.

On August 3, 1968, I flew on the Governor's F-27 Fairchild Wayfarer to the Republican Convention in Miami. The country was more deeply divided than at any time since the Civil War, and the face

79

America presented to the world was often contorted, its voice strident and shouting epithets. Yet among the delegates to the Republican Convention, a sweet serenity prevailed. The crowd's wholesome placidity suggested a giant church bazaar, a world untouched by the rioting and dissension swirling outside.

At a cafeteria-style dinner, I sat next to a cheerful Pennsylvania matron wearing a Nixon button. "I thought your delegation was supposed to be in our corner," I said in friendly provocation.

"Oh, but I like Nixon," she beamed.

"You mean you support Nixon," I said. "You admire and respect Nixon."

"That too," she answered. "But I like Dick Nixon." This New York liberal had never heard of people who *liked* Richard Nixon. My smug naïveté began to dissolve.

My dinner companion proved to be well in the majority. It was all over in one ballot—Nixon, 692; Rockefeller, 277; Reagan, 182. Nelson's campaign had cost the Rockefellers $28,881 per delegate. He said later that he knew why he had failed. Characteristically, his account dwelled on the mechanics rather than the character of his defeat. He always found safety in numbers. "Reagan had the solid South, until Mr. Nixon and Mr. Mitchell made a little arrangement with Strom Thurmond." Technically, it was true. Nixon had squeaked by with only twenty-five more votes than needed for nomination. Had Reagan not lost support in the Nixon-Thurmond pact the game might have been protracted another ballot or two. But the assumption that this prolongation would have worked in Nelson's favor was too facile. Something far deeper underlay his defeat. Republican heartlanders were uncomfortable with Nelson Rockefeller. His sophisticated social concerns, his chic eastern internationalism, his grandiose visions and grand spending did not sit well with those Republicans who knew what it was to sweat out a bear market.

A more plausible explanation for his failure is that Nelson Rockefeller was in the wrong party. When asked at a moment of exhaustion-induced candor why he had failed again in 1968, Nelson raised his eyebrows and answered, "Have you ever been to a Republican Convention?" Had he become a Democrat, as Franklin D. Roosevelt was, he would have been that attractive irony, a people's aristocrat. Once over lunch, I had asked if during his service to Roosevelt, FDR had ever encouraged him to change parties. "Yes," he said. "But I never considered it. Harry Truman tried to get me to change at one time when I was down there working for him, too. This was until he fired me from the State Department." Betraying his opinion as to where the Republican Party stood on the continuum of progress, he added, "I would rather try to pull a group forward than hold a group back."

Between the Republican and Democratic conventions, while Nelson Rockefeller was vacationing at his summer home in Seal Harbor, Maine, he received an unusual proposal. Dwayne Andreas, a wealthy friend and confidant of Senator Hubert Humphrey's, acting at Humphrey's direction, called to ask if Nelson would consider running as Vice-President on the Democratic ticket. Rockefeller answered, "You tell Hubert I'm terribly flattered. But I've been a Republican all my life. I can't change now."

Never had he so much as voted for a Democrat: "To tell you the honest truth, I just didn't vote when I got up against it that badly." Nevertheless, he recognized what this congenital party loyalty had cost him. A year after the convention, from the safety of six thousand miles distance, speaking in Spanish in a foreign country, he had this exchange with an Argentine journalist.

REPORTER: "Señor Rockefeller, why were you never elected your country's President?"

ROCKEFELLER: "I was in the wrong party."

He blamed no one else for the 1968 defeat. Flying back from Miami Beach, he wandered down the aisle of the plane consoling his despondent supporters. "You were fine. I just wasn't good enough. I let you down." It was gallant, and largely true.

After Nixon's inauguration, I gave the Governor a few lines that he used in speeches when Henry Kissinger was present: "Three times Henry and I worked on presidential campaigns. And in 1968, we finally made it. Henry went to the White House." Kissinger's career offers the ultimate example of native potential catapulted to its highest possible trajectory by the Rockefeller booster rocket. The story of their meeting is by now familiar—Kissinger was one of several academics whom Rockefeller gathered around him in 1955 when he served as President Eisenhower's special assistant for foreign affairs. The intriguing question is why Kissinger, among that assembly of talents, was able to connect so enduringly with Nelson. The likely answer is that he wanted it most and was best equipped to make it happen.

Henry Kissinger had a respect for power understandable in a refugee from Nazism who had experienced firsthand the fate of the powerless. And he was unlikely to find a more powerful patron than Nelson Rockefeller. He also possessed, in abundance, the combination of brilliance and egotism that Nelson always found entrancing. Kissinger's hard-eyed vision of a world order maintained by counterbalancing powers suited Nelson perfectly, and a romance of foreign-policy soul mates bloomed. In 1956, Kissinger became director of America at Mid-Century, a Rockefeller Brothers Fund Special Studies Project that was one of the more remarkable private efforts ever to influence American international policy. The brothers had pooled their resources and engaged nearly a hundred authorities to explore the next decade. The panel's 1958 report, *Prospect for America*, is extraordinary in that during the 1960 presidential election, both parties lifted from it for their platforms. The very emblem of the Kennedy Administration was taken from a section of the Rockefeller Brothers' report entitled "The New Frontiers."

Henry Kissinger handled foreign policy for Nelson in all his presidential quests. In between, Dr. Kissinger remained on the Harvard faculty, where a professor's modest salary was augmented by Nelson's retainer. The initiatives through which Kissinger made history as Richard Nixon's national security adviser and secretary of state were all foretold in his service to Nelson Rockefeller. On China (from a speech that he drafted for Rockefeller during the 1968 nomination campaign): "We can compete with closed systems best by freely communicating our essential qualities. We need not fear contact with any people—including those from Communist countries . . . we gain nothing by encouraging Communist China's tendency toward self-isolation." And foreshadowing the Nixon era détente (from the same speech): "Our policy should seek to encourage serious and genuine relaxation of tensions. . . . We can afford to lower barriers to encourage the exchange of scientists, educators, journalists, and business-men."

Other Kissinger practices in Washington also dated from his Rockefeller apprenticeship, the "dead key," for example. Nelson Rockefeller's secretaries used the dead key, an earpiece through which they monitored his telephone conversations. I once passed a secretary who was doing the monitoring. She rolled her eyes: "And they call women gossips!" Henry Kissinger, at the National Security Council and as secretary of state, went Nelson one significant step further. He had his stenographers take down his telephone conversations.

Whenever Governor Rockefeller spoke on international affairs, I worked with Nancy Maginnes, his foreign-policy aide. She usually sat engulfed by overspilling file drawers, her long, unpampered blond hair framing a patrician face from which an ever-present cigarette dangled, depositing ashes over her desk. On more formal occasions, she could be elegant, even regal. She was a serious woman, utterly eschewing Kissinger's devices of irony and egocentric wit. I liked her directness and integrity, though her politics were more suited to the British Empire in the nineteenth century than the United States in the twentieth. I particularly admired Nancy's composure during Kissinger's early White House days when the press pantingly reported him escorting a succession of famous beauties. Throughout this period, she behaved with utter indifference. Whether her demeanor rose from a certainty in the strength of her relationship with him or was merely good form, she performed convincingly as a completely secure woman.

In 1973, on the twenty-fifth anniversary of Israel's statehood, I had to draft a congratulatory message for the Governor to send to Tel Aviv, a *pro forma* communication. Rockefeller, however, had gotten it into his head that his message had to be cleared by the White House. I transmitted the language to the National Security Council, then waited for days without an answer. As the deadline for delivering the message neared, I went to Nancy Maginnes to see if she could expedite the matter through her White House connection. She agreed to help, adding, "But I went through Henry's briefcase over the week-end. And I know he doesn't have it."

In March 1974, Nelson Rockefeller was to deliver a speech on inter-American relations, and I began looking for Nancy. Her assistant, Ann Boylan, insisted, unconvincingly, that she had no way to contact her. Time grew short and I grew anxious. Then a grinning Nelson Rockefeller solved the mystery. Henry Kissinger and Nancy Maginnes were on their way to Acapulco, flying to their honeymoon on a jet provided by Nelson.

The bond between Rockefeller and Kissinger went beyond their respect for each other's qualities, the one's intellect and toughness, the other's power and toughness. Above all, they represented to each other the possibilities of America. Kissinger's success, until their meeting, was, for one who had begun as a refugee, solid enough, but not unprecedented. His spectacular rise was achieved after his linkup with Rockefeller. Seen from the historian's perspective, the Rockefellers too had begun in humble circumstances, barely yesterday. America had been the making of them. And one of them, in turn, was now enabling an immigrant college professor to realize his vast potential. Each man was an affirmation to the other of the country's infinite promise. Out of this mutual recognition and respect grew a closeness that Kissinger accurately compared to that between an older and a younger brother.

Much later, in 1977, when both were out of public life, Nelson made sure that Henry would have a place to land, should he need it. Mrs. Whitman showed me through an elegantly refurbished West 55th Street, unrecognizable from its paint-peeled past as the Governor's New York City office. The third floor had been handsomely paneled; luxuriant plants warmed the corners, and Nelson had provided paintings from his collection. All this was for his friend Henry, in case he should ever need an office in New York, which, it turned out, he did not.

When Kissinger published the first volume of his memoirs, the dedication read, "To the memory of Nelson Aldrich Rockefeller," and the first chapter opened appropriately with the account of how Nelson had altered his life.

Richard Nixon's election as President in 1968 allowed Rockefeller to shed the uncomfortable cloak of Vietnam critic. Politically, there was neither need nor advantage in his taking sides openly in the debate over the war, but from time to time, he revealed his sympathies. The matter of Congressman Daniel E. Button is instructive. Button had become the first Republican elected to Congress from New York State's Albany County in almost fifty years. A former newspaper editor, Button had fashioned victory by attacking Albany's O'Connell machine and espousing moderate Republicanism. Early in his first term, he was the chief beneficiary of an Albany fund-raising dinner starring Rockefeller. The Governor spoke first, effusively praising Button as the man who had signaled "a new Republican age" in Albany County. Then Button spoke, including in his remarks the mildest criticism of President Johnson's intensification of the war in Vietnam. Button had barely finished when Rockefeller jumped up and regained the microphone. "Ladies and gentlemen, let's make no mistake," he said with hard, sidelong glances at Button. "At a time of great trial such as this we have got to support our President!"

Thereafter, Button's request for funds from the party's treasury for his re-election campaigns went unanswered. In 1970, he was redistricted by a state legislature controlled by his own party so that he found himself running against a virtually unbeatable Democratic congressman, Sam Stratton, an unremitting hard-liner and a senior member of the House Armed Services Committee. Button lost his seat in Congress.

Rockefeller's attitudes on Vietnam grew out of a reflexive anti-Communism and had deep roots. Before the Second World War, Nelson had begun educating himself in Communist theology. He urged his associates to read a book he had discovered, fascinating, he said, *Das Kapital*, by Karl Marx. The whole nefarious business was spelled out there. He spoke with the wide-eyed earnestness of someone who had just discovered sin. While serving in the Roosevelt Administration, he heard General Stanley D. Embick, who had been chairman of the Inter-American Defense Board, speak on the balance of power in the postwar world. Only two powers, Embick said, would then possess sufficient land mass, manpower and resources to wage a major war—the United States and the Soviet Union. Nelson was indelibly impressed.

He completed his petrification as a Cold Warrior during his service as President Eisenhower's special assistant for foreign affairs. During this time he enjoyed an intimate knowledge of and developed a lasting taste for CIA covert operations. His sympathies did not pass unnoticed at the CIA. Years later, in an unrelated context, I interviewed James Angleton, the agency's mystical high priest in charge of counterintelligence. Angleton confided to me that he had offered to place Nelson in touch with his international labor and Israeli connections should they be useful to the Rockefeller presidential ambitions. To Angleton's disappointment, Nelson had not responded.

Early in his career as governor, Nelson had had the kind of encounter that historians especially savor—when this prince of capitalism met the czar of the proletariat. It was 1960 and Soviet Premier Nikita Khrushchev had come to visit New York City. Nelson, as governor, paid a courtesy call on him at the Soviet Consulate. Afterward, much stimulated, he told the staff about it:

"I went in alone. He must have had seventeen people with him, his children, two psychiatrists. They sort of wanted to study me. The Russian ambassador started out and proposed a toast. They even knew that I didn't drink hard liquor, so they had soft drinks there for me. So, I thought they had done a pretty good job of homework. Then Khrushchev said, 'I want to propose a toast of coexistence.' I said, 'I won't drink to that. I don't believe in it.' And he said, 'What do you mean you don't believe in it?' Well, after that we had a very frank talk. I told him that we had a half million of his people who had come to New York to seek freedom and opportunity, and he said, 'Don't give me that stuff. They only came to get higher wages. I was almost one of them. I gave very serious consideration to coming!' "

At this point in his narrative, Rockefeller leaned back, grinning. "I told Khrushchev, 'If you had come, you would have been the head of one of our biggest unions by now.' "

He discussed the nature of Soviet leadership with a group of visiting White House interns with all the moral certitude of an American Legion keynoter. "They believe that the individual is not a spiritual human being. They don't believe in human dignity and respect for individual rights and equality. We do." For Nelson, the world's political camps divided neatly. Of Egypt, he noted, "It had been under Communist subjugation for eighteen years, and then President Sadat had the courage to throw the Communists out." So much for Arab nationalism of the Gamal Abdel Nasser brand.

Nelson even felt compelled to clarify Henry Kissinger's pursuit of détente, lest the world assume that his protégé had gone soft. "The word 'détente,' relaxation of tensions, has given a false impression that the Soviets are changing or might change their basic concept of world conquest. Of course, this isn't true," he warned.

On Vietnam, he never wavered, even over the widening of the war. In April 1970, Richard Nixon invaded Cambodia, not an event on which a state governor was required to speak out. And, with his own 1970 re-election campaign looming, there was scant profit for Nelson in taking a stand. A key adviser turned in a memo to him urging tactful silence. Nelson tossed it back unread. Instead, he spent a half hour on the phone sympathizing with Nixon over the public's failure to comprehend the wisdom and courage of the President's action. Albany, New York, became possibly the only state capital to issue a statement of public support for the Cambodian invasion. "The gravity of the world situation has been brought into sharp focus by the President's forthright speech tonight," Nelson's statement began, and closed: "Our prayers will be for success and the rapid achievement of a lasting peace."

I heard him render a final judgment on Vietnam a few months after American troops had been withdrawn from the war. We had been discussing, over lunch at the Executive Mansion, the reasons for the antiwar movement, particularly resistance to the draft. "That's easy," Nelson explained. "Those guys just didn't want to get killed." So this was what lay behind the long agony of riot, convulsion and national division, a want of patriotic sacrifice in some of the young. Vietnam was evidently that simple to him.

His hard-lining would undoubtedly be more fashionable today than it was during most of the seventeen years in which he held public office. During that time, he occasionally found his views in style, but more often, he was out of step as national Administrations cooled or warmed in their relations with the Communist sphere. Nelson, meanwhile, remained essentially the constant Cold Warrior.

Chapter VI

THE PRINCE OF POCANTICO

ONE MORNING IN 1971, the conversation in the Governor's conference room turned to acupuncture. The press had reported that James Reston, of *The New York Times*, had undergone an emergency operation while visiting China and had been treated with this ancient therapy at Peking's Anti-Imperialist Hospital. "My grandfather built that hospital," Nelson remarked with a rueful smile. It was true. The hospital had originally been constructed by John D. and given to the people of China as the Peking Union Medical College.

One had a sense that all the world was Nelson's province. The scope of his fortune, an estate of approximately $182 million, including property, investments and trusts, barely suggested his reach. To measure him by the money alone would be to imagine the power of the Catholic Church as the sum of its Sunday collections. Consider this day. Governor Nelson Rockefeller leaves his Pocantico estate at 8:30 A.M. for Manhattan. If he were not immersed in paper work, he would see, through his limousine window, the morning sun splashing on the Hudson River Palisades. These staggeringly beautiful shafts of basalt would have disappeared long ago were it not for his father. John D., Jr., had been horrified to see the Hudson Palisades ground into crushed stone to build Manhattan's towers, and so he bought the surrounding land and gave it to New Jersey. Now the Palisades are preserved forever within the protective boundaries of Palisades Interstate Park.

Nelson glances at his newspaper, which headlines the latest FBI caper. The FBI, in large part, grew out of crime research financed long ago by the Rockefeller family's Bureau of Social Hygiene. For that matter, Rockefeller money underwrote Dr. Alfred Kinsey's study of human sexuality, the Lynds' sociological landmark, *Middletown*, and Margaret Sanger's research of birth control.

Nelson has in his reading file a report from the Brookings Institution, which his family also helped to create. And there is an article he hopes to get to in *Foreign Affairs*, a journal published by the Council on Foreign Relations, which the Rockefellers also helped found.

The car passes a steep hill at the northern tip of Manhattan crowned by The Cloisters. It would pain his father to see the decay into which much of the neighborhood has fallen since Junior built this oasis of urban tranquillity.

Later, at 55th Street, Nelson's first appointment is a courtesy call by the new French consul general for New York. The diplomat is well briefed, and expresses gratitude for the Rockefellers' part in perpetuating the glories of his homeland. Nelson knows that he is referring to the vast Rockefeller contributions that helped reconstruct Versailles and the Cathedral at Rheims after World War I.

He receives a call from Happy. "Yes, Sweetie. Of course, I knew he'd love it." A member of the family has just returned from a visit to California's Redwood National Park, then Jackson Hole, in the Grand Tetons, and finally Tennessee's Great Smoky Mountains National Park. The young Rockefeller, Happy reports, was treated royally everywhere. Why not? Rockefeller philanthropy saved these natural wonders.

In the afternoon, Nelson is to make a speech commemorating U.N. Day. He searches the text in vain for mention of how the U.N. headquarters came to be where it is. He loves that story. The speech writer is probably unaware of it. In 1946, the nascent United Nations was on the point of abandoning all hope of a permanent home in New York City. In a frantic eleventh-hour feat, Nelson found a tract on

Turtle Bay and convinced his father to buy the land for $8.5 million and to donate it to the world organization. The old man was relieved to get out of the matter by money alone. His impetuous son had already offered the theater at Rockefeller Center for meetings of the U.N. General Assembly and had urged the family to donate Pocantico as the permanent U.N. site.

Returning up FDR Drive after the U.N. ceremony, Nelson glances briefly at the stream of planes approaching La Guardia Airport. Several bear the markings of Eastern Airlines, the line brother Laurance helped to found. Laurance is Eastern's major individual stockholder.

Nelson's driver expertly cuts ahead of a Lincoln Continental, all the while admiring the car's contours. His passenger could tell him something about that classic design. In 1934, Nelson worked briefly at the Paris offices of the Chase Bank. While there, he was dazzled by a French automobile of flowing sculpture. The next summer, at Seal Harbor, he described the car to his neighbor Edsel Ford. "Could you get just the body sent over for me and mount it on a Ford chassis?" he asked. Ford agreed, and the result became the prototype of the Lincoln Continental. Nelson still had the original at his place in Maine.

Back at the office, Nelson has to handle a hot potato. He wants to use surplus revenues from the public authority that operates New York's toll bridges and tunnels to help relieve the subway deficit. But the bank that is trustee for the bondholders of the authority has brought suit declaring that this diversion would violate the bondholders' rights. Nelson will have to talk over this ticklish matter with the bank's chairman. He asks his secretary to get the banker, his brother David, at Chase Manhattan.

It has been a long day and it is not yet over. Nelson has promised to take Happy to the theater this evening. He is easily bored and always restless there, but he loves the setting, the enchanting airiness of Lincoln Center. Although Lincoln Center is really brother Johnny's show, the rest of the family contributed nearly $30 million to build it, and Nelson managed to wangle another $15 million out of the state for the Center's New York State Theater. Later the limousine glides away from Lincoln Center and makes its way crosstown.

He is relieved that they do not have to drive all the way back to Pocantico. Tonight they will be staying at their three-story apartment on Fifth Avenue.

We were having a dinner meeting at the Pocantico estate. After dessert, one of the staff pulled a candelabrum close and lit his cigarette from it. Nelson peered over his glasses. "We have matches for that." His tone lowered the room temperature perceptibly.

Pocantico was his refuge, and Kykuit, the main house, Nelson Rockefeller's castle. His dominance in the family is suggested by the fact that Kykuit had originally been his grandfather's home, then his father's, and finally, of the five brothers, Nelson's. There were seventy-one other homes at Pocantico. Most of them, modest dwellings occupied by Rockefeller associates and employees, were clustered in the tiny hamlet of Pocantico Hills, part of the estate. The ten Rockefeller family homes were located within 150 acres called the Park, set off by an eight-foot wrought-iron fence topped by two feet of barbed wire. Nelson's Kykuit overshadowed all the other homes in size and grandeur. John III lived in a French château, handsome, yet reflecting its owner's diffidence. Laurance, the most modern Rockefeller, built a contemporary home, Kent House, of white brick. David occupied Hudson Pines, which he had bought from his sister, Babs, after her divorce. Winthrop, riding against tradition and paternal pressure, did not have a home at Pocantico.

New York suburbanites are forever comparing the horrors of their commutes into the city. It would have been difficult to improve on Nelson's thirty-five minutes by chauffeured limousine from midtown Manhattan to 6.5 square miles of sculptured parkland along the Hudson River. His estate was one place where the pragmatic Nelson exhibited a sense of history. When he elevated Joe Canzeri from advance man to manager of Pocantico, he told him: "My father built this place for his father. There is nothing like it anywhere in America. Your job is to keep it that way."

When John D., Jr., began Kykuit in 1907, he gave his architect a challenge of subtle complexity. "I want a residence so simple that any friends visiting my father would be impressed by the homelikeness and simplicity of the house. While those who are familiar with and appreciate fine design and beautiful furnishings would say, 'How exquisitely beautiful.' " The architect got it half right; one searches in vain for the homelikeness and simplicity.

The cadence of life at Pocantico during the lifetime of John D., Jr., suggests both the solidity and the absence of spontaneity in the family. As long as Junior lived and occupied Kykuit, his sons took turns in having Sunday dinner at the big house with him. Marriage and the arrival of their own children did not alter this custom. They then brought their families, following the same order of visitation as regularly as the seasons follow each other.

Pocantico proved a boon to the fortunes of the Republican Party in New York. Every fall, Nelson invited members of the Governor's Club to lunch on the estate, their reward for putting up a $500 annual membership fee, which went toward supporting the state GOP organization. Though the Governor's Club was purely a fund-raising device, the Rockefeller association gave it a distinct social cachet. I remember my amusement when a business acquaintance asked me if I could wangle him an invitation into the club. "I'll do my damnedest," I had replied, "if you've got five hundred dollars."

At one of these Pocantico outings I skipped the post-luncheon rhetoric and took the opportunity to explore the grounds. The formal gardens around Kykuit revealed the cultural gulf between Nelson and his father. Junior's acquisitions—a Renaissance fountain by Giovanni da Bologna and powerful sculptures by George Grey Barnard, *The Hewer, The Rising Woman* and *Adam and Eve*—stood alongside Nelson's choices—coolly modern works by Brancusi, Arp and Calder. The farm roads that had once laced Pocantico had long since been obliterated and relocated. I soon realized why. I followed a lane that disappeared into a forest; then, suddenly, the road opened again atop a high ridge, spreading Long Island Sound at the viewer's feet. With another turn it dove between thick hedges before bursting onto a vista embracing miles of the Hudson River. Another sharp curve and the towers of Manhattan rose. These visual delights had been ingeniously engineered into the seventy miles of roadway.

The Governor's Club members had been served lunch that day in the Playhouse. Have no fear of grown men and women crouched over toy furniture. The Playhouse dining area seated three hundred comfortably. Also under the same roof were an indoor tennis court, pool, gymnasium and bowling alleys.

Jim Cannon, a Rockefeller colleague, remembered his family's Pocantico summer. The Cannons had been invited to use one of the main houses in the Park while Jim worked on a special project with Nelson. Cannon's children and various young Rockefellers spent their days horseback riding, swimming, playing tennis. Nelson also provided a Datsun roadster so that the older children could be taught to drive. His two youngest sons, then twelve and ten, had already learned in this way on the estate's roads. At noon, the Pocantico staff set up a snack bar where the young people ordered cheeseburgers, Cokes and shakes, just like on the outside, except that at the Pocantico Burger King no money changed hands.

Carl Spad's family occupied another Pocantico house while Carl worked to defeat Congressman Ogden "Brownie" Reid, a Westchester neighbor who had offended Nelson by shifting from the Republican to the Democratic Party. Spad found it a pleasant assignment. When he had to entertain local politicos, he called Joe Canzeri, and a bar and barman appeared along with trays of refreshment. Should Spad's eye become jaded, workmen replaced the paintings in the house with others from Nelson's collection.

Pocantico was hardly the model of simple elegance that Nelson's father had envisaged, but life there took on surprisingly simple touches. When those of us on the staff came to work at Kykuit, no phalanx of servants appeared. The door opening, coat taking, drink mixing and meal serving were all accomplished by one houseman. Nelson employed no valet and Happy had no personal maid. The small staff performed almost invisibly, moving in, completing their tasks noiselessly, and quickly withdrawing. Nelson spoke French to the houseman and Spanish to most of the maids. At home, he took a stubborn pride in looking after himself in certain matters. He insisted, for example, on packing his own bags, and took great pride in a method he had learned from his father that promised two relatively wrinkle-free suits.

During one Pocantico lunch, as the houseman poured the wine

and I eyed the bottle with evident curiosity, he obligingly peeled back the napkin to reveal the label, Calon-Ségur, '67, a highly respected Médoc third growth, but not inordinately expensive.

Anne-Marie Rasmussen, the Pocantico maid who later married Nelson's son Steven, recalled a Christmas tradition at Kykuit when she still had the downstairs perspective on the Rockefellers. All the servants lined up in the front hall sitting room, where they could admire the Christmas tree. Each member of the family then thanked them personally, and the servants were presented with an envelope. Anne-Marie, new to the staff in 1956, found $10 in her envelope. Older hands received $20.

Pocantico was virtually the only place where Nelson Rockefeller *played*. He had given up tennis years before, and now, on weekends, he played the estate's eighteen-hole golf course, usually with Laurance or his two young boys. Occasionally, his partner was Bobby Douglass. "He was pretty good, but erratic," Douglass found. "We played for silver dollars. His brother David told Nelson just before silver dollars went out of circulation that they would probably go up in value. So he and Laurance bought a few bags. They used them to settle their golf bets. Nelson was a tough competitor, but not so tough that he didn't want a few strokes after I began to take some of those dollars." Whenever Nelson had to give up any of the coins, he would remark grudgingly, "Do you know what yesterday's quote on these was? Three dollars and twenty-nine cents each!"

He took his recreation in short bursts, two hours at the most on a weekend. Then it was back to the house to lay down a barrage of telephone calls in preparation for the week ahead. He had a thick black address book and put through his own calls whenever at home.

Life became simpler for him at Pocantico. Not simple, but simpler. He had, at various times, Chrysler, Lincoln and Cadillac limousines on the estate and thirty-seven restored antique cars in running order. One year Nelson gave Happy a Rolls-Royce costing, at the time, $33,000. The car hardly ever left Pocantico, serving essentially to get her from one Rockefeller house to another. A bit extravagant, wasn't it, an aide teased him. Nelson shrugged. "We're getting along, you know. It's time to start having a little fun." For himself, he preferred driving the grounds in his favorite, a '65 Mustang, for which he dressed appropriately. "I thought he was a laborer," Norm Hurd, the state budget director, recalled of one Pocantico visit. "I walked right past him." Nelson's outdoor weekend dress was a forty-year-old sport jacket, shapeless slacks and gnarled shoes.

But the man with the threadbare elbows and baggy pants remained ever the Hudson River patroon. "He'd walk me around and never stop," Joe Canzeri recalled. " 'Deepen the pond. Transplant the hedges. Sharpen the boys' ice skates. Seal the windows in the orangery. And remind me to call Henry Kissinger.' I scribbled it all down in a notebook because he never forgot anything."

I watched Nelson perform as squire at his Washington home on Foxhall Road. He had thrown a party there for the Washington press corps. More than a hundred journalists roved the pampered lawns, nibbling canapés and swiftly emptying trays of drinks, while a roving trio of Latin musicians serenaded. Between handshakes, grins and winks for his guests, Rockefeller was muttering to Canzeri, who had arranged this seemingly flawless evening. Evidently not all that unflawed, for Rockefeller was pointing angrily to something in the distance. He then melted among his visitors. A harried Canzeri dispatched an assistant in the direction of Nelson's unhappiness. Joe turned to me with a hopeless shrug. "He says a goddamned *log* is showing!" I peered out across the carpeted acres, across a pond and into the trees, and sure enough, I could barely distinguish the tip of a felled tree. It was the "five-percent rule" in action. Nelson was forever reminding Canzeri of the maxim passed on to him by his father. "The first ninety-five percent is always easy. It's the last five percent that produces perfection. And that's what I'm after."

Kykuit was apparently not enough home for Nelson at Pocantico. He had long admired the architecture of the East. In the early 1970s, he brought Junzo Yashimuro from Tokyo to design a Japanese house. In his quest for fidelity, Nelson also arranged for eight Japanese carpenters to emigrate temporarily to build the house. The workers arrived with improper documentation and had to be deported, which briefly spawned a spate of "Japanese wetback" stories around the office. Nelson arranged their re-entry, and the house was completed for a relatively modest $650,000. The Rockefellers used it principally for guests and occasional entertainments. Nelson's contention, all along, was that he had built the house for Happy. Thus they continued to live at Kykuit, and she did not move into the Japanese house until after Nelson died.

Soon after the new house had been completed, Harry Albright, who served Nelson in several key posts, was invited with his wife, Joan, to have a drink there with the Rockefellers and other friends. Nelson had set up a guest book and asked everyone to sign it. Albright scanned the signatures and spotted the name of one earlier guest particularly qualified to judge the house's authenticity, the Emperor Hirohito. Anwar Sadat, Lord Louis Mountbatten, King Hussein, the Shah's wife, Empress Farah Diba—all of them came as his personal guests, not as state visitors.

Nelson was an attentive host to less exalted callers at Pocantico. Al Marshall and Norm Hurd arrived there exhausted and freezing at two-thirty in the morning after abandoning their state car nearby during a blizzard. Nelson alerted his servants to stay up to tend to the needs of his two associates. At eight o'clock the next morning, he bounded cheerily into their bedroom, his arms heaped with spare clothes, razors, toothbrushes, soap and towels. He held up a pair of belled corduroy pants before his scholarly state budget director. "Try these, Norm. I got them at Brigitte Bardot's boutique in the south of France last summer. They're too tight on me now. If they fit you, keep them." Hurd happily did.

In November 1976, the President of the United States visited Pocantico. At his side was his Vice-President and lord of this manor. Jerry Ford had come, at Nelson's prompting, to dedicate Pocantico as a National Historical Landmark. The designation did not mean that tourist crowds could now troop through Kykuit as they did Mount Vernon or Independence Hall. Pocantico was to remain the Rockefellers' private preserve, but now it had been recognized as a monument of American history.

Pocantico resembled a subdued Eden with its discreet abundance and the instant fulfillment of wants which the staff met with an unobtrusive competence. One might well wonder if being reared in these gardens of unfailing peace and plenty affected one's religious needs and outlook. In Nelson's case, the case of the astronauts' visit was instructive.

On December 24, 1968, Frank Borman, James A. Lovell, Jr., and William Anders, the Apollo 8 astronauts, became the first men to circumnavigate the moon. The nation, weary of war in Vietnam, hungry for undiluted heroism, eagerly embraced these conquerors of the heavens. New York City welcomed them with a parade up Fifth Avenue. Nelson Rockefeller ordered a state dinner in the astronauts' honor at the Waldorf Astoria Hotel. The staff plunged into frenzied effort, and within two days, more than two thousand invitations were mailed to a blue-ribbon guest list. The task was expedited by a master card file of names that the Governor maintained, indicating addresses, phone numbers, spouses, children, and level of intimacy (General Almerin C. O'Hara: "Dear Buz").

The matter of footing the bill, estimated at $60,000, was resolved with Nelsonian flair. The occasion was to be a state dinner and consequently, Nelson reasoned, a state expense. His only obstacle was the required advance approval of the state comptroller, Arthur Levitt, who had cultivated a reputation for a tight fist. Rockefeller called Levitt to inform him that he had just approved a pending increase in the comptroller's expense allowance. And, by the way, wasn't it marvelous what these three brave men had done for the country's prestige and spirit and, of course, shouldn't the Empire State pay them a fitting tribute? Levitt swiftly agreed.

On the day of the dinner, I was called into the Governor's office to go over the text for the event, which I had prepared. "You left out God!" he said in the now familiar accusing tone which suggested that a staff member was deliberately out to sabotage him. With another man, I might have raised an issue I found intriguing—whether space exploration strengthened or weakened the basis of conventional religious belief. A case could be made that these cosmic probes demystified the universe, made it more explainable in terms of chemistry, mathematics and physics, rather than by theology and faith. But this kind of philosophical soul-searching bored Nelson Rockefeller. And so, I merely waited for him to think out loud. "What these men have done shows the power of God, what He's created." His eyes filled with wonder. "That's just as important as the exploration business. Work up something like that for tonight."

That evening, in the glittering ballroom of the Waldorf Astoria, he spoke with deep emotion: "Above all, this voyage has done more to restore our faith in God than any event of our time. For it has demonstrated the divine order of the universe. God has given us the privilege of understanding a little more than we did before about the order that prevails out there."

Chapter VII

MISSION FOR NIXON

In 1968 JIM CANNON was a senior editor at *Newsweek*, an astute political observer, Alabama-born, handsome, with infinite charm and the raconteur's gift. A good ole boy with class. He first covered Rockefeller for a *Newsweek* cover story in 1958, then in presidential campaigns and at governors' conferences. He was intrigued at the way Rockefeller dominated his family, his fellow governors, his political associates, yet stumbled so badly on the presidential trail.

That winter, shivering in the New Hampshire snows as he covered the presidential primary, Cannon made a decision. This was to be his last political hurrah from the stands. The time had come to get down onto the field. As a well-connected journalist, Cannon easily arranged an appointment with the Governor some months later and told Nelson he wanted to work for him. Rockefeller made a guarded commitment. Weeks passed during which Cannon heard nothing. Then, just before Christmas, Cannon and his wife, Cherie, were invited to dinner with Nelson and Happy at 21 in Manhattan. The evening was cordial, even casual. Still, Cannon had a sense that he and Cherie were being auditioned. As the dinner concluded, something else amused him. When Nelson Rockefeller dined at 21, nothing so vulgar as a check intruded.

Matters thereafter moved quickly. One Friday in January 1969, Jim Cannon, still a senior editor at *Newsweek*, was invited to fly to Watertown, New York, with Rockefeller. By Monday morning he was a special assistant to the governor of New York at a desk at 55th Street, with an odd assignment for a state official.

Three days after his inauguration as President, Richard Nixon had called Rockefeller and had asked him to undertake a special mission. The President had just talked to Galo Plaza, secretary-general of the Organization of American States, and had asked him the single best move that he could make to develop a successful policy toward Latin America.

"Send Nelson Rockefeller there," answered Galo. "His name is magic."

Rockefeller was cautiously flattered by the unexpected request. He had, in one way or another, served every American President in his day, except for Jack Kennedy. Now his old nemesis was calling on him. But Nixon might have ulterior motives; suspicious staff aides wondered if the President wanted Rockefeller to taste the hospitality that Nixon had known in 1958 as Vice-President, when he had been stoned and spit upon in Latin America.

Though he approached the proposition warily, Nelson Rockefeller was not a man to turn down the President. On that plane ride to Watertown with Jim Cannon, Rockefeller drafted the terms under which he would accept the assignment. The trip must be designated a "presidential mission." He was to be provided with presidential aircraft. He would tolerate no State Department interference. Indeed, Rockefeller was to have total control over who accompanied him and whom he saw in Latin America. He asked Cannon to give him a hand in drafting his letter to Nixon. Then, much to Cannon's surprise, when this task was completed, Rockefeller started to write the reply that the President was to send to him agreeing to Rockefeller's terms. Thus was Cannon introduced to Nelson's operating style.

"Keep it small. Keep it small," the secretary of state warned repeatedly when Rockefeller met with Nixon to discuss the final shape of the Latin-American mission. Rockefeller was undaunted by Nixon's newly named man at State, William Rogers. His entrée to the White House on foreign policy was his own protégé, Henry Kissinger, now national security director. "If I'm going to do this right, I'm going to need enough expert advisers" was Rockefeller's stubborn counterrefrain to Rogers' cautions. Nixon kept his own counsel. But on one point, he and Rockefeller gleefully agreed as they rivaled each other in defaming the State Department in front of the man whom Nixon had just named to head it. "Mediocre." "Unimaginative." "Spineless." The two old battlers pounced on a handy common prejudice as they strove mightily to like each other.

Nixon, however, was unprepared for Rockefeller's grand vision of the mission. He had imagined a single airplane touching down at half a dozen major capitals, where Rockefeller would confer privately with key Latin leaders and report back to him. The whole business should take two weeks at most. Rockefeller, however, assigned Jim Cannon to organize an invasion. Experts were recruited from agriculture, education, economics, women's rights, and sixteen other fields. Nelson intended to visit every one of the twenty-three nations between the Rio Grande and Tierra del Fuego.

Cannon, for the first time, experienced the vicarious clout of the Rockefeller name. Mexican Foreign Office bureaucrats emphatically rejected his request that President Gustavo Díaz Ordaz meet Governor Rockefeller on the Sunday on which he was to arrive in Mexico City. The Mexican leader's Sundays, they said, must be kept free. Cannon fretted for a while and then had his secretary place a call directly to the president's office. "Mr. James Cannon calling for Governor Nelson Rockefeller." Díaz Ordaz came on the line. Of course, he would be honored to meet Governor Rockefeller on his arrival.

Nancy Maginnes' crew, out-of-work ballerinas, aspiring actors and budding playwrights, produced thick fact books for each country, studded with crop statistics and industrial output and explaining the nice distinctions between the Partido Radical Conservador and the Partido Conservador Radical. An advance team of seventeen fanned out weeks before the mission to remove every pebble in Rockefeller's path. They worked places like Tegucigalpa, Quito and Managua with a thoroughness suggesting that Nelson Rockefeller was campaigning for *jefe del estado*. I traveled with the advance team and was given cram courses by U.S. embassy staff on each nation's culture, mores, heroes and history, to enable me to write Rockefeller's arrival speeches. "Bolívar was right when he said, 'If the world chose a capital, it would have to be Panama.'" "In the Nobel Prize awarded in 1967 to Miguel Angel Asturias, the world justly honored Guatemalan letters." "We saw your growing economic might when the two millionth Brazilian-made vehicle rolled off the São Paulo assembly line." We could have gone to the State Department to have the speeches translated, but that was unnecessary. Flor Brennan, the family's own translator at Rockefeller Center, did the job.

Nelson Rockefeller's love for Latin America was genuine and rare among major American political figures. The raw vitality and wild beauty of this world had won him during his early manhood. So much of Latin America was unfinished, rich in resources and people, a continent virtually begging for development. Here Nelson's penchant for practical dreaming, for grand schemes of uplift-via-free-enterprise, could enjoy full sway. And Galo Plaza was right. His name was still magic to the oligarchies, the *latifundistas*, the conservative, U.S.-educated, old-family ruling classes in Latin America. But to the Latin left, his name was anathema.

The presidential mission to Latin America got off to a shaky start. In Guatemala, the CIA warned Rockefeller not to stay overnight in the capital and not to ride around the streets. Nelson and numerous advisers thus were forced to meet their Guatemalan counterparts in a tropical boondock.

In the Dominican Republic, his Secret Service bodyguards told him to keep his windows rolled up during the motorcade through the capital city of Santo Domingo. Local anti-gringos had a habit of lobbing grenades at such tempting targets. "Absolutely not," Rockefeller retorted. "The last thing I'm going to do is hide from the people behind bulletproof glass like dictators I've known down here." He ostentatiously rolled down the window, and Jim Cannon, riding with him, involuntarily shared his bravado. Up front, the Secret Service men's windows remained firmly shut.

In Honduras, the police killed a demonstrator among a mob of anti-American students. Rockefeller was determined to talk directly to the crowd. The Secret Service tried to hold him back, but he shook off his protectors and moved into the tense throng alone. He debated animatedly in Spanish with the students. Afterward, he remarked, "See. Nobody laid a hand on me. But somebody lifted my wallet."

"In all the years I worked for him, the hardest thing I ever had to do was deliver the word on Venezuela," Jim Cannon later recalled. "We were in Trinidad and the next stop was Caracas. I'd just been informed by the Venezuelan government that they could not guarantee his safety. They were uninviting him. He was having lunch at the time. He looked up at me as though I'd struck him. Then he said, 'After all that country has meant to me. And all I've done for them?' He shook his head. 'This is a terrible blow.' "

The American press maintained a drumfire of criticism about the trip, and Nelson faced rising pressure to break it off. But this combative personality would never cancel the mission. Nelson Rockefeller tended to become more intractable in the face of criticism.

Argentina proved the worst. As the Rockefeller party arrived, seventeen IBEC-owned supermarkets were still smoldering. The fires had been ignited by urban guerrillas who placed incendiary devices in the caps of toothpaste tubes and hair spray and shaving-cream cans on the store shelves. Ten thousand troops stood guard in Buenos Aires. A labor leader was machine-gunned as Rockefeller met with Argentine officials. When Nelson told the Argentines that he intended to meet with opposition and student leaders, they objected vociferously. The Secret Service had also ruled out a meeting he had planned with left-wing students. Rockefeller, however, slipped out a back corridor of his hotel with a handful of aides and spent an hour with six young leftist leaders in a private apartment. They studied him with disbelief, as though unable to accept that the living symbol of all they abhorred was actually with them in a small middle-class living room. He spoke in Spanish, which helped dissolve the tension, as he answered their politely phrased but increasingly probing questions. He and the students parted as philosophically distant as ever, but with friendly handshakes. Outside, this great city of three million lay under a pall. Streets were dark and deserted, and the atmosphere was of a nation on the brink of civil war.

The hostility toward him from the Latin left was not without foundation. His first service in Latin America years before under President Franklin Roosevelt had been intended to help quarantine the hemisphere from Nazism. Yet, as the Allies triumphed, it became clear that it was not so much totalitarianism that Nelson opposed but regimes or ideologies hostile to the United States. With the war won, he dismissed the claims of some State Department advisers that Latin fascists were regaining influence. The danger, he believed, was not resurgent fascism, but communism, and he had not altered that view in the intervening quarter century.

Innocent of his tolerance of rightist Latin regimes, I was to be badly burned. In Panama, I had been given a quick course in the country's history by Panamanian employees of the U.S. Information Service. They were, at first, uncomfortably deferential, peddling a Pollyannaish vision of harmony between Panama and the Yankee giant with its foot planted across their isthmus. When they came to trust me more, they urged that Governor Rockefeller, in his arrival speech, say something supporting an eventual return to democracy in Panama. Not criticism of the current regime, but just a quiet brief for political freedom. I checked the suggestion with embassy officials who concurred.

Thus, in the draft, I included: "Under the firm pledge of your present government to return to the blessings of democracy, I know that Panama will progress even more swiftly and surely in the future." I cabled the full text to the Governor, in New York.

On the next stop, in Rio de Janeiro, I had dinner with Brazilian friends whom I had known from my tour there as a USIA foreign service officer years before. The husband was a businessman, his wife, a high-level, longtime employee of the American embassy. Hardly bomb tossers, they were roughly the equivalent of middle-of-the-road Republicans. They surprised me with their vehement opposition to the dictatorship then ruling Brazil. They cited harrowing cases of friends who had been tortured or jailed without explanation or who had simply disappeared. They too urged me to have Rockefeller, as the American President's representative, say something favoring democracy. And again I included the point in my draft remarks, this time in Nelson's speech for his arrival at Brasilia.

When he saw the Panamanian and Brazilian drafts, he was furious. "Don't you understand? That's exactly what these people resent, our sticking our noses into their business, Americans trying to tell them how to run their internal affairs." I assumed that he referred to the resentments of those in power rather than those in the political prisons. The passages supporting a return to democracy were removed from the speeches.

During the Panama visit, he was utterly charmed by the young *caudillo* Omar Torrijos. He liked the Panamanian strongman's energy, his up-from-the-people authenticity. Torrijos wanted one thing from the United States at that moment, helicopters, so that he could get around the country more easily. The U.S. State Department had earlier refused, believing that Torrijos would only use them to tighten his grip on the country. Nelson Rockefeller, with a sly grin, disagreed. Panama needed the helicopters for its rural medical programs, he told the State Department people. Omar Torrijos got his helicopters.

"Let me say a word about the gentleman who has been referred to as a tinhorn dictator," he said later. "This is a self-made man, a poor boy who went into the army because that was the only way he could get an education. There is no more sincere person in terms of his own country and his objectives."

In a later stop, at Haiti, our embassy officials pleaded with me to omit any mention of the country's bloody-handed dictator, François "Papa Doc" Duvalier, in Rockefeller's speeches. When I told them that I had to include the man's name somewhere in the text, one attaché suggested, "Well, just have Rockefeller say how delighted he is to be here at beautiful Duvalier Airport." In the final text, Papa Doc was mentioned only slightly more prominently. I also mentioned at our initial meeting with the U.S. Embassy staff that the Governor's practice in each country had been to meet with the opposition as well as the government. The ambassador answered, "In Haiti he'll have to do it in the cemetery." What the newspapers and television did feature of the mission's arrival in Haiti was Nelson Rockefeller on a balcony, a wide grin on his face and his arm around that luckless nation's "president for life."

Nelson believed that political norms in North and South America had to be judged by different standards. As he told a reporter: "By working with the group that is in power, we can do more to encourage the restoration of democratic institutions than we can by having nothing to do with them or openly talking against them." Long afterward, speaking in a closed session with a group of U.S. military wives in Washington, he was more blunt. "A great many of my friends down there say that democracy is really impossible today in those countries because in a democracy you cannot control the organized subversion, guerrilla activity and so forth. . . . So they either go communist or to a military dictatorship."

On September 3, 1969, seven months after the mission had been announced, Nelson Rockefeller presented his Latin-American report to Richard Nixon. Considering the chaotic course of the trip, the product that emerged from it was surprisingly sound. The report represented Nelson's pragmatism at its keenest. He had come away believing that the old pillars of the status quo—the Latin church and the military—were changing, moving along progressive and reformist lines. Since military regimes were apparently congenital in Latin America, he urged that the course of reason was to learn to live with these governments rather than isolate them. He did not spare American businesses whose exploitive behavior stirred Latino antagonisms. He called for more open U.S. markets for the region's products and recommended preferential trade advantages and generous refinancing of Latin America's foreign debt.

Shortly afterward, he told the National Press Club, "To quote the press reaction of last summer, the trip was 'ill-conceived,' 'ill-timed,' 'a personal humiliation' and should have been canceled. But, since my report came out in October, the press has described it, and I quote, as 'deserving high marks,' 'expert counsel,' 'most helpful' and 'a sharp analysis of the situation in the Western Hemisphere.' I therefore congratulate you. Any American institution that could learn that much in just a few months can't be all bad."

Richard Nixon, however, barely raised a finger to implement the Rockefeller recommendations. It was not, Rockefeller ruefully concluded, entirely Nixon's fault. Nelson had never been able to infect his friend Henry Kissinger with his own passion for Latin America; and Henry was now largely shaping the Nixon foreign policy.

It was late in the year, and Nelson's interest was necessarily turning to 1970 and the need to decide whether he should run for an unprecedented fourth term as governor of New York. He had committed his reputation and $750,000 of his own money to this effort to create a fresh U.S.-Latin American rapport. The result was stillborn. In the end, the IRS informed him that even his expenses in this cause were not deductible.

Two years later, I witnessed part of the reason for his love of Latin America. My wife and I had planned a vacation on the Caribbean coast of Venezuela, and when the Governor learned of the trip, he suggested, "Why not visit the ranch for a few days?" Why not, indeed.

We spent some days on the beach, then went to the Hotel Tamanaco in Caracas to await a man who was to take us to Monte Sacro, Nelson's spread. While at the hotel, we received a call from Bill Coles, who had been described to me as "Nelson's man in Venezuela." Coles was a Dartmouth classmate of Nelson's, swept up early in the Rockefeller wake and deposited in this country to look after Nelson's interests. Coles and his wife had lived most of their lives and had raised their children in Venezuela. He invited us to visit him at his home in an elegant Caracas suburb.

That night he told us how, years before, Nelson had proposed something different for their college class reunion. The whole Dartmouth class of '30 was invited to come down to the ranch, as his guests, of course. A good number of alums made it and had a grand old time. In the meanwhile, their host was caught up in a competing enthusiasm at home. Nelson picked up the tab but missed his own party.

The Rockefellers had Bill Coleses all over the world, people whose lives had crossed their paths at some point and thereafter never left their orbit. In Brazil, or Hawaii, or Tehran, there was always Nelson's man or Laurance's or David's. I once heard a speech delivered by a man who gave as his professional title "Associate of Laurance Rockefeller." An odd umbilical, I thought.

The day after our visit to Bill Coles, we met Sam Scillitani, who had come up from the ranch to get us. We drove through jagged, verdant mountains into the Venezuelan interior where, three hours later, we arrived at Monte Sacro, located on a site where the Great Liberator, Simón Bolívar, had once lived. The nineteen-thousand-acre ranch was a sharp-toothed bowl, ringed by mountains and flat at the bottom, except for a small rise in the middle. On this high center ground, Rockefeller had built a Spanish-mission-style home. From the house, one looked out over a 360-degree panorama of cultivated fields to the surrounding mountain wall that defined his property.

Sam Scillitani was the ranch's business manager and lived with his family in a house nearby. Our full-time host now became George Baker, the ranch manager, an affable aggie type, twenty-five years on Nelson's South American payroll. Baker lived in a wing of the main house at Monte Sacro with his wife and children. We were given another wing as our quarters.

Early the next morning, Baker took us on a Jeep tour. The ranch was no rich man's plaything, but rather an avocation designed to pay. Rockefeller was a serious *latifundista*. There were herds of Brahman cattle, and vast fields planted in corn and potatoes. Nelson's latest and most promising crop was chili peppers. We entered a storehouse piled high with casks from which rose an eye-searing miasma. The casks held pressed peppers then being sold in competition with Louisiana growers to the McIlhenny firm for its Tabasco sauce.

Dotting the ranch were wooden cabins, neat and white, built by Nelson for the *campesinos* who worked on Monte Sacro. We visited the school that Rockefeller provided for the peasants' children, and nearby saw a trainer working with Happy's horse in preparation for her next visit. On the way back up the hill to the main house, we passed a simple stucco chapel. "It's for the workers," George Baker explained. "Every Sunday we bring in a *padre* from the village near here to say Mass." The interior, scrubbed white, had the austerity of a New England meetinghouse. Great fifteenth-century wooden candelabra brought from Spain flanked a small altar. Early-eighteenth-century religious canvases hung from the whitewashed walls. Its absent landlord had decorated this tiny part-time chapel with more valuable art than most towns in the United States possess.

In the evening, we sat by the pool in the courtyard of the house, sipping Bloody Marys piquant with Rockefeller tabasco sauce. When I expressed my surprise to George Baker that the ranch was so serious a commercial venture, he told us that Monte Sacro was just one of four ranches that Nelson owned in Venezuela. On them, agricultural history had been made. At one, Rockefeller had introduced the cultivation of rice to Venezuela; on another, he was raising the capybara, a dog-size rodent valuable for its hide.

It was all in the Rockefeller tradition. A working farm fulfilled a streak of economic puritanism in the family. Make your pleasures pay, or at least provide tax losses. Oil, Manhattan real estate, banking, tabasco peppers, and leather from super-rats. Diversification indeed. And back at 30 Rockefeller Plaza somebody was counting it all up, the chili peppers, the rat hides.

The eaves of the courtyard were ringed in lights, chockablock, covering the entire perimeter. I asked Baker why they were not turned on. He smiled. "Nelson had the architect Philip Johnson down here once. They were sitting out the way we are now and Johnson got talking about hanging a 'curtain of light' around the courtyard. So Nelson had all these lamps put in. It must have cost him fifty thousand dollars. And every time we turn on the damn things, the power drain knocks out the generators."

The house as well as the ranch was fully staffed, cooks, maids, gardeners, the trainer for Happy's horse. Nelson Rockefeller could have shown up on fifteen minutes' notice and have received the same solicitous care here as at his triplex on Fifth Avenue or at Pocantico. At the time of our visit, he had not been to Monte Sacro for nearly four years.

Chapter VIII

THE PEOPLE
AROUND THE MAN

RETURNING FROM A TRIP to the Lyndon Johnson White House, Nelson leaned back in his seat on the plane and grinned contentedly: "LBJ said he wished he had a staff as good as mine." Years later, after taking a similar road show to perform before President Nixon on drug legislation, he beamed: "Nixon wanted to know why he can't get the kind of people I have."

He fairly salivated in the presence of talent, and he collected people with the same acquisitive zeal as he did Chinese porcelains. His staffs, throughout his various incarnations—as federal official, political candidate, New York governor and Vice-President—were conceded to be first-rate. It is simplistic to say that he got the best because he could afford them. Often he recruited people into government at unimpressive public-service salaries. Another magnetic force was at work. As Jim Cannon saw it, "Nelson Rockefeller gave you the feeling that you had become part of an enterprise larger than yourself."

The experience of Edward Logue is illustrative. Ed Logue began 1968 a contented man. He was the most admired urban developer in

America, virtually the first to vindicate the urban theorists who preached that the rotting cores of northeastern cities could be redeemed. Logue did it first in New Haven, where he transformed a fading Italian neighborhood and tumbledown nineteenth-century factories into a balanced community of new homes, new plants, new jobs. The largest downtown development in America—the $2 billion enterprise that gave Boston its Government Center, the Prudential Center, and a revived waterfront—was the child of Logue's practical genius. He had, however, been unable to convert his development credits into political success and had been beaten the previous September in Boston's 1967 Democratic mayoral primary.

Logue was now doing well as a consultant. He had joined the Boston University faculty and found a new love in teaching. His family lived on Beacon Hill, his favorite part of his favorite city, and they had a summer place on Martha's Vineyard. The scars from his political defeat were healing, and although his campaign debt still bothered this scrupulous man, he had already paid off nearly half of it. For the Logues, life in Boston was good. Three months later, Ed Logue had moved to New York and was working for Nelson Rockefeller.

Logue received his first telephone call from the governor of New York State in January 1968. "The charm," as he remembered, "fairly oozed through the phone. He paid me the highest compliment. He knew my work. He also knew that I was happy in Boston. He said that he was just asking me to come down to New York to take a look at an urban-development bill for him."

Logue went to the 55th Street office and met in the fourth-floor conference room with Rockefeller's counsel, Bob Douglass; an assistant counsel, Stephen Lefkowitz, son of the state's attorney general; and Charles Urstadt, a housing official. Logue, with a Yale law degree, quickly read through the bill's legalisms and grasped its daring thrust. This legislation would create a government agency of unprecedented sweep and power. Its proposed Urban Development Corporation could break through the logjam blocking the construction of new housing for New York's poor, its ghetto blacks and Puerto Ricans. The corporation was empowered to sell bonds to finance its own construction and would be able to develop whole new towns and industrial parks. This was dream legislation to a man of Logue's ambitions, but he spotted a fatal flaw.

Douglass telephoned Rockefeller and asked the Governor to join them. On being introduced to Logue, Rockefeller turned up the charm to near lethal voltage. He quickly established his own knowledge of urban development and his passion for building. The two men spoke the same dialect. Logue warned Rockefeller, "The way this bill is drafted, Governor, you're at the mercy of John Lindsay." Lindsay was then the mayor of New York City, and the relationship between him and the Governor generally had the feel of Dry Ice. The bill, Logue went on, allowed any local government to throw zoning and building-code obstacles across the Governor's development plans. This fellow knew how to play the game, Rockefeller could see that right away, especially his example of Lindsay as the potential villain. He measured Logue with increased appreciation. "Let's go down to my office." The two men departed alone.

Harry Albright, formally Rockefeller's appointments officer, functionally his chief talent scout, recognized the move. Logue was about to experience the one-on-one, Nelson's style of wooing. As Albright explained it, "His approach was to deal with people he wanted privately, just Rockefeller and you in a room. Being alone with this man of fabled wealth and power was heady stuff. He compounded the effect by his behavior. He was graciousness itself. He poured your coffee. He told his secretary he was not to be disturbed by phone calls while he talked to you. Nelson Rockefeller's time was your time. All the time in the world, and his rapt attention. Everybody knew what his time was worth. And he was giving it all to you. This created an irresistible effect."

The usually guarded Rockefeller flattered by letting down his hair, drawing his prey closer into his confidence. He had told Albright, with an intimate gaze when he was recruiting him, one-on-one, "I'm not afraid to have people around me smarter than I am. I've done it all my life. I need you. I want you to work for me."

In his private conversation with Ed Logue, the Governor admitted that he would have difficulty passing an urban-development bill that gave the state power to overrule local governments. But, with his habitual ebullience, he told Logue, "I think I can get it passed." On that note they parted, with Rockefeller adding, "And when I do, I want you to come to work for me."

Rockefeller began to twist the arms and cut the deals necessary to marshal support in the legislature for his bill. Then Martin Luther King, Jr., was assassinated, and riots erupted in black ghettos across the country. Rockefeller used the emotional momentum to put across his proposal for rebuilding New York's decaying inner cities.

Although Logue had been mildly infatuated after that first meeting, his heart, as well as that campaign debt, was in Boston. In March, Rockefeller invited him back to 55th Street and offered him the presidency of the most powerful urban-rebuilding instrument in America. Logue asked about the salary. It would be equal to his own as governor, Rockefeller said, then $50,000. What about the campaign debt, still amounting to over $30,000? He could not just walk out on it. Rockefeller told him not to worry. Logue did not know exactly what that meant, but there was utter assurance in Rockefeller's voice. Logue also had his beloved home on Beacon Hill. And he was damned if he was going to commute into Manhattan every day from Glen Cove or Nyack. "Ed, you ought to think about an apartment in the city." Logue explained that he could not afford to buy an apartment. He sensed Rockefeller's growing impatience with these quibbles. With the nation's leading urban developer within his grasp, Nelson Rockefeller wanted to discuss housing for the millions, not one house for the developer. "Look, Ed, take all that up with Harry Albright afterward."

Albright had long since observed that "Rockefeller was not scared off by high prices for people. He admired someone who struck a hard bargain. He always told me to get the best person. Price was no object."

Logue had one last concern. He was a practicing Democrat. How did he go to work in the enemy camp? Albright was able to tick off a list of Logue's party colleagues in the Rockefeller Administration who had managed to overcome the same reservation.

Thus Ed Logue came to New York. The campaign debt was

erased by Nelson and a $31,389 loan was made to Logue, enabling him to buy a Manhattan apartment. The loan would subsequently cause far greater headaches for Nelson Rockefeller than for Ed Logue.

Some of Nelson's acquisitions never got out of the packing crate. William Watts, a talented Ford Foundation official, had taken leave from his job in 1968 to join Rockefeller's presidential campaign staff. Afterward, Nelson wanted Watts to remain on his gubernatorial staff. With urban discontent then at a flash point, Nelson simply created an Office of Urban Innovation and made Watts its director. Then nothing happened. Nelson was too occupied elsewhere to decide what he wanted of either the man or the office, and Watts languished in baffled inactivity for months, another victim of a passing Rockefeller enthusiasm. Watts, who could have been the right arm of any governor in the nation, wearied of being a Rockefeller spare part and left to join Henry Kissinger on the staff of the National Security Council.

I was often amused at the wealth of talent the Rockefeller staff squandered on the simplest problems—four highly capable college graduates, for example, huddled together to decide whether two or three government limousines would be needed to meet the Governor's party at the airport.

Nelson Rockefeller ran an authentic meritocracy. It can be argued that the ethnic and social diversity of his staff served his political purposes. But the general rule in politics is to place the exotic and unpronounceable names and the blacks in positions of high visibility, where they can do some political good. Even Nelson's personal staff, however, displayed as much creed, class and color diversity as his high-profile appointments.

He had arrogant people around him, ambitious and self-aggrandizing people, but there were few professional sons of bitches, no Chuck Colsons or Bob Haldemans, no vindictive hunts by "plumbers" for sources of leaks, no informer planted among us. A Rockefeller ship, if never easy, was generally a happy ship. Inescapably, there were rivals for Nelson's ear and for his proxy power. But the contests were conducted, at least outwardly, with sporting élan. The social lubricant among Rockefeller people was a deceptively casual bonhomie overlaying their well-developed ambitions.

I was flying late one night from New York to Albany with Al Marshall, a rare hour of inaction which allowed Marshall to ruminate on the nature of our chief. "You and I are friends," he said. "But if he told me to cut your head off, I would. God knows, he's had me do it to enough others." Marshall said it with a grin, and we laughed. And he would have. Nelson preferred the role of recruiter and delegated the function of headsman.

He liked healthy, comfortable people around him, staff members who worked uncomplainingly and wore well. Few of his people displayed evident emotional or physical disabilities. It was not an ideal environment for hiring the handicapped. Obesity particularly offended him because it suggested a weakness of the will. He was no cool judge of horseflesh. His verdicts on people were visceral, subjective, what he preferred to call "intuitive." Because he trusted his intuition so completely, his opinion of someone, once fixed, was virtually irreversible. There were few second chances to impress Nelson Rockefeller favorably. One subordinate could offer the wisdom of Solomon and be ignored, while the fair-haired could mouth bromides and have them greeted as revealed truth. He would impatiently dismiss a good idea suggested by one of the outgroup and two minutes later credit it to a favorite: "That was a hell of a suggestion, Bill."

Because he dealt with many people, he card-indexed them mentally: Hugh—press; Bobby—legislation; Norm—money; Ed—housing. If Ed said something perceptive about drugs, his words would be greeted by an unregistering stare. His card-file categorizations of people were sometimes liberally stretched. He was to tape a television message at 55th Street and snatched me as I was passing by in the hallway and asked me to sit in on the taping. Joe . . . speeches . . . words . . . TV, some such association must have flashed through his mind, since I was utterly innocent of television. I sat just off camera as the director set up for the take and rolled the tape. When it was over, Nelson looked at me expectantly. Without hesitation, I turned to the director. "Let's do it over. This time we'll have the Governor speak with more force." The director glared. There had been nothing wrong with the take, but I had long since learned what Nelson Rockefeller prized in his people—authority and certainty.

For all his arbitrariness, subjectivity, and snap judgments, I always had a sense that while Nelson Rockefeller could be dead wrong about the personalities of his subordinates and utterly oblivious of their private lives, he was a rather shrewd judge of professional capacities. But then, that was all he really wanted or needed to know about them.

I had worked in the Governor's office for two years before setting foot in the seat of the family's empire—Room 5600. Room 5600 was misnamed. It was not a room at all, but the entire fifty-fourth, fifty-fifth and fifty-sixth floors of 30 Rockefeller Plaza. The cryptic designation was in the diffident family style. The central switchboard operators answered simply, "Circle seven three seven hundred." The office letterhead read only "Room 5600, 30 Rockefeller Plaza, New York, N.Y. 10020." The aura of Room 5600, particularly after the seedy improvisations at 55th Street, was jarring. Leaving the elevator at the fifty-sixth floor, the visitor faced thick glass doors behind which a security man, invariably a retired New York City policeman, sat at a bare desk. The atmosphere was rarefied, airless and as mute as the William Couper bust of John D. Rockefeller staring from a pedestal next to the reception desk.

The fabric-covered walls, the rugs, the ceilings, were in that most neutral and unfelt color—beige. The carpet silenced one's steps. Indeed, the dominant sound of Room 5600 was silence. No Muzak sedated the visitor. No mail-room radio blared. No knots of employees chitchatted at water fountains. The corridors were gently curved and hung with subdued abstracts, creating the effect of a deserted art gallery. Most doors to the individual offices were closed, adding to the lifelessness of the place. Room 5600 appeared uninhabited, though behind those doors, some two hundred people served the Rockefellers.

From Room 5600 the endowments of the Rockefeller Foundation, Rockefeller University, the Rockefeller Brothers Fund and the private family investments were directed. Here the staff managed the personal affairs of more than eighty family members. Was it tax time? The accountants prepared family returns. Was a young Rockefeller's support sought for a new cause? The philanthropic staff evaluated it. Was a Rockefeller to be divorced? The legal staff handled the case.

Was a trip planned? A travel office made the arrangements. Was the press stalking them? The public-relations office dealt with reporters. For Happy Rockefeller's forty-first birthday party, John Jackson, director of stage operations at Radio City Music Hall, went up to decorate and light Pocantico.

When an artist friend of mine, William Wilson, wanted to show his work to Nelson Rockefeller, I placed him in touch with Carol Uht, Nelson's personal curator. When I wanted to inquire about a Caribbean vacation at the height of the season, I went to the Room 5600 office whose function it was to make special bookings at Rock-resorts. At the time, arrangements were being made for a U.S. senator and his wife. The capacity to put up people on short notice at Caneel Bay, the Dorado Beach or the Mauna Kea was the kind of favor that won Nelson Rockefeller quiet support in unlikely corners.

When I had a small sum of cash accumulated, I went for advice to the 5600 expert who invested for the family. His advice, like their portfolios, was cautious, not particularly imaginative. The most daring suggestion was Big Macs, the bonds of the state's Municipal Assistance Corporation, which were then staving off New York City's threatened default.

The people with whom one dealt at Room 5600 differed from Nelson's governmental staff, not so much in ability as in demeanor. Nelson's government aides were more effusive and individualistic. The staff members at 5600 appeared to have been affected by the aridly decorous air that they breathed all day. Their style was a muted deference. Attractive people on the whole, friendly, able, even serene. As one of their astute number pointed out, "The difference between working here and somewhere else is that most offices are trying to sell something, insurance, bonds, fashions. Here, it's the other way around. People are always trying to sell us something, pitching for the Rockefellers' support or money. That turns the psychological climate around. We always have the upper hand. That gives us a kind of tranquillity."

For one year, between Nelson's resignation as governor of New York and his appointment as Vice-President, I was on the family payroll at Room 5600, still writing his speeches. I found the Rockefellers generous and considerate employers, but the paternalism of the manor house was ever present. In mid-December, we were invited to the annual office Christmas party. It was held in what the public knows in the evening as the Rainbow Room, on the sixty-fifth floor of 30 Rockefeller Plaza. By day, it is the Rockefeller Luncheon Club, where family executives dine and do business.

For the Christmas party, we were each given tags showing our names and family affiliation. Thus, "Mr. Smith—Mr. Laurance's staff." Or "Miss Jones—Mr. David's staff." My tag read, "Mr. Persico—Mr. Nelson's staff." The party, in the Rockefeller style, was flawlessly executed, offering well-stocked bars and roving waiters bearing trays of caviar, smoked salmon, oysters. But like every Rockefeller social affair, the event was more tasteful than fun. Midway through, Nelson's son Steven, serving as master of ceremonies, did a surprisingly amusing monologue reviewing the past year at 5600, but the audience reacted stiffly, as though unsure at how to laugh with or at a prince of the manor. At one point, standing amid a circle of colleagues, I pointed to my name tag and said, "Ah belongs to Massa Nelson." Cold stares were turned on me; that was not the 5600 style.

Chapter IX

FOURTH TERM

In 1970, Nelson Rockefeller was completing his third term as governor. He had held this post as long as any New Yorker in the previous 165 years. Although the thrill was long gone, he chose to run for an unprecedented fourth four-year term. He simply could not let go. New York, though no longer the nation's most populous state, still provided a huge stake at the presidential gaming table. Just two years before, Rockefeller had seen Richard Nixon—a political itinerant who had gone from California to Washington, back to California and then to New York—win the nomination with no real home base. But Nixon was different; he was a creature of the Republican Party, accepted everywhere, a blood relative, taken in no matter at whose door he knocked. Rockefeller still remained, if not a party outsider, a not entirely trusted in-law. Nelson needed New York as an assurance that the party needed him. Thus he believed that he had to run for a fourth term.

Among potential contenders for the Democratic nomination that year, most feared by our camp was Arthur J. Goldberg. Nelson was in his usual precampaign slump, with only 34 percent of the voters supporting his re-election, and Goldberg represented the most formidable rival he had yet faced. Arthur Goldberg was neither a remote aristocrat, like Averell Harriman, nor a forgettable face, as Nelson's last two victims had been. A former justice of the Supreme Court, he was a self-made man, exuding rectitude, and heaped with honors. He had also been secretary of labor in the fabled Kennedy Cabinet and U.S. ambassador to the United Nations when that job still meant something. Most intimidating, he was an authentic labor man, the longtime general counsel to the AFL-CIO. Goldberg, running in a strong union state, could be expected to reclaim Nelson Rockefeller's magic weapon, the Republican governor's extraordinary endorsements by labor unions. Thus, when Goldberg was nominated, an unease settled over our staff. I was unperturbed. I had heard Goldberg make a speech.

The smoothly meshing gears of a Rockefeller state campaign began to slip into place. Stage one was to answer the traditional plaint at election time: "But what have you done for us lately?" To provide the answer, Al Marshall summoned the heads of all state agencies to the Governor's office. He asked me to be there. I arrived to find the conference room buzzing with commissioners chatting over sherry. Marshall's office adjoined the conference room, and I went in to let him know that everyone had arrived. Marshall was his customary hearty self as he shuffled his papers into final order, but as we went through the door, his manner changed abruptly. He bent his head, locked his eyes on his folder, and greeted no one. He took his place at the head of the table. The babble of conversation trailed off. The commissioners, like chastened schoolchildren, took their places. When all were seated and the room utterly silent, Marshall slowly raised his head. He peered around the table face by face and spoke in a low growl. "You sons of bitches have had your asses in butter long enough." He stared menacingly. "Now it's time to get on the road and start selling Nelson Rockefeller." The commissioners fell over one another in their haste to describe what they would do to preach Nelson's gospel. I always admired a Marshall performance.

The staff moved into the Governor's fourth state campaign with the assurance of a man winding his watch. The scheduling people took possession of Nelson's waking hours, accommodating his small stock of idiosyncrasies. Under no circumstances was he to stay overnight in Buffalo. Why? No one knew, and he never explained. Advance men were never to put him into a hotel's presidential suite, because the presumption, or the irony, made him uncomfortable. Constituencies were identified with pinpoint precision, as entries on the campaign payroll suggest—"Coordinator, Jewish Black Youth for Rockefeller, $250 per week" and "Writer, Anglo-Jewish, $200 per week."

Rockefeller was always a better campaigner than a politician. Yet the inbred family distaste for casual familiarity often assailed him before stepping into crowds. "God, do I really have to do this?" he would moan, eyes rolling and shoulders shuddering. But once immersed, he responded with adrenal zeal. He hand-shook, back-slapped, kissed and winked his way through the throng. He downed blintzes and pizzas, and coined his own all-purpose greeting for mass-produced intimacy: "Hi ya, fella!" He reveled in adulation and reacted to antagonistic audiences with hearty combativeness. The roar and feel of the crowd tapped something elemental in his nature.

As the campaign plane arrived at a stop, he first combed his hair. Then, if it was cold or raining, he stood in the aisle and reached his arms back, knowing his coat would be there. He never carried anything. The inevitable briefcases and folders were lugged about by advance men. His advance team had firm instructions—they were never to touch him, to push him, to interpose themselves between him and the people. A point man, arm raised, went ten to twelve feet ahead to show the way, and a bodyguard and another advance man served as Nelson's flankers, a few feet off each shoulder, whispering the names of upcoming notables. His advance staff spared him the seeming clumsiness of a Jerry Ford stumbling down steps or banging his head on airplane hatches. "You can't concentrate on meeting people, greeting dignitaries and still know where your feet are," Joe Canzeri explained. "I'd walk alongside him whispering, 'Up two steps here. Duck your head now. Curb here!' All the while he'd be smiling, waving, talking to the people."

Canzeri, who succeeded Joe Boyd as the chief of advance, had a signal for extricating the candidate from the clutches of bores and badgerers. Nelson would tug at his earlobe and Canzeri then moved in to steer him to "someone you promised to see, Governor."

His handshake was no casual gesture. When Charles Lanigan campaigned as candidate for state comptroller, the Governor instructed him: "Put your hand out." Rockefeller then jammed his own hand hard between the V of Lanigan's thumb and index finger. "See. You've got to hit in close, deep, where they can feel it. Connect first, before they do. That's the way to make them feel the power." With a proud smile, he showed Lanigan the callus on his palm.

Soon after Labor Day, the Goldberg campaign suffered an unexpected blow. The New York State AFL-CIO turned its back on the former counsel to its parent organization. The champions of the workingman chose the grandson of John D. Rockefeller over the son of an impoverished Jewish immigrant. To those with a memory of history, Nelson Rockefeller's ability to command the political support of labor was puzzling. Nearly sixty years before, miners of the Colorado Fuel and Iron Company, in which Nelson's father held the controlling interest, had been locked in a bitter strike against their employers. The strike was marked by bloody clashes between the workers, strikebreakers and the Colorado militia. On April 20, 1913, a shot of unknown origin sounded, and militiamen with machine guns opened fire on the tents where striking miners and their families had taken refuge. More than fifty men, women and children were killed in what came to be called the Ludlow Massacre. Long thereafter, the Rockefeller name was the most hated among workingmen in America.

How Nelson managed not only to escape this opprobrium, but to earn labor's embrace, is a story that leads back to Rockefeller Center. During the 1930s, when Nelson was helping his father build the Center, he worked with George Meany, then business agent for the Bronx plumbers' union. Nelson proved reasonable and attentive to union sensibilities, and the giant construction project lost not a single day to a strike. The two men remained mutually respecting friends as Meany rose to the pinnacle of the American labor movement and Nelson entered public life. Later, as governor, Nelson Rockefeller put billions into construction, which translated into thousands of jobs for union members. He compiled a pro-labor legislative record, including regular increases in minimum wages and workmen's compensation and the establishment of collective bargaining for public-employee unions. In the 1970 election he corralled the endorsements of eighty-three unions totaling 1.3 million workers, and when he managed to snare the support of the state branch of Goldberg's own AFL-CIO, he said coyly, "Arthur could never understand it. I am not so sure I do either."

Much of his success was explained by Victor Borella, a pleasant, deceptively tough little man working out of Room 5600. A poor orphan, Borella had won a scholarship to Dartmouth, and there he made the pivotal acquaintance of his life, Nelson Rockefeller. During the mid-thirties, while working in a New York public-relations firm, Borella received a call from Nelson, whom he had not seen since Dartmouth days. Rockefeller hired Borella as his man at Rockefeller Center to deal with labor unions. Borella became executive vice-president of Rockefeller Center, and by the time Nelson ran for governor in 1958, his likable and respected lieutenant had become the friend of virtually every union figure worth knowing in New York.

Beyond Borella's role and Nelson's own friendships and labor record, a factor less intangible helped make Rockefeller the unlikely darling of organized labor. His rapport with John DeLury, president of New York's Uniformed Sanitationmen's Association, is instructive. In 1968, shortly after Nelson had managed to settle a New York City garbage strike, there popped out of his office a peppery rooster in a vested blue-serge suit, a cigar dominating his face. "Gimme a car," John DeLury ordered, without removing the cigar. Three of the Rockefeller staff jumped to his command. DeLury stuck his thumbs in his vest and gave a preening smile. Something had gone on behind those closed doors that confirmed what John DeLury had always suspected about himself. He was quite a guy. What headier, loftier, more unalterable proof? He had just come out of a man-to-man, equal-to-equal, leader-to-leader exchange with Nelson Rockefeller, the hero of the sanitationmen and the Prince of Pocantico. And he had won, or at least he had taken his share of the hands played.

In large part, Nelson Rockefeller succeeded with labor because, if one stripped away the fortune, made him a poor boy rather than rich, placed him at the starting line equal with all others in the race of life,

he might easily have emerged a labor leader. He had the pugnacious-
ness, the uncluttered pragmatist mind, a meat-and-potatoes taste in
almost everything except art. He looked the part—solid, rugged, with
a jaunty confidence in his stride, a gravelly voice, a handsomer John
L. Lewis. His first-naming, back-pounding manner allowed the chieftains of labor to believe that "there, but for a few million, goes one of
us." They got close to him, called him "Nelson" and not the false
intimate's "Rocky." He could urge them along paths against their
wishes and be forgiven, even assisted. I sat with one of them having
a drink in a Buffalo motel bar as he derided blacks, "who don't know
which end of the hammer to grab." But this union leader was there to
help implement Rockefeller's plan for minority employment in the
construction of a new state university campus.

Was Rockefeller a social chameleon, pandering to the knights of
labor? To a degree, yes. But he slipped into the part naturally. He
told Joe Boyd that he liked the union people because they laid out
what they wanted with a minimum of hypocrisy. He found them
more congenial than the businessmen, the spine of his own party,
who viewed him as a rich man who wanted to give away their money.
He might come out of a meeting with union leaders shaking his head
and raising his eyebrows in the unspoken message, "My God, the
people I have to work with." But his manner suggested not so much
the aristocrat forced to consort with the yeomanry, but rather a yeo-
man at heart who recognized that he had been more fortunate than
they largely through an accident of birth.

The 1970 campaign had opened with Nelson inviting Goldberg to
Pocantico, a civilized gesture that may have deluded the politico tyro
into confusing the campaign with a civics debate. But he quickly felt
Nelson's ermine-wrapped knuckles. On Columbus Day, two Hispanics, presumably from the Goldberg camp, heckled Nelson at a rally
in a Puerto Rican neighborhood, and others pelted his party with
eggs. At the next stop, a parade reviewing stand, Goldberg came
toward Rockefeller, hand outstretched, apologizing for his supporters'
bad form. Rockefeller, spotting the TV cameras on them, refused
Goldberg's hand. Instead, he lectured his opponent loudly and with
an accusing finger: "I cannot accept your apology. You, of all people,

a justice of the Supreme Court! You should be most concerned about freedom of speech. And you let this happen?" Goldberg was visibly shaken. Nelson later confessed, "It was sort of silly . . . but, well, if you want to play in this game . . ." He trailed off with a shrug.

In 1970, Nelson Rockefeller won an unexpected supporter. The model for many speech writers has been Ted Sorensen, who worked for John F. Kennedy. The hero of the previous generation was Judge Sam Rosenman, whose writing gifts shaped much of Franklin Roosevelt's memorable oratory. In the summer of 1970, Judge Rosenman appeared at a press conference in Nelson's 55th Street office to endorse the Governor for re-election. My surprise was not only that this charter New Dealer had chosen Rockefeller over Arthur Goldberg but also that the octogenarian New Dealer was still alive.

He was a fine-looking old man obviously savoring the spotlight after so many years in the shadows of private life. Rosenman's presence, his wit, his aura of one who had strode with giants, held the reporters long after the news value of the conference passed. After a lofty explanation of why he had bolted his party to back the Republican Rockefeller, he added another point, with bemused petulance, which may have come closer to the truth. Said Judge Rosenman, "I invited him [Goldberg] to become a member of my law firm. I regret that he decided to go elsewhere."

Later, with the campaign at fever pitch, the judge submitted a speech to Nelson on the drug issue, an election-year perennial. He had cleverly managed to tie drugs to another Rockefeller campaign staple, "bossism" among New York City Democrats. The text was rich with eloquence and irony, and had an unmistakable cadence. My God, I thought, this sounds like Franklin Roosevelt speaking. Then I realized, of course, it was Franklin Roosevelt speaking.

Unfortunately, Judge Rosenman's text arrived at a time when our increasingly exhausted and testy candidate had issued a dictum: no speeches longer than ten minutes. The Rosenman script ran nearly an hour, and as I began trying to cut it, my hand faltered. It seemed sacrilegious to tamper with the language of a man who had christened the "New Deal" and who wrote so much of the quotable Roosevelt.

In a note to Rockefeller clipped to his draft, Rosenman had written, "Immeasurable of my masterworks have never been heard beyond a rustle in the wastebasket," and he would not be disturbed "if this speech met the same end." That, unfortunately, was the destiny of this text, which did not fit into the final hours of the campaign.

In 1970, as in his other campaigns, one newspaper alone mattered to Nelson Rockefeller. Press officers who showed him lavish praise from the pages of the New York *Daily News* or the Rochester *Democrat and Chronicle* were rewarded with a polite "Hmmm." *The New York Times* was his official register, his report card. As the campaign progressed, the newspaper was making Nelson nervous. The *Times* had roughed him up during the previous two years, accusing him of bending "to conservative pressures for cutbacks in welfare and Medicaid formulas," describing his drug program "a costly failure," and criticizing him for driving "gaping holes in the constitutional walls between church and state." The South Mall, the capital complex being constructed in Albany, was, in the judgment of the *Times*, "a monumental extravagance."

Rockefeller was cornered at a dinner by the editor of the *Times* editorial page, John Oakes, and said testily, "What have I done now to displease you?"

Oakes mentioned a housing policy affecting New York City and said, "Why couldn't you just have done what we said?"

"Listen, Johnny, I don't think you people understand I'm the one who got elected," Nelson answered.

With the polls projecting a close race, a *Times* endorsement could decide the election, and now, with election day nearing, the *Times* was giving enviable play to a series of thoughtful, solidly researched position papers issuing from the Goldberg camp. Nelson decided that he too must have position papers. Less than a month remained in the campaign, and sixteen major speeches were due the week he made the decision. The speech writers had been told, in effect, to stop fighting the forest fire and to start planting saplings.

That the *Times* intended to endorse Arthur Goldberg was a foregone conclusion among our staff. Still, we went into a fevered production of twenty-one position papers, ranging from Agriculture to Culture, from Aging to Youth. Each paper had to contain fresh initiatives, no mean feat for an activist Administration already in power a dozen years. This scramble for the new included proposals for a state program to reduce loneliness among the elderly, financial incentives to get junked cars out of sight, noise limits on jackhammers, penalties for bringing explosives onto college campuses, and a railroad link to Kennedy Airport.

On October 21, thirteen days before the election, Nelson Rockefeller arrived at the *Times* executive offices on 42nd Street to meet with the editorial board, an election-year ritual at which the newspaper's tribunes weighed major candidates. Nelson clutched, like a life preserver, a massive notebook of position papers defining the next four Rockefeller years. Four days later, the *Times* endorsed him as "far better qualified than either Mr. Goldberg or the Conservative nominee, Dr. Paul L. Adams, to head New York State in the four difficult years that lie ahead." Nobody was going to convince Nelson that his big black notebook had not turned the tide at the *Times*.

On election eve, he gave a previctory party for 150 friends and staff at 812 Fifth Avenue. The celebration was hardly presumptuous. His private pollster, Lloyd Free, had ruled out defeat. The guest list reflected his curiously eclectic social circle. Among those present were Joey Adams, Cleveland Amory, Louis Armstrong, Tom Braden, Bennett Cerf, Gardner Cowles, Henry Ford, Arthur Godfrey, Lionel Hampton, Kitty Carlisle Hart, Vincent Impellitteri, Jacob Javits, Henry Kissinger, Joseph Levine, David Merrick, Robert Moses, William Paley, Cliff Robertson, Jackie Robinson, Samuel Rosenman, Dorothy Schiff, Spyros Skouras, Arthur O. Sulzberger, Darryl Zanuck, and labor leaders Jacob Potofsky and Harry Van Arsdale.

Rockefeller as governor had been expensive but effective. Goldberg was untried and dull to boot. When it was over, Nelson had won his most emphatic victory, defeating Goldberg by a 730,000-vote plurality. He also became the only American governor ever elected to four four-year terms.

The 1970 campaign reduced the Rockefellers' fortunes by well over $4 million. Family gifts were intriguing in size and source. Nelson's stepmother, Martha Baird Rockefeller, again came through unstintingly with $2,779,000. His brother Laurance gave him $544,000;

David, $421,000; Winthrop, $3,000; and John D., III, $500. Nelson also spent $77,500 of his and Happy's money to be re-elected. The total campaign cost had been $7.2 million, a new American record for any election except for the Presidency.

If money alone determines the outcome of elections, Arthur Goldberg might as well have stayed home. He had 35 paid campaign employees; Nelson, by election day, had 476. Goldberg's campaign cost an estimated $1.8 million; Nelson had spent four dollars for every dollar of Goldberg's. The lopsided result suggested that given Goldberg's sleepwalking performance, the Rockefellers could have had a victory, if not a landslide, for far less money.

Did Nelson ever feel any qualms that financially he started his political hundred-yard dashes at the seventy-five-yard line? He once talked about money and politics over a staff lunch before announcing for his fourth term. "In the old days, you used to be able to go and campaign on the village green . . . and if you didn't do it on a village green, you did it on the back of a railroad train . . . and everybody came down to the depot to see the train and listen to the candidates. You could reach people. Today the only place you can get a village green is to buy time on television . . . so my objective has been to get on television. So you maybe say, 'All right. We ought to give everybody a half hour.' When do they give it? Sometime nobody is looking? You've got to get on prime time, when the people are there."

No Sunday-morning TV ghetto for Nelson Rockefeller. Nor did he overestimate the public's attention span. "If you're on for more than a minute or two, they're probably going to turn it off, because they're bored with politics, and politicians stand in very low esteem at the moment, unfortunately. And so I've tried to always get on prime time, short spots, so I could get on, get my message across and get off, before they turn me off. Now that takes money."

Agreed. Prime-time exposure took money—both for him and his opponent. Except that he had more of it. In 1970, his Democratic rival, Arthur Goldberg, proposed that he and Nelson limit their radio and television spending to seven cents per voter. This would have cut Rockefeller's media budget by 86 percent.

If pressed hard, he would accept in principle the fairness of publicly financed political campaigns. It was a beautiful idea in theory, he thought, but murdered by a gang of ugly facts. "How do they decide," he asked, "how much to put in? . . . The Democrats in New York State are registered about 800,000 more than the Republicans, so maybe they should have more money than we do because they have more people registered? . . . Does that make an equal race? . . . What do we do about the Liberal and Conservative parties? Do they get the same amount? And if I go out and set up another party, can I get more money from the government because now I'm a candidate on another ticket? Or somebody else, he's sitting in his living room. He's getting bored. So he decides 'I'm going to run for governor.' He goes out and forms a party . . . does he get the same amount of money?"

The one election reform Rockefeller unreservedly supported was mandatory public reporting of campaign contributions and expenditures. "Openness is important. . . . I think every cent should be known, and the source of it should be listed." But as for giving up his financial edge: "I think that is second most important." Indeed he saw clear-cut advantages to the nation in the election of wealthy candidates. As he put it, "There is a lot of merit in the fact that somebody who does have funds and doesn't have to be dependent and have strings on him is going to be more responsive to the people and less responsible to the special interests of any kind."

Besides the hands-out-of-the-cookie-jar virtue of the rich candidate, Nelson cited yet another advantage of wealth, one revealing his attitude toward self-made successes, especially white ethnics: "Those who have come up the hard way have had to fight other people to get there. They have prejudices. At least there are many who belong to other minorities who feel that they have prejudices. They feel people who have not been through that struggle are liable to be more broadminded, more progressive, more open than those who have fought one group against another." People who had lifted themselves from poverty were often narrowed in outlook, he said, "by their working-class resentments."

He suffered no compunction. He was ready to spend what it took to win. In fact, he spent more money trying to shoo a pesky political fly from his own backyard than most candidates can afford for their own campaigns. After he lost the presidential nomination to Richard Nixon in August 1968, he went home and remembered someone else whom he did not like—Richard Ottinger, the Democratic congressman representing the district which included Pocantico. The heir to a plywood fortune, Ottinger was running for re-election and using Rockefeller as his foil. He accused the Governor of trying to force construction of a highway along the Hudson River in order to spare Pocantico from intrusion by new roads. Mocking Rockefeller's environmental record, he labeled him a greedy ally of Consolidated Edison, willing to desecrate the land with thoughtlessly located power plants. Congressman Ottinger, in short, bugged Nelson Rockefeller, and the Governor was ready to make a substantial commitment to virtually anybody who ran against him.

It was a slow political autumn, and Nelson's armies had little to do beyond garrison duty. Seeing an opportunity to pluck the annoying Ottinger from his hide, he supplied Ottinger's Republican opponent with a campaign manager, a speech writer, an advance man, and a press officer, all from his own staff, their expenses and salaries paid from an anonymous account at Room 5600. He also made a large cash contribution to the campaign.

As a member of the loaned staff, I asked Nelson if we could have a poll taken to measure his candidate's strengths. I asked to have his pollster, Lloyd Free, do a name recognition, main issues, and trial heat survey. Nelson approved this $15,000 project instantly. The poll showed his man so far down that Free stated, "He's dead, no matter what you people do for him." I reported his conclusion to Rockefeller, along with my own unflattering estimate of the Republican candidate and my eagerness to pull out of this campaign. Nelson's face took on a belligerent fixity. "I've come from almost that far behind and still won."

"Yes," I answered, "but this guy's no Nelson Rockefeller," which placated him. I was learning. Nevertheless, he asked our band of well-heeled *Kamikazes* to stay on until the bitter end. When the Republican was crushed, I wondered if Ottinger had the satisfaction of knowing that he had beaten not only his opponent but Nelson Rockefeller as well.

One adjusted perhaps too easily to living within Nelson's means.

In the final days of his 1970 gubernatorial campaign, I took my speech-writing staff of seven out to dinner at the East Side restaurant that our headquarters had informally adopted. Dinner over, I casually asked, "What's fifteen percent of five hundred and twenty-five dollars?" and signed the tab in the name of the campaign treasurer.

"Where's it all coming from?" I asked one of our fund raisers. "God bless Martha Baird," he answered. As the second Mrs. John D., Jr., she controlled the central Rockefeller fortune after Junior died. No boy ever had a more generous stepmother than did Nelson Rockefeller. By the end of the 1970 campaign, Martha had given Nelson $11.7 million for his political ambitions. His brothers and sister had contributed another $3.6 million. When federal campaign-spending controls were passed in 1971, Nelson remarked, "My family is grateful. They've got me off their backs for the first time in twenty years."

A time bomb was unwittingly set during the 1970 campaign. On July 17, John Wells, a politically astute and influential lawyer, was on Nelson's schedule for a brief meeting during a busy day. This sly old owl of Manhattan Republican politics had an idea for puncturing Arthur Goldberg's stately balloon. He suggested to Nelson that a book about Goldberg be written by that literary hit man of the right, Victor Lasky. The plan needed "an investor," Wells explained. Nelson was noncommittal, but after Wells left, he sent a note to his brother Laurance asking if he could help find backers for the book. As we shall see later, four years were to pass before this bomb detonated.

As the Wells incident suggests, Nelson was not overawed by the writer's function. He had a cavalier attitude toward books and the people who write them. The Library of Congress card catalogue shows several books credited to him, but his authorship took a curious form. His first book, *The Future of Federalism*, reprinted the Godkin Lectures that he had delivered at Harvard in 1962. When a visiting academic complimented him on the work, Rockefeller responded airily, "Oh, my staff did that."

During his 1968 bid for the presidential nomination, another book was published under his name, *Unity, Freedom and Peace*. The next

Nelson Rockefeller title appeared in 1970, *Our Environment* Can *Be Saved*, timed to work the then fashionable issue into his campaign for re-election. These last two books had been ghosted for him by Rodney Campbell, a prodigious researcher and speed writer who worked under Hugh Morrow's direction and completed each book in a few weeks.

When *Our Environment* Can *Be Saved* was finished, Morrow took it to Nelson. Rockefeller, then caught up in his re-election campaign, begged off, saying, "Hugh, I just don't have the time to read it." Thus the book achieved a fairly rare distinction even for a ghosted work—not only had it not been written by the putative author, it had never been read by him. Nelson, however, did have a certain sense of literary integrity. After *Our Environment* Can *Be Saved* came out, he was scheduled to speak before some conservationists, and I had included in his text, "I've just written a book on the environment." He rewrote the line to read: "I've just put out a book . . ."

When I once asked him if he had ever really wanted to write a book, he said, "To tell you the truth, I tried once, and I just drew a blank. I really did. I got all tied up in trying to put one sentence together."

Nelson Rockefeller, realist, pragmatist, statistics addict, worshiper of charts, appointer of more than eighty state fact-finding commissions, relied on a guru. His sage was no Oriental wrapped in a white sheet; he was a middle-aged doctor with a German accent as thick as *Schlag*. The staff long wondered about his specialty—was it psychiatry? psychology? divinity? He was, it turned out, an internist who had treated Nelson's first wife, Tod. It was not, however, the anatomy that he plumbed for Nelson Rockefeller, but the soul.

His name was Franz Winkler, another of the sometime satellites in Nelson's orbit. Dr. Winkler was also an "intuitive genius," Nelson said, and thus a natural soul mate for him. Further, the doctor had gathered around him a circle of young disciples, which, in the political environment of the late sixties and early seventies, heightened his attractiveness and value to Nelson.

I first encountered the doctor at a meeting in Nelson's townhouse on West 54th Street. Around the table sat a half dozen of Nelson's aides on whom he depended to keep the state budget from going through the roof, to control pollution without driving industry out of the state, and to pressure banks to put more loans into New York ghettos rather than Florida shopping centers. These people were now engaged once each week with Nelson, under Dr. Winkler's tutelage, in divining the condition of America's soul. Winkler sat quietly for the most part, his hairpiece slightly askew, bright eyes measuring us, as these harried state officials enjoyed the rare luxury of waxing metaphysical. Nelson had set a tape recorder in the middle of the table, since these sessions were to form the basis for a book prescribing a cure for the sickness of spirit that Winkler had now convinced him afflicted America.

The discussions served another purpose of which I had been warned. They gave Winkler the opportunity to use his intuitive gifts to size up staff members for Nelson. For my first meeting I adopted a posture describable as Sixties Relevant. From time to time I interjected thoughts like, "But does a purely technological advance necessarily signal human progress?" I have no idea of my grade.

Al Marshall, possibly the ablest man around Nelson Rockefeller and an administrator of massive capacities, could, nevertheless, not fool Dr. Winkler. Brilliant administrator, perhaps, but Winkler confided to Rockefeller that Marshall was essentially a "negative spirit," unreceptive to new ideas. Marshall returned the compliment. Winkler might be intuitive, but his answers to the real world problems with which state officials grappled were "infantile."

Still, what counted most during that period was Nelson Rockefeller's opinion of Dr. Winkler's opinions. "I've known that man for fifteen years," he confided to me, "and I've never known him to be wrong about anybody." Then with a conspiratorial wink he added, "Do you know what he thinks about Blank [one of the state's highest-ranking officeholders]? He says he's prematurely senile." Winkler rated Nelson too and told him that the public perceived of him as a "mother hen," tiring people with his nagging concern for their well-being.

Dr. Winkler played an influential role in drafting Nelson's fourth inaugural address; indeed, he became the hidden conduit through which we inserted pet proposals into the speech. One had first to catch Dr. Winkler at his office between patients, convince him that an idea was sound, and then have him sell it to Rockefeller. One of his own hobbyhorses appeared in a memorable passage in the Governor's 1971 inaugural address. A few days before the speech was to be delivered, we were at the apartment at 812 Fifth Avenue hammering out final details after weeks of work. Nelson put his stamp of approval to the last paragraph and turned an exhausted smile on Dr. Winkler, who had remained disconcertingly quiet. "What do you think?" Nelson asked.

Winkler spoke in his habitual tone, that of a gently chiding teacher. "What about the little animals?" Rockefeller's face went blank. The doctor continued: "You say nothing about what is happening to helpless creatures in the schools today in the perverted name of science. Our children are becoming brutalized by so-called scientific experiments." Nelson suddenly looked tired and, turning toward Hugh Morrow and me, said, "Take care of this, will you." We filed out of the apartment sharing puzzled frowns.

I made some phone calls and found that a movement did indeed exist composed of people who were appalled at the slicing up of frogs, rabbits and mice in classrooms. But how to introduce this issue into an inaugural speech? Where to fit it among the calls for federal revenue sharing, more jobs in the private sector and the rescue of mass transportation?

On inauguration day, my wife came to the Capitol to attend the ceremony. I had a few last-minute phone calls to make before we went to hear the Governor deliver the speech. "Here, take a look at this while I get things wrapped up." I handed her a copy of the address and continued my calls. Sylvia suddenly began signaling me to get off the phone. "There's something terribly wrong. Somebody's slipped something in by mistake." She pointed to a passage that read: "Our overwhelming increase of intellectual knowledge and technical power can be matched by a corresponding growth in the human spirit. One illustration of the need to achieve such a balance may be found in the increase of cold-blooded experiments on live animals in secondary schools, staged in the name of science without regard for the brutalizing effect on the children participating in them. And now, in the field of conservation . . ."

"It's no mistake," I answered wanly.

Why did Nelson have such faith in a man so removed from his own pragmatic and unreflective turn of mind? Why was he tolerant of Winkler's intellectual maundering when such behavior in another staff member would have been rewarded by instant exile? "He wanted to escape being dominated by bureaucrats. He wanted to get out of the prison of logic, of charts, facts and deductive reasoning," Al Marshall concluded. Nelson Rockefeller wanted to believe that somewhere someone possessed something better than the purely rational tools of the human mind. He craved intuitive flashes. He yearned for shortcuts through the tedious, painstaking, logical resolution of problems at which, in truth, he excelled.

Soon after his contribution to the 1971 inaugural speech, Dr. Winkler died. Nothing further came of the book to cure America's spiritual malaise. In fact, Nelson was by then so bogged down in conventional solutions to problems that he did not attend his mentor's funeral.

His missing the Winkler rites illuminates his customary reaction to death. His attitude was not so much stoic, which suggests a disciplined muting of grief, but fatalistic, in which one accepts death's inevitability with a minimum of emotional fuss. He had been unreservedly saddened by his mother's death in 1948, when he was thirty-nine. He grieved deeply over the loss of his son Michael, fourteen years later. Thereafter, he took the death of intimates and associates with an infantry commander's that's-the-way-it-is shake of the head. When his stepmother, Martha Baird Rockefeller, died, he seemed, one of the staff remarked, "most interested in what was to happen to her furniture."

In time, I became inured to the ritual charm, the arbitrary demands, the casual arrogance, the ever-present odor of power. But the money? Never. After delivering his 1971 State of the State message to the legislature, the Governor invited those of us involved in preparing it, along with spouses, to the Executive Mansion for lunch, something of a recompense for lost family time. It was a rare moment, not to be dining with Nelson, since we frequently worked over meals, as food stains on numerous speech drafts attest. The rarity was that for once Nelson Rockefeller had nothing to do. The lunch offered an opportunity to talk to him about something besides fiscal federalism. I had once read that he had had a role in the production of *Citizen Kane*, and I asked him about the story. He frowned for a moment, as though peeling through layers of memory. Then he smiled wistfully. "I was working in Rockefeller Center at the time. They told me this fellow just had to see me about making a movie. He came in, a big, good-looking guy. He started carrying on about how important his movie was. Very emotional. He was practically on his knees. I thought he was going to kiss my hand. He made me terribly uncomfortable. The thought passing through my mind was, How do I get him out of here? So I agreed to give him some money, mostly to get it over with."

"So you helped Orson Welles finance maybe the greatest American movie ever made?" I said it in genuine admiration.

"I guess so."

"I'm curious, Governor," I asked. "Have you ever seen *Citizen Kane?*"

"No." His voice conveyed a total lack of interest.

Chapter X

THE IMPERIAL GOVERNOR

"THEY HAD THEIR THROATS CUT and their cocks stuffed in their mouths," the press secretary came out of his office and reported to us, eyes bulging. It was Monday morning, September 13, 1971. We had gathered at the West 55th Street office where telephone reports were coming in on the storming of Attica prison by the State Police. The state's maximum-security fortress, housing its most hardened criminals, had been seized by inmates five days before, along with thirty-nine guards as hostages. This latest lurid detail referred to hostages who had been found dead after the troopers recaptured the prison. I had an immediate sense that something was wrong. The genitalia atrocity is one of the oldest in the lexicon of barbarism. Whether Turks are slaughtering Armenians or savages murdering missionaries, it always surfaces. I began to wonder about the reliability of information that we were getting out of Attica.

I had seen Nelson Rockefeller forgo force as a solution nearly four years before when he refused to call out the National Guard to break the New York City garbage strike. His knowledge of what had happened to his father after the Ludlow miners' massacre was, I assumed, too deeply etched ever to be forgotten. And I was right, then. I had been sure that he would not sanction the use of massive force at Attica. And I was wrong. Russell Oswald, chief of the state's prison system, telephoned to say that four days of negotiation had failed. It was necessary, in Oswald's judgment, to retake the prison by force. The Governor agreed.

Bob Douglass was the Governor's man on the scene at Attica on the morning the prison was stormed. He had an open telephone line to Nelson at his Fifth Avenue apartment and reported as each hostage was freed. Ultimately, twenty-eight of the thirty-nine men were safely recovered. Ten had died along with twenty-nine inmates when the prison was stormed. One hostage had died of injuries earlier. State officials initially reported that the ten dead hostages had been murdered by prisoners. The Governor judged the attack a success, and said that he was "amazed" that so many hostages had been saved.

The next day the bottom dropped out. The Monroe County medical examiner studied the bodies of the hostages and concluded that they had not died by their captors' hands. The atrocity reports were untrue—they had been killed by State Police gunfire during the assault. State officials on the scene disputed the medical examiner's findings.

Back in Albany by now, I had been instructed to call Attica, get the facts, and prepare a statement that would, if possible, put the state in a defensible light. These conversations soon turned grisly. As the corrections officials described the hostages' bodies, I found myself uncomfortably pressing for more detail. Wasn't there anything else? Just a scratch on the neck? A contusion on the arm? Don't you see anything besides the gunshot wounds? There was little evidence of the atrocities that I was supposed to recount. One hostage had required fifty-two stitches, but he was one of the survivors.

Soon after, the Governor called. One of his counsels wanted to discuss the medical examiner's report with him, and I was told to listen in on an extension for whatever information might prove useful. In describing the medical examiner, the counsel said, "Of course, he's a known leftist." Rockefeller muttered, "Sure. It all fits." His position throughout had been that in Attica he faced no isolated, spontaneous prison revolt but a manifestation of the international terrorist conspiracy. Attica did, in fact, hold numerous militant blacks who saw themselves as political prisoners, and their demands for amnesty and free passage to a nonimperialist country had the ring of radical rhetoric. Still, I was surprised at how eagerly the Governor seized upon the rationale of extremist conspiracy, including the medical examiner's presumed politics, to explain the tragedy.

Later, the Governor asked me to draft several letters—as he put it, "Joe, you're good on the sensitive stuff"—praising state officials who had been on the scene. These included Russell Oswald, the commissioner of correctional services, as the current euphemism had it, and the State Police major who led the assault. Letters of appreciation signed by the Governor also went to all troopers who made the charge that day. I drafted messages to some of the thirty-two "observers" who had gone to Attica to help negotiate a settlement, Congressman Herman Badillo, for one, whom the Governor particularly admired. Finally, I drafted the most difficult letters—those he would send to the families of the hostages who had been killed in the attempt at their rescue.

One question troubled me then and long afterward. A key consideration in putting down the revolt had been to save the lives of the hostages. They and their inmate-captors were crowded together in the prison yard, and the situation appeared to call for the most precise and discriminating application of force. But that most imprecise of weapons, the shotgun, had been used by the "rescue squad." Why? And had Nelson Rockefeller known that shotguns were to be used?

Commissioner Oswald made a questionable case for the 12-gauge guns that the troopers carried, stating that "only the shotgun commanded the respect and the firepower to deter or prevent seizure of the State Police weapons by determined inmates." But the Governor later admitted that he had not known shotguns would be used. Would he have vetoed their use had he known? "As a politician and as a civilian," he said, "I did not think I ought to get into technical matters."

In the wake of Attica, controversy swirled about the conduct of the Governor and state officials. A hinge of the debate turned on Rockefeller's refusal to come to the prison as the prisoners had demanded and as several of the observers had urged. Would it have made a difference? The inside hardly affords the best vantage point for objectivity. Still, it struck me that Rockefeller's presence would only have raised the level of spectacle without necessarily ending the uprising less bloodily. The seed of the tragedy grew from a series of decisions each of which was out of synchronization with the state of the uprising at the time. The two crucial misjudgments were, first, to temporize in the beginning when swiftly applied firmness could have choked off the riot before it took root, and, second, to resort to overpowering force when more time would have cost nothing. From up close, Attica appeared not the calculated act of the powerful to crush the powerless, but rather a bloody botch, a tragedy of errors.

Attica's last casualty was the state's prison chief, Russell Oswald. Oswald had attempted to practice the progressive penology that had motivated his professional life, which was why, instead of using force at the onset, he had chosen to negotiate with the prisoners and had allowed them to bring observers of their choosing into the prison. His putting his beliefs into practice at Attica succeeded only in placing him in a cruel vise between reason and force. Whenever I saw him during those months in which he remained in his job after the uprising, he presented a touching figure. He had always been an affable man. Now, his manner had become almost frantically cheerful, while his eyes spoke of ineradicable horror.

Nelson Rockefeller never afterward displayed any emotion over the experience. Whenever Attica came up, he dealt with it in mechanistic terms: "See, there was this cross fire . . ." or as a clash of institutional forces: "The prisoners' demands transcended prison reform and had political implications." He never treated the subject any differently, whether speaking to us privately or to the public. The reaction of his father to the Ludlow Massacre nearly sixty years before had been largely the same.

Nelson, who paid so dearly within his party for a liberal reputation, was the author of possibly the toughest criminal legislation ever enacted in this country outside of capital punishment—the 1973 New York State Drug Law. In the fall of 1972 the staff met in the basement floor at Kykuit, beneath the ornate nineteenth-century formalism of the main story. It was like breaking through a time barrier. Below, in the area Nelson called the Gallery, thick, cream-colored carpeting absorbed our footsteps; the walls, covered with white fabric, were alive with De Koonings, Pollocks and Picassos. We were there for an annual ritual. On the comparative quiet of election day, Nelson liked to gather the staff at home to preview his program for the upcoming year. No elections loomed in 1973, presidential or gubernatorial, and we anticipated a light session.

Michael Whiteman, who had become the governor's counsel after Bobby Douglass left to enter private practice, led us through a list of routine programs, which Nelson heard with scarcely concealed boredom. Suddenly he leaned forward, chin thrust out. "On drugs, anyone who pushes gets life in prison. And I mean life—no matter what amount. No more of this plea bargaining, parole and probation." He sat back, legs crossed, arms folded. Nervous smiles appeared around the table. He looked to Mrs. Whitman. "What do you think of that?"

"It may be a bit drastic," she answered uneasily.

Nelson shot back, "Maybe you don't understand the seriousness of the problem." He continued to study us with a remorseless eye, as though daring further disagreement. There were no more smiles, nervous or otherwise, only the gurgle of throats being cleared.

Hours later, the agenda covered, several of us boarded a helicopter and headed back for Albany. I sat reviewing my notes from the meeting on which I was to base the first draft of the message to the legislature. "What do you think I should do about that drug idea he mentioned?" I asked Whiteman.

He shrugged nonchalantly. "We'll beef up some of the other proposals I gave down there. That should satisfy him."

Several days later we met again with the Governor at 55th Street to review the first draft of the message. All went uneventfully until Nelson reached the section on drugs. "Where's my program?" He spoke with cold anger. "I told you exactly what I wanted." Whiteman looked stunned as Rockefeller again described the life-without-escape plan.

Richard Wiebe, a longtime key staffer, with a sharp mind and blunt manner, started to explain, in terms of penology, practicality, and simple justice, the illogic of putting someone in prison for life for selling an ounce of hashish.

Rockefeller's head snapped to the source of resistance. "What do you know about it?" Wiebe muttered defensively, "Well, I read." Rockefeller responded with a look of unalloyed disdain. Whiteman at last accepted that the Governor was serious and put his staff to work translating Nelson's intent into the form of legislation.

Howard Jones, chairman of the state's Narcotics Addiction Control Commission, had not yet been consulted about the Rockefeller proposal. When he learned of it, he asked for an appointment with the Governor. The two men met, with some of the staff, in a small room in the Capitol. Rockefeller's expression of settled concrete did little to encourage dissent, but Jones pressed on manfully. He pointed out that the courts were unlikely to hand down such harsh sentences, that the jails could not hold all the prisoners that this law would generate, and that pushers would recruit minors to carry their dope. Most tragically, the bill left no hope for rehabilitating an offender guilty perhaps of a single mistake in life.

Rockefeller heard his leading drug-control official in stiff silence. When Jones, like a man sinking in quicksand, finally trailed off, Rockefeller said only, "Is that all?" After Jones left, Rockefeller remarked, "He's just worried about his people." Howard Jones was a black.

That evening, at the pool house behind the Executive Mansion, another meeting was held to review the legislation. Whiteman's staff had drafted a drug bill that left room for minors and first offenders to escape the steel trap of life in prison. The Governor turned on him. "You are determined to destroy this bill. You insist on having your own way!"

For the young lawyer, this confrontation in the pool house was shattering. Michael Whiteman was a Harvard Law School graduate, highly intelligent, sensitive, thoughtful. Virtually his entire professional life had been devoted to Nelson Rockefeller, and he had risen through the ranks of the Counsel's Office to hold, at the age of thirty-three, one of the most powerful positions in New York. Nelson Rockefeller had made him, and he was not disposed to defy his benefactor. Still, he believed his job was to give Rockefeller good legislation and steer him from bad legislation. What Nelson now wanted was undeniably bad. When Whiteman left for home that night, he recognized that he had reached a professional crossroads in his long journey with a man whom he regarded as something of a father. The next morning he asked Mrs. Whitman for a private meeting with the Governor, who received him with chilly formality. The lawyer explained what he believed to be his responsibility, indeed his value to the Governor. "I am trying to be constructive. But if you doubt my loyalty or integrity, you should not have me around." They were among the hardest words Whiteman had ever uttered.

Whiteman's position virtually constituted the good soldier's creed at the policy level of government. Debate and disagreement are permitted until a decision is reached. You then carry out the decision. But Nelson, conditioned to ever-nodding heads, had trouble distinguishing honest dissent from disloyalty. However, he now appeared mollified by his counsel's frankness. Thus Whiteman would proceed with a bill that he did not like. And Rockefeller would recognize that Whiteman's distaste indicated no lack of fealty.

The counsel next had to deliver the Rockefeller proposal to the legislative leaders. Their disbelief matched his own original shock. "What's he sending up next?" Capitol wags asked. "Death for overtime parking?"

On January 3, 1973, Nelson Rockefeller proposed to the legislature "making the penalty for all trafficking in hard drugs (defined as heroin, amphetamines, LSD, methadone and hashish) a life sentence in prison." And to close all avenues for escaping the full force of this sentence, he went on, "The law would forbid acceptance of a plea to a lesser charge, forbid probation, forbid parole, and forbid suspension of sentence." The Governor further proposed "a $1,000 state cash reward for the person or persons providing information leading to the apprehension and conviction of each hard-drug pusher."

Liberals were aghast. *The New York Times* kept up an editorial counterattack, condemning Rockefeller's "prosecutorial prose" and simplistic "lock-'em-up-for-life" solutions. But editorial howls were no match for Rockefeller's evangelism and craft. In the end, he made the necessary strategic retreats. Hashish was exempted from the hard-drug penalties, and offenders aged sixteen to nineteen were made eligible for parole after spending a minimum of fifteen years in prison.

The elemental level of the debate left lawmakers scant choice—were they for or against drug pushers? The bill passed with ease and became law in May 1973.

Where did Nelson Rockefeller get this idea? Had penologists and jurists urged him along this course? Was it the product of professional investigation and research? In March of the previous year, Nelson had been chatting at a party with William Fine, then president of Bonwit Teller department store. Fine was also chairman of a drug rehabilitation program called Phoenix House, a commitment growing from his own son's struggle against drug addiction.

"Would you like to do something for New York State?" Nelson asked. Fine agreed, and Nelson said, "Then go to Japan for me." The Japanese had the lowest addiction rate of any major nation, and Nelson Rockefeller wanted to know why. Fine agreed to go and financed the trip himself. He flew there and spent a weekend conferring with Japanese health officials. He came away with the apparent secret to the Japanese success against drugs—life sentences for pushers. He returned and submitted a report to Governor Rockefeller.

For two months, he heard nothing. Then he met Nelson at another party at which Ronald Reagan, then governor of California, was also present. Fine intrigued Reagan with his account of the trip and his report on the experience. Reagan wanted to know if he might have a copy. Fine crossed the room to check with Rockefeller, who delivered a firm no. This thunderbolt was to be hurled by him. The $1,000 bounty was an idea that one of Happy's children had picked up at college. Thus the law under which thousands of narcotics cases would be tried in the courts of a great state had been something of a family affair, a neighborly improvisation without the deadening hand of oversophisticated professionals.

The 1973 drug law illuminated a salient Nelsonian quality: his are-you-with-me-or-against-me test of loyalty. How did members of the staff who knew better justify their efforts to advance this congenitally deformed scheme? Whiteman reasoned that an idea so fixed in the Governor's mind had gone beyond his capacity to alter. "Society and its elected leaders," he concluded, "have the right to be wrong."

And what of the staff member who wrote Rockefeller's overblown rhetoric promoting the bill? ("Are the sons and daughters of a generation who survived the Great Depression, and who rebuilt a prosperous nation, who defeated Nazism and Fascism and preserved the free world, to be defeated by needles, powders and pills?")

I never fully understood the psychological milieu in which the chain of errors in Vietnam was forged until I became involved in the Rockefeller drug proposal. This experience brought to life with stunning palpability psychologist Irving Janis' description of groupthink: "the concurrence-seeking tendency which fosters overoptimism, lack of vigilance and sloganistic thinking about the weakness and immorality of outgroups."

We begin by accepting as desirable a general objective. Thus, swallowing the distasteful parts of this objective becomes more palatable. Add to the situation that we are working for a figure whom, on the whole, we admire and respect. Add further that this beleaguered figure at the head of the table no longer wants to know whether you think his policy is right or wrong. He has already made up his mind on that point; he now only cares to know who is with him and who is against him. Who is part of his answer and who is part of his problem? When this state-of-siege mentality is reached, the constructive critic has a thankless, indeed hopeless task. His alternatives are to concur in the policy, shut up, or resign. The gadfly role is made even less attractive when one has witnessed the fate of those who dissent. Two members of our staff who initially resisted Nelson on the drug bill marked the descent of their stars from that moment. When you are an officer on the bridge of the *Queen Mary* and the skipper occasionally acts daft, you don't stomp off and sign on with a tugboat. And so I fell back on that stale rationale of the morally uncomfortable—the decision had already been made. Who wrote the words promoting the policy was irrelevant; if I didn't do it, somebody else would. There are narcotics other than heroin.

Six years after passage of the Rockefeller drug bill, Hugh Carey, then New York's governor, stated that the law had "resulted in injustices in numerous cases and has made courts, prosecutors and jurors reluctant to enforce its provisions." The Rockefeller program had "not been effective in reducing drug traffic in New York." Subsequently, its most ironfisted provisions were removed.

Nelson Rockefeller consumed people, their energies, their loyalty, occasionally their judgment. In common with many strong leaders he did not suffer critics gladly. He could be an Olympian grudge bearer, and bore his grudges with the silent snobbery of the super rich. The victims of his disfavor were usually left ignorant of their offense. Nelson's approach was the reverse of the right of *habeus corpus*. The alleged offenders were locked out, not locked up, without knowing the charges against them. At various periods in his service, I was at the vital center of his operations, exiled to the Siberian fringe, or somewhere in between, never really sure of what I had done to deserve each change in my fortunes. Others on the staff reported similar confusion.

While covering him as a journalist, Jim Cannon had known Nelson Rockefeller as the most affable and gracious of men. This opinion seemed to be confirmed when, soon after he went to work for Nelson, Cannon and his wife were invited to vacation at the ranch in Venezuela with Nelson and Happy. The holiday was so pleasurable that Happy wanted to extend it one more day. She raised this possibility at a time when Nelson was away from the ranch. Cannon took the initiative. He phoned Mrs. Whitman in New York to find out if there was any reason why the party could not return a day later. She told him that there was no urgent business requiring the Governor's attention.

When Nelson learned what Cannon had done, he said, "I really appreciate that."

"He spoke," Cannon later remembered, "with a coldness in his voice that I'd never heard before. Happy tried to help by saying it was her idea. That only made him madder."

"You work for *me*," Rockefeller reminded him.

Cannon recovered from that case of frostbite, but he came to know well the climate of alternating thaws and freezes. One Easter he left on a family vacation, sure that he had forewarned Rockefeller. "But after I left, he pushed my button one day, and I didn't pop up. When I got back, it was no more staff lunches. No more staying at the Governor's Mansion. No more rides on the flying royal barge. I had to get from New York to Albany on my own hook. Stay in motels. I wasn't invited to the State Republican Convention. Finally, after three months of this, I asked Ann Whitman to get me an appointment with him. I told him that in the news business, when my reporters got a story wrong, I explained the problem and how to fix it. He heard me out without a word or a change of expression. Finally, he said, 'Yes, that's one way to do it. Another way is to put some distance between you and them. They'll get the picture.' " The prince does not explain.

It is unfair to say that he demanded yes-men; rather, one learned to say "no" obliquely to Nelson Rockefeller. In his presence, the ordinarily blunt Al Marshall became wondrously elliptical in his dissents. He explained to me why he had learned to do so. "He had another drug program he liked when I first became secretary. He was going to sweep all the junkies off the streets, put them away for mandatory treatment. I told him we couldn't do it. Where were we going to put them? He got mad and told me I was just looking for excuses because I didn't like the idea. We went down to Washington, and the Feds shot his plan full of holes. On the way back in the plane he was mad as hell. He glared at me. 'All right, Marshall, maybe you won that time.' And I was thinking, What the hell did I win?"

In February 1972, after years in his employ, I saw someone take him on for the first time in a direct, personal clash. We had gone to Washington so that Nelson could testify on a bill calling for a federal takeover of welfare costs. Since New York's welfare program had ballooned from $400 million to $4 billion while he was governor, Rockefeller understandably favored the measure. In his testimony he recounted with relish the steps he had taken to uncover fraud in the welfare system.

Senator Abraham Ribicoff of Connecticut, a member of the Senate Finance Committee, spoke to Nelson with a harshness rare to Rockefeller ears. "I want to pin you down, Governor Rockefeller, to a sense of responsibility. . . . Let's not accuse fourteen million Americans of being cheaters. . . . I followed your activities in welfare and your restrictive practices in the last two years and . . . you imply that twenty percent of the people are trying to cheat." Ribicoff drilled on with an unrelenting prosecutorial style.

Witnessing for the first time this lack of deference, I was curious. How did Nelson Rockefeller react to unmoderated hostility from a professional peer? He responded like a neighborhood tough who gets an unexpected punch in the nose from the quiet kid on the block. He swiftly adopted an exaggerated respect and amicability. He looked to the committee with an eager smile. "Senator Ribicoff and I are friends. We've always been friends for years." Ribicoff had not sounded at all friendly.

From his staff he expected an uncomplaining sublimation of self. Indeed, a mortal sin in the Rockefeller court was "to go into business" for oneself, as Joe Boyd's experience illustrated. Boyd had worked for Rockefeller for twelve years, and Nelson had treated him like a son. He had brought Boyd along from Young Republican leader to chief advance man to patronage director. He had lectured Boyd through the years on the nature of power, the mystery and mastery of the leader's art. Boyd finally wanted to try it for himself. He decided to run for Congress from Suffolk County. Nelson opposed the idea; Boyd insisted. The reluctant Rockefeller was persuaded by the staff to hold a fund-raising reception for his departing protégé at his Fifth Avenue apartment. But there were to be no more lectures on power, no more lessons in leadership, no more secrets of winning politics. Joe Boyd had gone into business for himself.

I had once wanted to write an article for *The New York Times* op-ed page about the huge discrepancy in salaries then existing between the public and private sectors. (To cite one example: The physician in charge of the care of one million patients in the country's Veterans Administration hospitals was then making $40,000 a year, while in private practice virtually any surgeon who could hold a scalpel without cutting himself was earning an average $70,000 a year.) I went to Nelson with the idea and told him that, if he preferred, I would be happy to submit the piece under his by-line. "No," he said generously. "Go ahead. Submit the article in your own name."

On October 6, 1975, *The New York Times* carried a front-page story on Nelson's attempts to secure federal funds for financially beleaguered New York City. The paper also carried a long report on his upcoming appearance before a housing inquiry, and a third article, with photographs, described his new Japanese house at Pocantico. But on that day Nelson's eyes fastened only on my article on the op-ed page, and he turned unhappily to Hugh Morrow. "What's this now, Hughie? Joe going into business for himself?" Morrow reminded him of his earlier agreement to the article, thus probably sparing me another unexplained banishment to Nelson's limbo.

Among the staff, Hugh Morrow managed best to remain within fingertip distance of the man all day long, produce a prodigious volume of work, yet retain an amused, detached sanity. His patient loyalty, however, did not save Morrow from occasional missteps in the Rockefeller minefield. On one occasion he accompanied Nelson to the New York Hilton where the Governor was to make a statement to the press on his controversial mission to Latin America. They had agreed, at Morrow's suggestion, that the matter was best handled by not answering questions. After Rockefeller had said his piece, they would leave quickly. But reporters dogged their steps, and Rockefeller began to complain noisily—"This is ridiculous. This is stupid." —with hard glances at Morrow to insure that the reporters knew the author of the stupidity. It was happening in front of his peers, the people whom Morrow had to face daily to do his job.

He bore it in silence until they returned to West 55th Street. Thoughts of a house full of children, tuition bills and a Westchester mortgage did not deter him from the decision that his pride demanded, and he went to his office and typed out a letter of resignation. He then confronted Nelson alone in the Governor's office and handed him the letter. "Goddamn it, Nelson," he exploded, "I don't have to put up with this bullshit to make a living."

Nelson eyed him, cool and unfazed. "Hughie, neither do I." Morrow burst out laughing. The letter was torn up and the matter dropped.

Chapter XI

SONS AND DAUGHTERS

I LEARNED HIS PRIORITIES early in the game. One of the first speeches I wrote for Nelson Rockefeller involved the architect Wallace K. Harrison, his friend for more than thirty years. Harrison was to receive the 1967 Gold Medal of the American Institute of Architects, and the Institute had asked the Governor to make the presentation. In researching the speech, I was staggered to learn of the buildings that Harrison had authored. So imposing were his credits that I was unsure which to mention first in the speech. I finally decided that I should lead off with the United Nations headquarters, the symbolic capitol of the world. The text thus ran: "The imprint of Wally Harrison's genius is seen in the United Nations, in Rockefeller Center, in two New York World Fairs . . ."

I watched uneasily as Nelson went over the draft, page by page, without uttering a word or marring a line. The two of us were alone in the room, and the silence was unusual and unnerving. Reaching the end of the still virgin text, he flipped back to the opening and made one quick motion with his pen. He tossed the speech back to me with a prim, dismissing smile. Stopping in the hallway, I checked the first page—he had circled Rockefeller Center and moved it up to first place, ahead of the United Nations.

Bill Ronan once told of a similar microcosmic lesson in priorities that he had received at his first private meeting with Nelson. "The Governor-to-be took coffee, and the young lady serving some goodies along with it came over with a tray that had a Danish pastry and one glazed doughnut. It was passed to me and I took the glazed doughnut. When I did, I thought she was going to drop the tray. The next day, when I appeared for the second conversation, there were two glazed doughnuts on the tray. This was the beginning of my association with Nelson Rockefeller."

Others quickly learned to step gingerly about the Nelson psyche. In his first months as president of the Urban Development Corporation, Ed Logue had met Nelson only on the sunny side of the street. Then one day Logue arranged a ceremony to publicize the ground breaking for a new state park to be built along a stretch of the Harlem River, previously home to junkyards and rotting wharves. As soon as the event was announced, Logue received a telephone call. He heard an unfamiliar Rockefeller; a once glowing fireplace had gone stone cold. "That happens to be *my* project, not yours. *My* son Steven discovered that spot, do you understand? While he was on a canoe trip." Logue tactically and tactfully backed off. The ceremony was redesigned to be hosted by the father of the park site's discoverer.

The family had implanted in Nelson a serene self-assurance, which made him virtually aweproof. Enthusiastic? Impressed? Admiring? Yes. But genuinely overwhelmed by others? Almost never. I once included a quotation from Teddy Roosevelt in a speech. As he read it, an old memory surfaced. "He visited us in New York when we were children." Nelson spoke offhandedly of Roosevelt's visit, the way the rest of us might recall a favorite uncle stopping by the house. "I was curious about how he brought the big game back from Africa. He said he shipped the stuff by train. So I wanted to know how he got the giraffes through the tunnels. President Roosevelt told me they had a pulley on the giraffe's head. And when they came to a tunnel, they pulled it down, and at the other end, they let it up."

My first awareness of his relations with his grown children came about through a speaking invitation. The letter was from the president of the International Basic Economy Corporation inviting the governor of New York to speak at IBEC's twenty-fifth anniversary celebration. Nelson had founded IBEC, and the sender of the invitation and current head of the company was his son Rodman. After the "Dear Father," Rodman's letter was indistinguishable from hundreds of other invitations we received from organizations like the American Banking Association or the United Jewish Appeal. An utter absence of intimacy characterized the correspondence between father and son. I read the letter with a chill.

Perhaps not surprisingly, most of Nelson's children craved experiences in which they could seek a degree of public anonymity and their own identity. The shy, quiet Ann, Nelson's second child, was for a time a social worker in London's East End. Steven, next in line, commented on his six months in the Army: "I enjoyed being a nobody, a PFC. It was nice having no responsibilities. It was a vacation." The younger daughter, Mary, spent a summer on a public-health project among the Navajos. She lived in a trailer, ate out of tin cans, went unrecognized and loved it. Her twin, Michael, went off to New Guinea to study and photograph Stone Age tribesmen in the Asmat, where the Rockefeller world was planets away.

Only the haughty Rodman slipped unresisting into the role of princeling. Not a young man much after his father's heart, he was closer in temperament to his mirthless grandfather, John D., Jr. He had, however, followed in his father's footsteps by taking over IBEC. But Nelson did not approve of his son's management of the corporation and did not spare Rodman this opinion. He had, in fact, at a crucial point, turned down Rodman's request for a substantial loan to aid the firm. The distance between them came in time to resemble a chasm between glaciers, as I gleaned from one brief transaction.

In the 1968 campaign for the presidential nomination, we were still trying to dilute the effects of Nelson's divorce and remarriage. Thus I was ghosting an article that was to show Nelson as a caring father. As a start, I called Rodman Rockefeller and asked him for anecdotes on growing up with Nelson. The call went through quickly. Rodman was evidently not about to risk missing out on a possibly important signal passed along via one of his father's lieutenants. But when he understood that what I wanted was not something he had to do, but rather a favor to aid his father's campaign, the voice went cold. "I'm not quite sure what there is that I could say. You'll have to excuse me." At least he had inherited Nelson's capacity for choking off unwanted conversation.

Steven Rockefeller, four years Rodman's junior, had the Aldrich warmth and an admirable streak of independence. While his father and Uncle Laurance favored the controversial Con Ed power plant on Storm King Mountain, Steven had allied himself with the environmentalists and spoke out publicly against the project. He spoke too against the war in Vietnam, which Nelson, in his heart, never doubted was a noble cause. It was not these differences, however, that created a certain tension between father and son. Steven, as he grew older, had become afflicted with soul-searching, questioning the purpose of his life, the meaning of existence, quandaries that his father seemed to have never given a moment's thought. To Nelson his existence had a simple premise—to use his great advantages to acquire power and thus place his talents at their fullest in the service of his nation and the world. Steven's spiritual flailing about was utterly alien to him.

George Humphreys met Steven during the 1968 presidential campaign and recalled a dinner conversation they had. Steven had been working in the rental office at Rockefeller Center, following in Nelson's footsteps, but had lately left to pursue a doctorate in philosophy at Columbia University, a highly un-Nelsonian course of study. He explained to Humphreys that he wanted to teach. "For Christ sake's," Humphreys mused later. "Here's a guy with the leverage to affect a million people's lives and he wants to work on one classroom!" Nelson could not have expressed his bewilderment any better.

The young man's fairy-tale romance and marriage to Anne-Marie Rasmussen, the Norwegian girl who came to work as a maid at Pocantico, had failed in part because this immigrant Cinderella had eagerly embraced the values of wealth, power and social status just as Steven was rejecting them. Nelson liked this daughter-in-law. At a time when Anne-Marie was taking an aggressive stand on an issue involving her divorce from Steven, Nelson admitted that he harbored a special warm spot for the girl. "She's tough," he said approvingly. This was high praise in his value scale, and an unspoken statement of what he believed his son, the scholar, lacked.

With his warmth and unaffected ease with people, the third Rockefeller son, Michael, was both the envy and a favorite of his cousins. He had admirably struck off on his own, and although his interest in anthropology was perhaps less foreign to his father than Steven's absorption in philosophy, the subject was hardly a passion of Nelson's. For Michael, anthropology provided a way of stepping back and putting the whole of human experience into a spectrum where Rockefellers did not loom so dominantly. Michael wrote to his parents of his investigations among New Guinea's Kurelu and Papaguan tribesmen in terms that politely but trenchantly rejected Nelson's bedrock beliefs: "The West thinks in terms of bringing advance and opportunity to such a place. In actuality, we bring a cultural bankruptcy which will last for many years. The Asmat, like every other corner of the world, is being sucked into a world economy and a world culture which insists on economic plenty as a primary ideal."

It is questionable how long these mordant views would have been treated by Nelson as evidence of youthful romanticism before they became family heresy. But Michael died before that divide was ever reached, and his death was a grievous blow to his father. Nelson spoke of it years later to his staff. "I was not crazy about his going back. I never told him this, of course, because I've always felt you've got to back your children's interests." Then, with that need to connect the most intimate events of his life to impersonal, grander themes, he added, "If we as a people lose the curiosity and willingness to explore, and the risks that go with it, our civilization will stop making progress." The thought itself epitomizes the gulf between him and his lost son. Michael, at the time of his death, was questioning the very assumption of ceaseless progress; Nelson never doubted it.

Young Rockefellers were allowed, even encouraged, to say their piece at home. Nelson's children could spout heresy or question orthodoxy. But there the intellectual interaction ended. He listened, he did not quarrel, and he did not change. He knew what he believed. As his daughter Mary put it: "My father, well, I love him for his warmth. But he stands for power." The semblance of a free forum around Nelson's table, however, appears to have released steam without loosening family loyalty. Nelson's children strayed intellectually and emotionally, but none of them ever completely bolted the reservation. Unlike David's daughter Peggy, who embraced Marxism, or Laurance's daughter Marion, who chose to live in a caboose and do social work, none of Nelson's children wholly rejected their heritage.

I was amused to find Nelson facing the same prosaic problems as other parents of married children. The governor of New York State called Ed Logue to ask if he might have a place in his Urban Development Corporation for a fine young man. In staffing his new organization, Logue had insisted on the power to hire and fire without political interference. He had brooked no exceptions until now, but in the case of Nelson's son-in-law, Logue violated his rule. The young man was likable enough, but not in the self-starting Ed Logue mold. When a budget reduction forced Logue to lay off staff, he found himself in an awkward position. Fire Nelson Rockefeller's son-in-law? "He was a nice guy," Logue later remembered. "But dropping him was important if I was going to have any credibility when I let others go." By the time Logue had to make the decision, however, the marriage had failed. Thus Logue's misgivings were substantially eased. He was only firing Nelson's ex-son-in-law.

I once remarked to the Governor how difficult it was for middle-class people, including those to whom the Depression was a personal memory, to teach their children the value of money, and I asked how he could possibly hope to do so. "They earn money," he answered. "They grow vegetables in the summer. They do chores for their mother. Also they get a weekly allowance. Nelson, Junior [then nine], gets ninety cents. Mark [then six] gets thirty cents. I made a deal with Nelson. I told him that if he could keep his accounts accurate for two months—without using those little computer things they have—I would raise his allowance. When they get a little older, they'll have to learn to make out a budget. So much for clothes, so much for this or that, you know. That's the way you have to do it. I grew up that way too."

He was concerned about teaching spiritual values as well, he said.

"I'm a great believer in family prayers. When we were growing up, we always had prayers in the morning and a reading from the Bible. Then after the Lord's Prayer, it was a little like a Quaker meeting. Anybody would say whatever came to their minds about their problems, what they were worried about. It was a moment of communion with God. If a child learns to express himself, it's a very beautiful thing. We grew up that way. So I've continued it. We have prayers every morning." Did his children pray for material things? "No. It's mostly related to goings on in their lives, awareness of others, relationships with the kids at school."

Nelson tried to give more of himself to the children of his second marriage than he had to his children by Tod. When asked how much time he spent with his two youngest sons, he would answer a trifle defensively, "It's not how much time you spend with children, but the quality of the time you spend with them." One December afternoon Bob Hope was to appear at West Point to try out material for his Christmas show for servicemen overseas. He asked Nelson to attend. Hope felt that Rockefeller owed him this one. The comedian had appeared at several events that were helpful to Nelson. Chuck Lanigan, then state Republican chairman, was with Nelson when Hope's invitation came. "I don't know what to do," Rockefeller lamented. "Little Nelson wants me to go to the Christmas play at his school that day." He handed Lanigan a sheet of paper covered with a child's scrawl and said, "Look. He wrote this to me himself." Rockefeller's eyes suddenly brightened. "Chuck, you go up to West Point. Represent me. And show Bob little Nelson's invitation."

Lanigan went to the Academy. Hope was clearly displeased to learn that the limousine with screaming siren and flashing lights bore not Rockefeller but a political aide. Much chagrined, Lanigan handed the comedian the child's invitation. Hope stared at it and returned it without a word or a smile.

Nelson tried to be closer too to his grandchildren, some of whom were older than his youngest sons. He dashed off letters to them at odd moments and sent thank-you notes for Christmas or birthday presents. The letters were replete with spelling and grammatical errors and half-finished thoughts, all of which Mrs. Whitman would repair before mailing.

From the children of the first marriage he had expected much and had been disappointed. But he knew that he had not given all that much. With the children of his marriage to Happy, he chose to give much, and he expected a great deal.

Chapter XII

A BROTHER'S
DEATH

Nᴇʟsᴏɴ's ʙʀᴏᴛʜᴇʀ Wɪɴᴛʜʀᴏᴘ ᴅɪᴇᴅ of cancer on February 22, 1973. Just before his death, I was surprised to see Hugh Morrow take Nelson aside at the end of a staff meeting to brief him on Win's failing condition. So much of their living and even dying was handled by staff. Still, I had expected that such intimate news would come from another family member.

I met Winthrop Rockefeller once. He has been described as the different Rockefeller, approachable, down-to-earth, modest, a regular guy except for the millions. One afternoon when Winthrop was flying to New York on business, I went to La Guardia Airport to catch a ride back to Albany on the same family plane that he was arriving in. Bob Douglass was going to come along, but at the last minute, Nelson wanted him to drive with him to Pocantico. Bob, therefore, asked me to have the plane make a quick stop at the Westchester County Airport to pick him up after he finished his work with the Governor. At the terminal, I approached a strapping giant in a Stetson, gleaming boots and a luxuriant red-streaked beard. I introduced myself and explained Bob Douglass' request. Winthrop leaned back and roared like a foreman dressing down a ranch hand: "Now you go and tell

Nelson, with a degree in economics and a Phi Beta Kappa key, is congratulated by his father, John D. Rockefeller, Jr., upon graduating from Dartmouth in 1930.

Nelson and Tod, the former Mary Todhunter Clark of Philadelphia, on their wedding day in June 1930.

Nelson's father chose him to be president of Rockefeller Center. Here, with Garreau Dombasle, he
raises the first flags over the Center's French Building.

The five sons of John D. Rockefeller, Jr. (left to right) Winthrop, Laurance, John III, David and Nelson. The bust is of their grandfather John D. Rockefeller, Sr.

Kykuit, the home John D. Rockefeller, Sr., built for himself on the Pocantico Hills estate. Kykuit later became Nelson's home.

Nelson, at age thirty-three, while serving as President Roosevelt's Coordinator of Inter-American Affairs, his first job wholly outside the Rockefeller universe.

President Franklin D. Roosevelt, Nelson's Hudson River neighbor, who appointed Rockefeller to his first Washington post and who also gave him an exalted vision of the Presidency against which he tended to measure all contenders, including himself.

Nelson in the fall of 1945. Although recently fired by President Harry S. Truman as Assistant Secretary of State for American Republic Affairs, Nelson managed to retain numerous Latin American admirers. Here, Chile's President, Juan Antonio Rios, embraces Nelson after presenting him with the Chilean Order of Merit. A beaming John D., Jr., stands by (left).

New York's First Family—elect poses on the night Nelson was elected to the first of his four terms as governor. He and Tod are flanked by their children (left to right) Mary, Steven, Mrs. Robert L. Pierson (the former Ann Rockefeller, partially hidden behind her father), Rodman, Barbara (Rodman's wife), and Michael.

Henry Kissinger in 1947, then a professor of government at Harvard, selected by Nelson to carry out the international security study of the Rockefeller Brothers project, "America at Mid-Century." The findings and recommendations of this report were appropriated by both parties during the 1960 Presidential campaigns.

A Christmas morning at the Rockefellers' Fifth Avenue apartment. Nelson and his first wife, Tod (seated right), daughter Mary (standing), son Rodman (next to his mother), Rodman's wife Barbara (partly hidden) and their two children, Peter (left) and Meile (right). The painting is Matisse's 1915 work *The Italian Woman*.

Nelson meets with President Dwight D. Eisenhower, soon after the Republican national convention had nominated Richard Nixon as its candidate for President in 1960. Although they were likely philosophical Republican soulmates, Nelson never enjoyed Eisenhower's support after he publicly criticized America's leadership that year.

Happy and Nelson, after their 1963 marriage, honeymoon at Monte Sacro, the Rockefeller ranch in Venezuela.

A brief truce during the Rockefeller-Lindsay feud. Nelson and Lindsay (right), then mayor of New York, pose in August 1968 over a model indicating the landfill where Battery Park City is to rise on Manhattan's Hudson River shoreline.

The 1968 assassination of U.S. Senator Robert F. Kennedy required Nelson, as Governor, to name a successor. New York City's mayor, John V. Lindsay, was initially thought to be a likely choice, but mutual antagonism scuttled the deal. Here Nelson is seen with the man he ultimately selected, Congressman Charles Goodell (center). At the left is U.S. Senator Jacob Javits.

UPI

UPI

Nelson and Richard Nixon at a Women's National Republican Committee Meeting early in 1968. They would compete for the Republican nomination before the year was out, Rockefeller's last Presidential bid.

During his 1968 mission to Latin America for
President Nixon, Nelson presents a letter from
Nixon to Haiti's president, François "Papa Doc"
Duvalier. The State Department argued in vain
for Nelson to keep personal contact with the Hai-
tian strong man at a mininum.

Hugh Morrow, Nelson's Director of Communications during the gubernatorial and Vice Presidential years and his closest adviser on public
relations.

Nelson stands before the vast project he launched to give New York the
nation's premier state capital, which was ultimately designated the Nelson A.
Rockefeller Empire State Plaza.

Donald Doremus/New York State Office of General Services

The Nelson A. Rockefeller Empire State Plaza completed.

UPI

During a break in his 1974 congressional confirmation hearings as Vice President, Nelson chats with Happy (left) and Nancy Kissinger (center), his longtime international relations aide and wife of Secretary of State Henry Kissinger. Happy at this point had undergone her first mastectomy a few weeks before and was waiting to gain strength for the second operation, which took place shortly afterward.

Four months after President Gerald Ford had first designated
him as Vice President and after the exhaustive scrutiny of
House and Senate committees, Nelson is sworn into office in
December 1974 by Chief Justice Warren Burger.

The Congress required four months to confirm Nelson as Gerald Ford's
Vice President. Here he is shown in the fall of 1974 testifying before the
Senate Confirmation Hearings.

Vice President Rockefeller presides over the U.S. Senate. Twice earlier he had rejected offers to run as a Vice Presidential candidate, with Richard Nixon and with Hubert Humphrey.

One of Nelson Rockefeller's five homes, a Revolutionary-era estate on twenty-seven acres in Washington, D.C. It was among the ten highest assessed addresses in the city. After Nelson left public life, the property was sold to a developer, who subdivided it.

At a White House reception with the Marine Corps ensemble. President Ford, Nelson and Henry Kissinger chat. A portrait of President John F. Kennedy looks down from the far wall.

Mark Godfrey/Magnum

The author and Vice President Rockefeller doing the final edit of a speech aboard *Air Force II*. On the bulkhead is the Vice Presidential seal which Nelson later had redesigned to have the wings pointing up instead of down.

Nelson meets in the Oval Office with President Ford in the early weeks of his Vice Presidency. In the center is James Cannon, a key Rockefeller aide, who became chief of the Domestic Council staff in the Ford Administration.

The other Governor Rockefeller, Winthrop, photographed at Jackson Hole, Wyoming, during the National Republican Governors Conference in 1967.

Nelson, with brother David, head of the Chase Manhattan Bank, and Happy near the Maine vacation home.

Goaded by heckling university students at a political rally near Binghamton, N.Y., Nelson displays a capacity to respond in kind. The incident occurred as Rockefeller accompanied U.S. Senator Robert Dole (left) Republican candidate for Vice President in 1976, on a campaign swing through New York State.

Happy Rockefeller enters Riverside Church in New York City for the memorial service for her husband. She is flanked by her sons, Mark (left) and Nelson Jr., (right). On the right is Robert R. Douglass, former counsel to the governor and close Rockefeller adviser. On the left are President and Mrs. Jimmy Carter.

your Mr. Douglass that it costs a hell of a lot of money—and fuel—
to put airplanes in and out of airports, in case he's not aware of it."
The approachable, humble Rockefeller moved off with a cowpoke's
amble. The plane did not make the Westchester stop.

In 1953, Winthrop had gone to live in Arkansas and found its soil
more nourishing to his character than that of Pocantico and the East.
He was soon regarded as an Arkansas resource. On this voyage of
self-discovery, he found a cragged, overgrown mountain, bought it,
and shaped it into his city on a hill. An army of workers sheared the
top off of Petit Jean Mountain, and there Win created Winrock, a
twenty-three-hundred-acre ranch, which stunned and flattered Ar-
kansans, because it represented tangible evidence of his citizenship in
their world. Eventually, fifty thousand visitors a year drove up Petit
Jean to visit Winrock, to marvel at its artificial lakes, named Abby
and Lucy for Win's mother and aunt, and its private airfield. Win had
a film produced on Winrock, complete with folksy narration. When
he ran it for the family at Pocantico one Christmas, his father put his
arm around him and smiled. "Win, you've done a wonderful job."
That was what making the film had been all about.

In 1955, Governor Orval Faubus asked Win to head the Arkansas
Industrial Development Commission. Rockefeller's success in luring
plants and jobs to the state launched his political career, and in 1966
he was elected governor of Arkansas, the first Republican to gain that
office since Reconstruction. This prize must have been especially
sweet when he contemplated long ago rivalries with his brother, the
governor of New York State. He was re-elected in 1968, and then it
all began to crumble, as though some dark seed, dormant under the
Arkansas skies, had begun to germinate again. In 1970, he ran a
shambles of a campaign and was beaten by an attractive young Democrat, Dale Bumpers. Defeated, divorced from his second wife, and
drinking heavily, Winthrop was dead within two years. Shortly afterward, the Rockefellers planned a memorial service at Winrock, and
Nelson, as the leader of the family, was to deliver the eulogy.

When a prominent person died, I automatically began writing a
statement for the governor of New York to issue. This time I hesitated, judging that customary staff procedure would not apply to a
death in the family. Wrong. Mrs. Whitman called to say that Nelson

was asking to see what I had prepared for Win's memorial service. I reflected briefly, then began pushing the usual buttons.

My first call was to Dr. Joseph Ernst at Room 5600, a Columbia University Ph.D. in history and the family archivist. The Rockefeller archives form a major historical collection and are probably the largest and most exhaustively catalogued repository of family papers in the country. Where were the original account books that John D. Rockefeller kept as a boy? Joe Ernst had them. How many merit badges did young Nelson Rockefeller earn as a Boy Scout? Ask Joe Ernst. Did Nelson ever contribute to the National Association for the Advancement of Colored People? Ernst knew—$76,250 between 1961 and 1971. I had once asked him what he could provide for a speech of Nelson's before the Legal Aid Society. Ernst produced a yellowed letter, written in 1916 by John D., Jr., making a contribution to launch that organization.

The morning after my request for material on Winthrop, Ernst produced a trove: letters from Win's mother, magazine profiles, his war record, his speeches. I also called Winrock Farm to ask the staff for anecdotal material and to get a deeper insight into him than I had gained during my one brief brush at La Guardia Airport. I took the first draft into Nelson the next morning, still feeling that I was intruding on a private sorrow. His eyes were red-rimmed and his voice uncharacteristically subdued as we set to work.

In my conversations with people at Winrock Farm I had learned that Win kept a wooden plaque in his office bearing these lines from Edgar Guest: "He started to sing as he tackled the thing that couldn't be done, and he did it." As a boy of twelve, Win had burned the words into the plaque by directing sunlight through a magnifying glass. I had mentioned the plaque in the text, since it afforded an obvious clue to the man's striving.

Nelson Rockefeller was a master at pursuing distinctions without a difference, but this day he outdid himself. First he wanted "The sun's rays burned the letters into the wood." Then, "The letters were burned into the wood by the sun's rays." As we juggled subject, object and predicate in pointless permutations, Nelson grew testier and I became more puzzled by his obsession with the inconsequential. When that knot was unsnarled to his satisfaction, we reached a passage in which I had described Win's heroism during World War II. Leading his infantry company ashore at Guam amid heavy fire, Win, by now a major, saw one of his men disappear into a shell hole and start to drown in the surf. He had reached for the soldier and swung him onto his shoulders, all the while wading toward the fire-raked beach. Again we began wrestling with invisible nuance. "Win reached out and grabbed the man." No. "Win reached under the water, grabbed the man and . . ." No. "With one hand, Win reached out and grabbed . . ." Christ! What conceivable difference could it make? The text became a field sown with verbal land mines blowing up at unlikely places. His absorption in meaningless changes was as maddening as it was inexplicable.

His behavior that impossible day began to make emotional if not logical sense later when I learned more of the Nelson-Winthrop relationship. Nelson blamed himself for much of Win's trouble. He knew just enough pop psychology to connect his childhood bullying and taunting to Win's later insecurities and self-destructive excesses. "I am responsible," he later said. Getting the eulogy exactly "right" seemed another reflection of his obsessive need now to do right by the brother whom he believed he had wronged for so long.

On the day of the memorial service, Nelson, his family, and a few members of the staff flew from New York to Winrock. So many private Rockefeller jets were headed for Arkansas that day that Nelson had had to rent a plane from an oil company. The service drew the Vice-President, governors, notables from throughout the nation. The day was grim, drizzling, gray.

Just before his departure for Winrock, Nelson told Hugh Morrow that he was afraid he would not be able to get through the eulogy. Morrow reassured him, telling him that if he could not speak, he should simply stop, wait for his composure to return, and then go on. When it was time for the eulogy, Nelson rose, looked out over the numerous progeny of John D. Rockefeller and the guests, and felt the very paralysis he had feared. When his voice broke, he stopped and then resumed. The pauses gave his words a simple eloquence. Of five sons, the prodigal had gone first. Nelson's pain was deep, for the loss itself and for what he believed was his part in causing it.

Chapter XIII

MONEY AND POWER

The talk-show host Mike Douglas once asked him, "What would you have done if you hadn't been born in the position you are in, with the fortune you have?"

Nelson Rockefeller answered unhesitatingly, "I would think of making one."

He carried less walking-around money than many a suburban teen-ager. "I usually have between ten and fifteen dollars in my pocket," he once revealed, and he never felt the necessity to apologize for his millions. A conservative southern senator once asked Nelson why rich men in politics so often adopt a liberal stance. He answered, "I think some people feel this is because of a guilt complex. I have to tell you, I have no guilt complex."

At a town meeting, a leftist radical attacked from the opposite direction. "Would you tell us how you feel about being in the position of owning billions of dollars in personal wealth while millions of people around the world are starving?"

"It's simple. I have no billions of dollars, therefore your question has no relevance."

His antagonist pressed on. "How about many millions of dollars?"

Rockefeller said, "That I do. I have tried to use those dollars to the best possible purpose so as to help people in this world and to make our private-enterprise, democratic, capitalistic system serve the best interests of mankind. This has been my family tradition, as you well know, sir."

His interrogator asked if he had ever considered sharing his wealth with the world's needy. Nelson replied, "You are talking Fabian socialism—or communism. I happen to believe in capitalism and private enterprise and democracy, based on production and not on dividing up something that exists into little pieces. Then what have you got?"

He came to the office one morning grumbling about what the schools were teaching. "If you want to know what worries me, it's the textbooks. I've got two little ones. Nine and twelve. I don't see anything teaching them about the American enterprise system. I don't see anything about what this system has done to give opportunities to Americans. The American people are growing up today without an understanding of the system that made this country great."

"Unlike a lot of liberals," Al Marshall recalled, "he wasn't turned off by somebody making a buck off a socially worthwhile program, like banks and bond buyers getting in on his housing projects. He was enough of a capitalist to wonder how good the motivation was if somebody couldn't make money on it. That was his philosophy of government. Take a project that private enterprise won't touch, and then make it commercially appealing."

Though saddled with the image of a big government spender, Nelson could speak fluent laissez-faire capitalism when the occasion suited him. In 1975, he agreed to help William Simon, Gerald Ford's treasury secretary, who was then casting longing eyes at the state house in New Jersey. Simon had gathered a large group of eastern pillars of commerce to his estate for a private meeting with Rockefeller. The press was kept waiting outside.

Nelson sat in the center of Simon's drawing room. His jaw jutted out like a concrete abutment, and his voice lowered to a husky growl. One had to strain to hear him. *"They"*—he spoke the word as though identifying an alien, invading force—"don't have our sense of values. *They* don't have our understanding of the role of capital. *They* don't have our love of country." The sinister "they" to whom he referred were the leaders of the Democratic Caucus in the Congress. A hushed silence prevailed as Nelson went on. "My position has not always been understood in the Republican Party. But let me tell you. I want to preserve this country. Who's got more to preserve?" He said it with a mirthless laugh, as his eyes played over the audience. The opulent setting, his conspiratorial tone, the aura of power pervading the room, suggested a capitalist cabal straight out of a Robert Ludlum novel. The man knew how to play to his class.

Any potential guilt over his money was further assuaged for Nelson by six decades of Rockefeller philanthropies. Why should a man apologize for wealth when his family had given nature lovers Jackson Hole, history lovers Colonial Williamsburg, Francophiles a restored Versailles, and humanity the benefits of Rockefeller-financed medical research?

At Nelson's confirmation hearings for the vice-presidency, a California congressman, Jerome Waldie, dismissed the philanthropies abruptly: "You are not entitled to adulation and you are not even entitled to anything except the responsible feeling that you have performed that which you are obligated to perform for people of this country. You have not performed anything in excess that an individual who works forty hours a week in a paper mill in Antioch, California, who goes home at night and takes care of a cub scout troop, and works on the weekends, contributes and sacrifices for public service." In a similar vein, out of curiosity I once calculated that Nelson Rockefeller giving a panhandler $1,850 and a typical middle class person giving him a dime represented roughly equal financial sacrifice.

These are carping observations. The more interesting point is not whether the Rockefellers' philanthropies meant any personal sacrifice to themselves, but the shrewd way in which they gave their money away, an approach that they liked to call "venture philanthropy." The Rockefellers subscribed to the old idea of teaching a hungry man to fish rather than buying him a meal. In the end, the seed capital that they planted in philanthropic endeavors gave them greater national and international influence than did their profit-making enterprises and was certainly more lasting in effect than had they blown the fortune on polo ponies and casinos. They were responsible enough, and wise enough, to underpin their own position by strengthening, through their giving, those institutions in society that they found worthy of perpetuation.

If Nelson felt no guilt and offered no apology for his wealth, a deeper problem remained. When a man is handed a gold cup at birth, how does he know if he is an authentic winner? I put the question to him, rather less bluntly, one afternoon. He answered, "I'm not sure that inheriting money is making good. You've got it and so you're lucky from that point of view. But that doesn't provide any inner sense of having made good, having achieved something yourself."

He was constantly asked by interviewers, in disbelieving tones: "Nelson Rockefeller, with all your money, why are you knocking yourself out, running all over the country trying to become President? Why didn't you become a playboy?" He usually fell back on explanations stressing "service," "responsibility," "love of country." All, no doubt, sincere, but at bottom lay the deeper reason. Nelson Rockefeller had a high opinion of himself. He believed that he possessed an extraordinary and natural gift of leadership. To him, his money was incidental—he was destined to achieve with or without it. And one does not prove that point by becoming a playboy.

If he felt no qualms over the money, neither did he feel removed from those with little of their own (though he once started to illustrate the effect of a tax proposal by saying, "Take an average family with an income of a hundred thousand dollars."). He surprised Ed Logue, chief of the Urban Development Corporation, with his sensitivity toward ordinary people. Logue had prepared a film to promote the Urban Development Corporation, and premiered it for the Governor. The film opened with a pan shot across interminable rows of look-alike homes in a suburban tract, with a narrator making clear that such failure of imagination was not to be the UDC style. Nelson watched restlessly, then said, "You'd better be careful, Ed. People live in those houses, and they like 'em." Cut. End of Logue's film.

He summarily rejected any notion that he was isolated from the masses of mankind. "I can step out of a car in Harlem or in any other place, Chinatown, or any part of this country, and feel perfectly at home. And I have. I don't think, frankly, what you have in terms of money determines what you are like inside and your ability to understand people or relate to their problems."

Indeed, he believed that he understood the plight of the poor better than they did themselves. I watched him one day during a four-hour session with angry New York City black leaders discussing the housing situation in the South Bronx. When one of them challenged his ability to comprehend their problems, he said, "Is it more difficult for me to understand the question of someone living in the ghetto than for someone living in the ghetto to understand the housing complexities I have just been explaining to you for hours?"

Although he admired people who had lifted themselves from poverty to wealth and power, Nelson believed that most self-made men could not share his breadth of vision. They were often intellectually inhibited by "bitterness from their early deprivation," as he put it. An upstate mayor, a man who had done extremely well after a humble beginning, once joined Rockefeller at a New York reviewing stand to watch the Pulaski Day parade. With great ceremony, the mayor lifted a hair from Nelson's jacket, observing, "Governor, you need to be neatened up a bit." Rockefeller smiled his coldest smile and brushed some dandruff off the man's shoulder. "You could stand a little tidying up yourself, Mr. Mayor." He had absorbed well his father's lesson: "Neither scorn nor fear the common man."

In the first draft of the eulogy for his brother Winthrop, I had written that Win's election as governor of Arkansas was all the more remarkable for his surmounting three obstacles: Win had been an easterner, a Republican and a Rockefeller. "Oh, no," Nelson spoke animatedly, delighted to lay an old ghost to rest. "That business about the Rockefeller name being a political handicap? That was what the papers, the intellectual types, always said. The American people never felt that way. You can see that with Win and Jay and I getting elected to public office." He relished the verdict of the people over the elitists.

He occasionally liked to sentimentalize the Rockefellers' origins. Through the years, John D., the founding grandfather, became, in Nelson's telling, a high-school dropout, first at age sixteen, then fifteen, then fourteen. Actually, he was graduated from Cleveland Central High School in 1855. Nelson sometimes told of roller-skating to school on the sidewalks of New York, omitting the fact that the family limousine was cruising alongside.

The Rockefeller brothers, especially Nelson, who was the least provident of the five, had rather eccentric ideas about thrift and simplicity. When he was running for the presidential nomination in 1968, Nelson summoned his chief advance man, Joe Boyd, to his motel room in a South Carolina city. Boyd found Happy stretched out on one bed and Nelson on another.

"Joe, sit down." Nelson spoke gravely. "I'm worried about expenses in this campaign."

Boyd nodded. "Yes, sir. It's an expensive business."

Rockefeller went on. "Now, I like Oreo cookies. But I only eat three or four." He sat up and rummaged in the wastebasket for an empty Oreo package. He then reached into a dish piled with cookies. "Here you've got two dozen." He began dropping the Oreos into the empty package. "Can't we get a refund on packages we don't use?"

Boyd nodded uncertainly and left. Thereafter he gave his crew fresh instructions. In the future, uneaten Oreos were to be taken along to the next stop.

His brother Laurance went out one afternoon at Pocantico and chopped his own firewood. He found the exertion bracing, and impressed by the rewards of the simple life, he decided to write on the subject. He roughed out a few thoughts for an article that he turned over to an aide to develop and polish. The first draft completed, the assistant boarded a plane with Laurance. They edited the piece on the joys of rediscovered simplicity while flying at forty thousand feet, the only two passengers in a $4.5 million private jet.

A reporter would occasionally ask us what Nelson did with his salary as governor which had risen by then to $85,000. Our press office replied that he kept it. His state salary provided his mad money. Nelson sent his paychecks to a private secretary at Room 5600 and would dip into the account for $5,000 or so in cash for an occasional shopping spree.

Being esteemed and liked apart from his money was emotionally vital to Nelson Rockefeller. After becoming Vice-President, he was invited to speak before that showcase of political humor, Washington's annual Gridiron Club Dinner. Representing the Democrats that year was Robert Strauss. Strauss, a gifted storyteller, had the audience in his palm with his double-edged style, Texas hype and Jewish sage. Nelson sat on the stage, savoring Strauss's performance along with everyone else. Strauss suddenly turned to Nelson and drawled, with a broad grin, "I want you all to know—party differences aside —that I like Nelson Rockefeller." He continued the dazzling smile. "And I'm going to tell you why." Nelson glowed with good fellowship. Strauss's voice suddenly dropped to a low growl. "I like Nelson Rockefeller . . . *because he's got MOOO . . . NNNEEY!*" Nelson's smile turned sickly. Later, when it was his turn to speak, he reached a Bob Strauss joke in his script. He stopped and said with a sad air, "You know, I just wish Bob had said he liked me because I was real."

Chapter XIV

THE LEADER

"THERE MUST ALWAYS BE a something which others cannot altogether fathom, which puzzles them, stirs them and rivets their attention." Had Nelson Rockefeller been more intellectual, he might have articulated this characterization of the leader. Actually, Charles de Gaulle said it. Nelson, nevertheless, lived by it.

He had a maddening manner of expressing his wants through fuzzy, half-articulated phrases. "You know what I mean," he would say with a dismissing wave, as an aide left his office, struggling to understand what he meant. He could change a speech or a guest list four times in a day. The staff was expected to adapt uncomplainingly, as though each instruction were being received afresh with no conflict created or time lost in carrying out the earlier inoperative orders. Peter Wallison, who served him as his counsel during Nelson Rockefeller's Vice-Presidency, evolved a rule. "There are two ways to become a nonperson with Nelson Rockefeller. The first is to fail to do exactly what he tells you. The second is to do it."

One had to learn the meanings of his conversational shorthand. "Where am I?" muttered while going over a staff paper, meant "You've described a problem, but you have failed to include the efforts and achievements of Nelson Rockefeller to solve it over the years. I want that in here." "I hear what you're saying" meant "Shut up and stop reiterating a point that I have already understood and dismissed."

Bob Douglass, alone among us, could best divine Rockefeller's intent, as though an unseen cable joined their minds. The rest of us often eyed one another for some clue to a vaguely expressed want. Afterward, Douglass translated. I once asked Mrs. Whitman how so apparently intelligent a person could be so opaque. "It's deliberate," she answered, "to keep you off balance." When a man can make vague and arbitrary demands, while others have to race around, struggling to decipher and fulfill them, this behavior sets that man apart and lends him that mystique of the superior being that de Gaulle described. Nelson thought consciously about such dynamics of leadership. He had once counseled Joe Boyd, "You can't be obvious or arrogant. But sometimes you have to use power just to make sure people know who has it."

He thus created an environment where one did not ask why the implausible was being ordered, but rather how to do it. Lawyers, as servants of logic and form, frequently misread Nelson because they were forever telling him why something could not be done. He would grumble, "Don't tell me we can't give state aid to parochial schools because it's unconstitutional. Tell me how we *can* do it."

Richard Dunham eventually won high trust as Nelson's budget director. But the plain-speaking Dunham almost ran aground early on because he had not learned how to separate clouds from silver linings for Nelson. Bob Douglass took Dunham aside and said, "Dick, when he asks you to do something improbable, don't tell him the obstacles. Tell him yes, right away. Of course, it can be done. Then casually mention a few problems. You're doing it backwards." Dunham adapted and survived. Rockefeller had come out of a private world where he got what he wanted, and he transported this expectation intact to the public sector. Aides who did not share his faith were guilty of negativism, an unpardonable sin in Nelson's eyes.

He generated constant striving among us by withholding total approval. We carried no credits over from one day to the next. He could exclaim "Fantastic" to someone who had worked through the night on an assignment, but this praise did not spare the same aide from a frosty rejection on another matter an hour later. We were forever starting back at ground zero, trying all over again to win his approval. Three of my colleagues who had each worked closely with him for more than fifteen years voiced virtually the same sentiment, "I never felt he entirely trusted me."

We were not to debase the Rockefeller currency by employing his influence casually. I once received a call from a friend, a high-level bureaucrat with the U.S. Information Agency telling me that the organization was being threatened with a stiff appropriations cut in Congress. Since I was a USIA alumnus, he asked if I could enlist Nelson to urge Congress to spare the ax. I took the matter to Jim Cannon, then handling our congressional liaison. Cannon went directly to the point. "If the director of USIA wants to call Nelson Rockefeller for a favor, that's different. Otherwise, forget it." We were not to cast pearls before GS 15s.

For all his outward gregariousness and exuberant bonhomie, Nelson Rockefeller created a certain aura of propriety around him. He eschewed that shortcut to masculine camaraderie—profanity. He cursed rarely and then mildly. I heard him tell one risqué joke in eleven years, and that about as comfortably as a schoolboy reciting a poem in French. I heard him use the all-purpose four-letter word once, and then only to quote John Lindsay. When asked, "Governor, did you hear what Lindsay let slip over an open mike?" he answered, "You mean when he said, 'Close the fucking door'?" He self-consciously slurred the word.

The surest giveaway that one's intimacy with Nelson was imaginary was to refer to him as Rocky. Only two members of the immediate staff called him Nelson, Bill Ronan and Hugh Morrow. Everyone else was more comfortable with Governor. Virtually the only staff member who could tease him was Bob Douglass, and he did so with extreme caution, the way someone might handle a pet porcupine. After Rockefeller had wangled an opposition legislator's key vote, Douglass chided, "You old rascal, you." He made sure to preface the remark with a broad, unmistakably admiring smile. Others failed to amuse. When Nelson introduced Chuck Lanigan, his new Republican state chairman, at a party luncheon, he inadvertently used the name of Lanigan's predecessor. Chuck rose and responded amiably, "Thank you, Governor Lehman." Amid the laughter, one face remained frozen.

Nelson could clarify personal relationships instantly by a shift in his tone of voice. Once, when we were flying the Grumman into Los Angeles, he said casually to the new steward heading down the aisle, "I wonder when we'll be getting in." The steward smiled back. "It won't be long now, Governor." Nelson's voice took on a glacial edge. "That's not what I meant. I expect you to find out what time we're getting in."

Rockefeller was a political leader to whom party loyalty was a sometime thing. Nelson was not only immune but almost allergic to the mother's milk view of political patronage. He appointed Harry Albright, an able lawyer with no strong party ties, as his patronage dispenser precisely because he wanted a buffer between himself and job-hungry pols. His sole instruction to Albright was "just find the best people for the job." He told the Republican state party chairman, "Look, if you've just got to place somebody politically, put them where they can't hurt me."

If he liked the Democratic better than the Republican candidate, he expected his party to go along with him. In 1966, he wanted the Republicans to endorse Arthur Levitt, the state's perennial comptroller and a Democrat, but this was too much for even his most supine party chiefs. However, the Republican candidate finally chosen to oppose Levitt was not permitted on the same platform with Nelson in Jewish neighborhoods; his presence, Nelson feared, might displease Levitt supporters.

An unlikely ally of Nelson's was Meade Esposito, an up-from-the-streets politico who ran the Democratic organization in Brooklyn. Esposito, son of a saloonkeeper, had warmth and a raffish charm. Nelson liked this uninhibited old pro enough to have Meade up to his Manhattan apartment occasionally. When the Democratic sachem paused before a Picasso lithograph and said, "That's nice," Rockefeller lifted the print from the wall, saying, "Here, Meade. It's yours."

His association with men like Meade Esposito helped serve a psychological need. Nelson never saw himself as an effete patrician, ripe for gulling by street-smart operators. He liked to believe that he could deal with, even best, the toughest characters on their own terms. The odd alliances paid off. When he needed Democratic votes in the state legislature, he could deal with Esposito and the required support materialized. One imagines the Brooklyn leader at his clubhouse, Picasso print on the wall, taking the call. "Nelson! H'wa ya? And Happy, and the little guys?"

In 1973, Nelson's last year as governor, he decided that Robert Wagner, New York's Democratic mayor from 1954 to 1965, ought to be Mayor Lindsay's successor. No matter that Wagner was a Democrat or that John Marchi, a perfectly respectable Republican, wanted the job. Nelson *liked* Bob Wagner.

He summoned Republican leaders from each of New York City's five boroughs to a West 55th Street conference where he intended to explain to them why they were going to love supporting a Democrat for mayor. He assumed that he could bend them to his will. What were they, after all, without him? They were barely seated when George Clark, the Republican Party leader in Brooklyn and thus the counterpart of Meade Esposito, said, "Governor, I want you to know that on this matter I will neither ask for nor accept a Picasso." Only Richard Rosenbaum, the new state chairman, burst out laughing at Clark's straight-faced teasing. Nelson glowered at Clark. In the end, the Republican leaders were spared the unhappy task of backing Wagner. Against Rockefeller's wishes, John Marchi filed for the Republican mayoralty nomination. When that happened, Wagner folded his hand and went back to practicing law.

Rockefeller's lack of interest in Party matters eventually began to weaken the state Republican organization's financial and political strength. For years, the Rockefeller family provided the bulk of party finances, and in the peak year, 1966, Nelson's contribution alone totaled $363,000. But eventually he asked George Hinman to get the party off his back. After his last re-election, in 1970, Nelson gave only $3,000. That year, the state Republican treasury was $1 million in debt. "The Republican Party existed, as far as the Governor was concerned, to nominate him," one of his state chairmen concluded. "He didn't have any real interest beyond that."

Chapter XV

ART, THE FAITHFUL MISTRESS

BOATERS SAILING PAST a coal wharf in Seal Harbor, Maine might well have been astonished to know what lay within that weather-beaten facade. Nelson Rockefeller had converted this unlikely structure on his summer place into a gallery for a half dozen Picasso tapestries and other art treasures. Nelson did not simply collect his art; he lived amidst it. When we went over speeches in the living room of his Fifth Avenue apartment, a Matisse looked down on us from the fireplace at one end of the room, a Léger from the other end. On the floor was a rug woven for Nelson by the artisans of Aubusson. The lamp shining over the Governor's shoulder had been designed for him by Giacometti, and was entitled *Lady*. A lamp with a title.

I remember with what cautiousness one of our circle crushed out his cigarettes in an ashtray, in order not to upset a Nadelman figurine of a bull. Small chance. The tiny bull weighed fifteen pounds. We all recalled the luckless tax commissioner who in an earlier meeting had stepped on a cloisonné ashtray that he had set on the floor. The Governor's face had turned white, but he had said nothing. At our next gathering, the cloisonné ashtrays were gone, replaced by plain glass. In this setting, the only one who looked genuinely at home was Nelson Rockefeller.

I watched Nelson function as art collector only once. The walls of the press office in the State Capitol in Albany were usually hung with Commerce Department posters depicting the joys of the Finger Lakes or the lure of the Adirondack Mountains. One January morning, they presented something fresh. Frank Litto, an Albany artist, had persuaded Bill Ekhof, an assistant press secretary, to allow him to hang his work in the press office. Litto's mixed-media creations fairly leaped from the walls. In the major work, *Funeral Caisson*, Litto had fashioned actual barn boards and links of chain into a stylized representation of the farm wagon and flag-draped coffin that had borne the slain Dr. Martin Luther King, Jr., through the streets of Atlanta. *Funeral Caisson* was a huge work possessing the simple dignity and power of the moment it celebrated.

Just before noon, Rockefeller came swooping into the Capitol and passed through the press room, exchanging handshakes and repartee with the reporters on the way to his office. He stopped stock-still before the farm wagon. "What's this? Who did it?" His eyes blazed.

Ekhof described Litto and his work.

"An unknown?" Rockefeller seemed to tremble in anticipation.

"I would say so," Ekhof conceded.

"Is it for sale?"

Ekhof said that he was sure the artist could be persuaded, all the while savoring Litto's good fortune.

"I've got a reception for the legislature over in the mansion in an hour. I want to have this hanging there by the time they arrive."

Ekhof raced to the phone and instructed the state's Office of General Services to get a truck over to the Capitol immediately. He then tracked down Litto and told the artist to put on a coat and tie and get over to the Governor's Mansion.

Rockefeller directed the placement of the heavy, unwieldy *Funeral Caisson*. "Let's put it here. No, there. No, farther to the right. Not that angle. Here, this way. Well, not *that* way." He settled on a location at the foot of the center staircase where Litto's work was the first thing to strike the visitor's eye on entering the mansion. When

Litto arrived, Rockefeller took him by the arm and steered him to a quiet corner. They talked animatedly. Then Nelson came over to Ekhof and winked. "He'll sell. See how much he wants. This is going to make the old place into a real people's mansion."

Litto was perhaps an unknown, but he knew the art world. "Look," he told Ekhof, "after Rockefeller buys something, its value automatically increases." He wanted $10,000 for *Funeral Caisson*. Nelson agreed, but he knew this world too. After all, no dealer had been involved, and a dealer would have taken a third of Litto's price. The artist got a check from Room 5600 for $6,666.66.

By the time Rockefeller left the Governor's mansion at the end of 1973, his interest in mixed-media folk art had evidently waned. He left the Litto work behind, a gift to the people of New York State.

Nelson's joy in art was genuine, his purest passion, his happiest refuge. His aesthetic was shaped initially by his mother, an early patron of abstract art. His father's taste was decorous and conventional. Junior never could understand those splotches and swatches on canvas that so excited his wife and son.

Where the sculpture garden of the Museum of Modern Art is located today, there once stood the Manhattan town house in which young Nelson grew up. In the Rockefeller family, the MOMA was known as "Mother's museum," since it was Abby's wish and the family's money that created it. "Mother wanted to start MOMA," Nelson explained, "to cut down the time between creation and appreciation, so a Van Gogh didn't have to die in poverty before his work was appreciated. Also, the idea was to help bring some guidelines to the public in a period when the artist is free by his own standards to move in almost any direction."

Nelson was just home from his honeymoon when his mother had him named to the MOMA Junior Advisory Committee. At about the same time, he gave the first hint of a lifelong itch to wed art to profit. With a friend as his partner he formed Art, Inc., to sell hand-painted postcards for twenty-five cents each in the newly opened Rainbow Room atop the RCA building. At a more elevated level, Nelson involved himself deeply in the direction of the Museum of Modern Art, and in 1939, he became MOMA's president. The office was quasi-dynastic, since subsequent incumbents included brother David and sister-in-law Blanchette, John III's wife. The New York City museum power structure, Nelson later admitted, "was where I learned my politics." He reveled in the world of well-bred Bohemians which the museum opened to him. The attraction of that world continued to elude his father. In 1950, after the museum had been in existence for more than twenty years, Junior finally asked Nelson to drop him from the MOMA mailing list. He just did not have the time for art that baffled him.

Nelson watched over MOMA like a nervous parent. In 1958, he received a call at Room 5600 that fire had broken out in the museum. He was around the corner and onto 54th Street with the first fire truck. He demanded a fireproof suit from the chief and dashed into the smoke-choked building. He was next seen, sweating and grinning, carrying out the imperiled paintings. It was, after all, Mother's museum.

The giants of the art world were not remote deities to Nelson Rockefeller. Rather, they were more like gifted subjects whom a young nobleman admires and patronizes. When his mother died, Nelson wanted a stained-glass window in the family chapel at Pocantico to honor her memory. He approached Henri Matisse to execute the window. The artist agreed to try, but later sent Rockefeller a letter saying that he had failed to find a satisfactory solution. The day after Nelson received the letter, Matisse died in France. "I was terribly upset," Nelson recalled. "He was very fond of me. And I had been very fond of him." Then Matisse seemed to reach from the grave to serve Nelson Rockefeller. A few days later, another letter arrived, written just before the artist's death. In it, Matisse said that he had finally worked out, on a wall of his studio, the solution to the window for Mrs. Rockefeller. There the scheme was found, and Matisse's posthumously completed design now illuminates a window in the Union Church in Pocantico.

Nelson Rockefeller could be spontaneously eloquent about art as with few other subjects. He told a group of art editors touring the Executive Mansion, "We are living in a mechanized society and people are looking for originality of expression. Aesthetics allow one to escape. We aren't subject to the conformity surrounding us on all sides. The reason art has such vitality is that you can have any concept, or have any kind of world you want. The freedom is absolute."

He was more amused than dismayed by visitors to the mansion, particularly state legislators, who snickered at the Rauschenbergs and Rothkos. No, he did not doubt that their grandchildren probably could paint better. In fact, a child's spontaneity was a precious thing, he said, and ought to be encouraged. Then he would patiently lecture them on abstractionism. "Look. Here's a subject where the composition, the color, the motion, the strength, constantly keep hitting you. If you are in a different mood than when you previously saw it, you are going to see a different painting, different proportions, with their fine points of variation in color, as though you're viewing it through slightly tinted glasses, or a different mood or attitude."

He devoured art catalogues the way other men read the sports page. On a plane or in his limousine he usually brought along brochures from galleries to scan at odd moments. He had worked out a quick procurement system with Carol Uht, his curator at Room 5600. Mrs. Uht put paper clips on catalogue pages describing works that she knew would interest him. He, in turn, marked the catalogue through a number code that told her what to bid on and the maximum he would pay.

His love of art was authentic, but he sometimes pursued it with a streak of the commodity trader. "I'm getting rid of all this sixties stuff," he once told his dinner guests, gesturing towards his Andy Warhols.

He also admired entrepreneurship in artists. His respect for Picasso increased after the artist taught him a lesson in the economics of creation. In the late 1950s, Nelson detected a curious anomaly in the art market. Prices for Picasso's paintings had become astronomical. Yet tapestries based on his works and done under Picasso's supervision were selling at comparative bargain prices, from $12,000 to $16,000. Rockefeller owned Picasso's *Three Musicians* and *Three Dancers*. He thought both would make brilliant tapestries. Through an intermediary named Mme. Couté, whom Nelson described as "a girl friend of Picasso's from way back," he arranged for Picasso to adapt the paintings as tapestries. Picasso first painted simplified versions of the canvases for the weaver to work from, since the infinite shades of oils could not be reproduced in the yarns. Picasso then selected the yarn colors himself. He supervised the progress of the work to its completion and put his signature on the back.

Unknown to Nelson, the weaver, Mme. J. de la Baume Durrbach, had agreed with Picasso to weave one tapestry for Rockefeller and one each for the artist and herself. Nelson stumbled onto this private arrangement accidentally. "That Picasso sure is a good businessman," he concluded with honest admiration.

One Christmas, Nelson's gift to his staff at 5600 was a book on Picasso's works. I opened my copy to find that the bookplate had also been done by Picasso. I asked the Governor about it. "My daughter was over to see Picasso," he explained, "and he scribbled something in a book for her as an inscription. When she got back, she showed this little sketch to the women in the office, and they had it done up as a plate." He grinned devilishly. "You don't often have your book-plate drawn by Pablo Picasso."

Nelson had no hesitancy in exploiting the marketability of his own name. In 1970, Chuck Lanigan sat opposite Rockefeller aboard his plane, watching Nelson leaf through a catalogue. Lanigan asked, "Buying more art, Governor?" Rockefeller gave him a conspiratorial wink. "No. Selling, to raise money for the campaign." Lanigan commented that it probably did not hurt sales when buyers knew that the work came from Nelson Rockefeller's collection. No, Nelson conceded. He often got up to eight times what he had originally paid for a painting. He added with a crafty grin, "When I want to sell my stuff, I always leave my stickers on the back."

He had been thrilled at the Montreal Expo by Picasso's six-piece sculpture, *The Bathers*, and told how he had leaped ahead of seventeen other buyers to acquire it. "I wired the dealer that I wanted to buy. He came back and said, 'There are seventeen people in line ahead of you.' But he gave me the asking price anyway, and he said, 'If you don't want it at that price, just say so. Then I'll work my way through the list, and if it's still not sold, I'll reach you.' Well, years before I'd missed out on something of his I wanted by this system. 'Forget it!' I told him. 'I'll take it at the asking.' "

Once his desire had been quickened for a particular work, he was implacable. He called Mrs. Whitman on a Saturday morning bubbling about a sculpture he had seen in the Parke-Bernet window on Madison Avenue. He had to know the price, he told her. He was oblivious to the fact that it was the Labor Day weekend and the gallery was closed, and she did not mention this to him as she began a desperate search.

His taste was uninhibited. Nelson could be smitten suddenly, anywhere, and exult, "These cost a dollar, *one dollar* a painting!" as he did over several watercolors he purchased at a county fair.

He was amusedly aware of the opportunities for charlatanism in art, particularly given the subjective standards of modernism. In a 1975 visit to Iran, he told the Shah that he and Happy were eager to visit the famed bazaar of Isfahan. The Shah ordered up his private jet, an aircraft of stunning opulence with an unexpected touch of thrift. The Shah of Iran, heir to the Peacock Throne, had bought a used plane from its original owner, Henry Ford II.

At Isfahan, the bazaar was cleared of all other shoppers. Nelson and Happy, with the place to themselves, moved from stall to stall, with Nelson fingering, feeling, exclaiming, relishing every moment. Accompanying the Rockefellers was the then ambassador to Iran and former CIA director, Richard Helms. Helms saw a Secret Serviceman staggering under an awkward burden. "Christ," the agent said to Helms, "he's bought a damned anvil. He just walked up to one of those craftsmen and bought his anvil!" He held out the chunk of iron, disbelieving.

Later, on the return flight, Helms asked, "Mr. Vice-President, what on earth do you want with an anvil?"

Rockefeller winked. "I'll say it was sculpted by Max Ernst and get thirty-five thousand dollars for it."

Rockefeller was among the earliest American politicians to promote government support for the arts. He wanted everyone, he said, to experience the pleasure and richness that art had given his own life. He believed that government had a responsibility to bring art to the people. He was initially burned for this belief. He once described an incident early in his public career: "I'll never forget it. I was Coordinator of Inter-American Affairs in the forties. We sent an exhibit of paintings to Latin America. I was called up before a congressional appropriations committee and was bitterly attacked. What was all this abstract stuff? Where were the religious pictures, they wanted to know." Later, as Under Secretary of Health, Education and Welfare under President Eisenhower, he tried to make a cultural angel of the federal government. His modest proposal for federal art subsidies was laughed out of Congress as "the free piano lesson bill."

These were the very kinds of experience that had soured him on appointive posts and led him ultimately to seek the authentic power of elective office. Almost his first act after being elected governor of New York State was to create the first governmental Council on the Arts in the country, an example eventually followed by most states and the federal government.

Though he wanted government to commit public funds to art, he had little faith in popular taste. He persuaded the state legislature to put up money for art in the new capital complex that he was building in Albany, the South Mall, but he had no intention of allowing benighted state assemblymen to intrude portraits of Mother Cabrini or statues of Abner Doubleday into his Pantheon-on-the-Hudson. As he delicately explained, "The participation of politicians in the selection of art would, shall we say, either retard the progress or put the criteria for selection on the basis of a political rather than aesthetic judgment."

He did go through the motions of creating a committee to review art for the South Mall. The committee forwarded a huge binder of suggested works to the Governor's office where it passed through the hands of the secretary to the Governor. Al Marshall looked at the collection, every work an abstract, and sent the book on to Rockefeller with a memo: "Guv, how do these grab you?" Rockefeller returned the memo: "Just fine, Al, I picked all of them myself."

He could be pragmatic in art as well as politics. He once invited Bob and Linda Douglass to Pocantico, where they admired a Miró in the dining room. Nelson smiled enigmatically, then confessed. He had wanted to create a tax benefit for himself by giving away a gift of art. He thus commissioned an artist to copy the Miró, and he donated the original to the Museum of Modern Art. The work they were admiring was the copy. If reproductions could give pleasure to Nelson Rockefeller, then why not to others, he wondered. The idea long simmered in his mind and eventually emerged in a form that was to enrage art puritans. But that endeavor was still years away. Indeed, it would prove to be Nelson Rockefeller's last vocation.

I once asked him how he felt about creating rather than collecting art. "I'm not an artist," he answered. "I would like to be a painter, a sculptor, an architect. I think creation is the most exciting and rewarding experience we can have." Had he ever tried? "I did try. But I was never successful. All I needed was to look at what I did."

Apart from art, Nelson Rockefeller's tastes were astonishingly unsophisticated. He was an impatient theatergoer and hated opera. As a young man he had enjoyed jazz, but he never became an aficionado. At the Governor's Mansion in Albany he kept a stack of records, many more than twenty years old, not collector's items—just old records. When someone mentioned the vitality of current popular music, Nelson agreed, expressing his liking for Chubby Checker, an artist whose apogee by then was already at least a decade past. His favorite song was "Sweet Georgia Brown," though I never recall him ever whistling or humming any tune. At public events, when the national anthem was played, Nelson always appeared to be singing proudly, but little sound actually emerged.

He rarely read books. When he did, it was usually something urged on him by one of his intellectual guides. He would mechanically absorb the major point, or his version of that point, often a one-sentence distillation. Thus *Without Marx or Jesus*, by Jean-François Revel, came out in Nelson's view as a defense of American capitalism. Robert Ardrey's *Territorial Imperative* made the case for a strong national defense. He had members of the staff prepare two- or three-page summaries of other current books, Peter Drucker's *Age of Discontinuity*, for example. The practice suggested those recordings like "Twenty-five of the World's Greatest Classical Melodies," with thirty seconds of "Swan Lake" squeezed between the "Anvil Chorus" and "Moonlight Sonata," and all the tedious, repetitious passages excised. Of newspapers, he read only *The New York Times* with care. He flipped through the *Daily News* and dipped into the *Washington Post*. Much of his news he obtained from evening television. He relaxed before the television set with two of his favorites, *All in the Family* and *Mannix*. He virtually never read for pleasure.

Once past the elegant service, almost any palate would have been uncomfortable at Nelson Rockefeller's table. His meals were for the gourmand not the gourmet: a meat course, with pot roast a recurring theme, potatoes, and another vegetable. Tasty, plentiful, unmemorable. The man who might have enjoyed truffles year-round appeared to have the tastes of a twelve-year-old. "He didn't dine, he ate," Joe Canzeri put it. "Let's have some more of that hard sauce," Nelson would say. It was a sweet, sugary paste that he liked to pile onto his desserts. But most of the time he appeared oblivious to what he was eating. At luncheon meetings his hand might absently reach for a sandwich on someone else's plate, his eyes all the while glued to the speaker. If thirsty enough, he would finish off someone else's Coke.

I asked a colleague what image came to mind when he thought of Nelson Rockefeller. "He's stirring his coffee with the arm of his eyeglasses." This ritual always followed his methodically producing a small gold case of saccharin tablets from his watch pocket. He used saccharin in his coffee after meals in which he stinted on nothing else.

On the road, advance men had instructions to supply his room with his two favorite snacks, Oreo cookies and Fig Newtons. Another stock item was a bottle of Dubonnet. Yet he was the sparest of social drinkers and easily became light-headed. When he behaved whimsically in an occasional after-dinner speech, the staff described the evening as a "two-Dubonnet performance." In his last years, he abandoned even Dubonnet after Happy told him it was high in calories. Thereafter, he took to sipping a little white wine or a Mateus rosé, hardly the choice of an exacting oenophile.

The plainness of taste was induced in part by the religious heritage of the Rockefellers. Rare among America's moneyed aristocracy, they were Baptists. This fundamentalist faith is associated more with southern farmers than eastern patricians and their Presbyterian and Episcopalian high church ways. Three generations into great wealth, this Rockefeller heir still displayed behavioral traces of the old-time religion.

Chapter XVI

WORKING FOR A ROCKEFELLER

"I'M TOUGH PHYSICALLY. I wear people down," Rockefeller explained to Harry Albright, when Albright was recruiting aides for him. Albright, who later went on to become state superintendent of banking and special counsel to the Vice-President, took Nelson's words as a warning to prospective subordinates. Rockefeller was indeed a hard worker, but perhaps unconsciously, an even harder taskmaster.

What wears down ordinary mortals is to spend oneself all day on the job, then to seek the solace of home only to find that the septic tank has ruptured, Jennifer's $3,600 orthodontia has to be redone, and an audit notice has arrived from the IRS. These distractions sap the will and tend to detract from total commitment to issues larger than oneself, and these were precisely the pinpricks of daily life which Nelson Rockefeller escaped. He might be frustrated by antediluvian legislators, or have a billion-dollar deficit in the state budget, or fail to be nominated for the Presidency, but at the day's end, the driver was waiting, the helicopter skipped him over rush-hour traffic. Dinner would be served flawlessly to five or fifty guests. And should there be an audit notice in the mail pile, the family's accounting staff at Room 5600 took care of it.

Nelson Rockefeller enjoyed the freedom to let his mind rove, to dedicate his considerable energy to elevated aims rather than exhaust it in the mechanics of daily survival. He was free to think grandly, and not always tolerant of the mundane preoccupations that diminished other people's vision.

Dick Dunham, after succeeding Dr. Hurd as state budget director, had the task one winter day of clearing the budget message with the Governor. Rockefeller instructed Dunham to meet him at the Albany airport at 7:30 A.M. The schedule that day included stops at Syracuse, Rochester and Binghamton. Between speeches, television appearances and ribbon cuttings, Nelson quickly resumed the thread of his previous discussion with Dunham. Thus the day passed, in the plane, in limousines, in hotel rooms, and in broadcasting booths. At 1:15 A.M., Dunham found himself parked outside Nelson's Fifth Avenue apartment putting the finishing touches on the budget. Nelson then turned to Dunham—who was now 150 miles from home without a clean shirt, toothbrush or hotel reservation—and bade him good night, with a cheery, "Let me see the revisions in the morning."

He was not deliberately thoughtless, but rather assumed a kingly indifference. The king cannot help it if footsore soldiers must march through the night—the kingdom must be saved. He saw his life in that crusading light and assumed that his subordinates shared his outlook. While he never failed to express thanks, it was not, "Thank you, I know you must be exhausted working straight through the weekend." It was simply, "Aren't you marvelous," with a wink and a smile. Then on to the next hill. "The first thing I learned working with Nelson Rockefeller," Jim Cannon recalled, "was how to find a Xerox machine and typewriters in the middle of the night in any hotel in America."

In August 1970, Nelson was in Rochester campaigning for re-election. He had spent the previous three days in political tub-thumping. The next morning he was to lead an environmental conference, and he looked forward to the shift to more substantive fare. Working with his environmental advisers, I had prepared a speech, but so far had been unable to get to him to clear it. He had finished his last stump appearance at a Puerto Rican festival and had arrived at the motel after 11:00 P.M. I was summoned to his room, where three other staff members and Henry Diamond, the state's commissioner of environmental conservation, were already with him.

Rockefeller had made a half-dozen speeches that day and had the punchiness of someone too long on his feet. He sat on the edge of the bed, an incongruous sky of cupids in flight painted on the motel ceiling. His pajamas could have passed for hospital issue except for the monogrammed breast pocket. He appeared to be falling asleep until something in the speech stirred him to life. He suddenly exclaimed, "That isn't what I want to say!"

"We haven't been able to get near you for days to find out what you did want to say," Bob Douglass offered tactfully.

Rockefeller muttered, "It's unsophisticated. I could give a better extemporaneous speech. Who's responsible for this?"

All eyes were turned away, some fixed on the ceiling, others on the floor, or on the Dubonnet bottle, or the Oreo cookies on the night stand. The environmental commissioner was too new to know the Law of Direct Eye Contact, and since he was the only one still looking at the Governor, he took the brunt of the assault.

We began a frantic rewrite as soon as the Governor dismissed us. Tim Smith, an advance man, went in search of a typist, returning after 1:00 A.M. with a dazed young woman recruited from the bar. She had an imperfect idea of what was expected of her, except that she was to be paid $25 for it. I fed copy to her as we completed each page of rewritten text. Her touch at the typewriter sounded like occasional sniper fire rather than a machine gun. She lingered long over a word. "It's 'environment'," I said. "How do you spell it?" she asked. We gave her the $25 and sent her home, as the advance man, Smith, took her place at the typewriter. At 3:00 A.M., while rushing down the motel hallway with more copy, I ran into a high-school classmate whom I had not seen for twenty-three years. We stared at each other blankly. I said, sounding the complete fool, "Good to see you again. I've got to run. I'm writing a speech for the Governor."

Nelson Rockefeller had a capacity to focus all his attention on the subject at hand, then cut away cleanly to the next issue, rendering the previous claimant on his time instantly invisible. This ability inspired my development of the Kleenex Theory, which I used to explain to curious friends what it was like to work for the man. Now a Kleenex tissue is a useful item with a definite, if limited function; it is not, however, a possession that is cherished beyond its immediate value. Others on the staff insisted that they had originated the Kleenex Theory, so common was the sensation among my Rockefeller colleagues.

He favored Sunday evening staff meetings. This time was, to Nelson, ideal for mapping the week ahead. To the staff, it meant further encroachment on what remained of weekends, since a seventy-to-eighty-hour work week was the norm. One evening, as we worked in the office at 55th Street, Al Marshall cautiously observed, "Governor, it's eight o'clock and it's Christmas Eve. Some of these people live a hundred and fifty miles away." Nelson raised an eyebrow, undecipherably, then nodded. And we went home.

American rites, like the Super Bowl, held no sacredness for him. Louis Lefkowitz, the state's attorney general, remembered, "I'd have to excuse myself every half hour to go to the bathroom to find out the score." Indeed, the passion of sports fans mystified Nelson. When the New York Mets rose miraculously from last place to take the National League pennant in 1969, he was persuaded to invite the team to the Fifth Avenue apartment. The next night, back in Albany, he had to make a political speech, to which I had added some humorous references to the Mets manager, Gil Hodges. In the car en route to the event, we went over the text. "Gil Hodges?" He looked at me baffled. "Who's Gil Hodges?"

The Mets went on to win the World Series. I brought a draft statement for him to release which began, "Gil Hodges and his Mets have performed a miracle." Nelson made only one change in the statement. Ahead of Gil Hodges' name he added that of Joan Payson, the club's owner. Others at such a moment might recall infielders and crucial double plays, hitters and soaring home runs, coaches and bold gambles. Nelson spoke of what he, a Rockefeller, understood best, Mrs. Payson's position, the patron's role, which, after all, made it possible for all these boys to play their games.

To conclude that his occasional insensitivity, the grueling hours, the neglect of family, were resented by the staff is to miss Nelson Rockefeller's hold over people. He created, in Al Marshall's words, a magnetic field. "You got caught up in it and made little effort to escape. The punishing hours, the sacrifice, were not just for him, he let you know. You were his partner in a cause larger than him or you. And he could make you believe that. There was an invisible flypaper around the man. People stuck to Nelson." Those uninfected with the shared enthusiasm that Marshall describes had short careers. One otherwise adequate Republican state chairman had been reported to Nelson as having said he "loved the job" because he had never had more time for his golf game. The man was soon replaced.

Nelson overworked people in style. One spring, Dr. Hurd had finally gotten away to Martha's Vineyard for a long-deferred vacation. Three days later, Nelson summoned him. Hurd made no mad scramble for an Allegheny commuter flight. The family's twenty-six-passenger F-27 Fairchild arrived at the Vineyard to transport him to Pocantico. When his task was done, the plane took him back, and Hurd watched amusedly as the crowd gathered "to see who the VIP was."

One spring Al Marshall proposed an executive retreat to Nelson. The Governor's staff, he argued, was growing stale from constant absorption in daily crises. Imaginations needed stretching. "We need to get away. Let our hair down. Think about what we were trying to accomplish. Just let the ideas flow." Nelson loved it. The executive retreat would stir the creative juices in his people and stimulate the "conceptual approach" that he so prized. He had the perfect setting too, the Dorado Beach Hotel, then one of Laurance's Rockresorts in Puerto Rico. He would arrange for the staff to stay in Laurance's quarters. "Al, I want you to start right away on an agenda. Put together a black book for each topic we'll cover, fact sheets, tables, you know what I mean." Marshall's heart sank.

Each day, the executive retreat began with a breakfast seminar and plowed through a tightly fixed schedule. The delicious distractions of Dorado Beach were held at agonizing arm's length, and the retreat became, if anything, more oppressive than the Albany routine. "He turned my spontaneous brainstorming into organized thinking," Marshall moaned. "Oh, yes, one day we got to hit some golf balls."

Jim Cannon recalled an August in Maine. "We were at maybe the handsomest home in Seal Harbor. Nelson had three terrific sailboats. Tennis court. Golf. We worked from Monday through Sunday, then started over, twelve hours a day, except for Nelson. He'd knock off about eight. From the window, my view was magnificent."

Nelson Rockefeller was incapable of sustaining a light touch. Every year, he gave a Christmas party for the Governor's office staff in the Red Room of the State Capitol. Typists, the mail-room crew and file clerks, who labored anonymously all year long, crowded around him while the Governor circulated, charming, smiling, approachable. Then he would climb onto the huge ceremonial desk to make an impromptu speech. I watched the performance year after year in amazement. No more than three minutes of amenities passed before he would shift gears: "I want to tell you, I couldn't be more grateful to you. And next year is going to be something too. We've got two hundred and three million in mandated increases alone. And that's not counting a billion five for the Big Six Cities." The secretaries' eyes began to turn glassy as he droned on. "Of course, as long as the federal government is carrying out more than a thousand categorical grants, of which we get back only eleven cents on the dollar . . ." Solving society's ills was fun, didn't everybody see that?

Some who shared the vision literally died in his service, willingly, it almost seemed. Frank Jamieson, Nelson's first public-relations adviser, was a fatherly confidant for more than twenty years. Jamieson, ravaged by lung cancer, dragged himself to Nelson's office virtually to the last day of his life. I witnessed a later example of this fierce devotion. Victor Borella had been instrumental in creating Rockefeller's astonishing rapport with organized labor. Then, old and unwell, Borella retired to his native New Hampshire after decades at Rockefeller Center and a half dozen Rockefeller campaigns.

A few years later, after Rockefeller had gone to Washington as Gerald Ford's Vice-President, I saw a ghost emerge from his office. Frail, fleshless, shuffling, Victor Borella had returned. We went to lunch at the White House mess and, with a glow in his eyes contrasting with his clay pallor, he said, "Nelson needed me. Nobody in the Ford Administration can talk to anybody in labor. So I'm going to come down from New Hampshire three days a week." The spent, sick face became newly animated as he spoke. Within weeks, Victor Borella was dead.

People might be frozen out or eased out but were rarely kicked out of Nelson Rockefeller's employ. One burned-out member of the Governor's staff was given a choice of four alternative jobs in state government. An acerbic assistant, whose very presence upset Nelson, was removed through appointment to a high-level state commission. The man was given a farewell party at 55th Street. As Nelson began to lavish praises, with the fellow and his wife beaming at his side, I began to wonder how our operation would now function without this paragon.

At one of my first staff meetings, a highly touted transportation expert made his debut before Nelson. The fellow, bullet-headed and mean of aspect, spoke with great force in scowling certainties. He closed on opening night, never seen again in Rockefeller's presence. He was not fired, just returned to the bowels of the bureaucracy.

The bad news for those cast off was not usually delivered by Nelson personally. His euphemism was "We're going to have to make some changes around here." It was left to Al Marshall or Norm Hurd to explain to the individual that a major feature of the change was his or her departure. Why the indirection? Softheartedness? More correctly, it was a matter of ego. Nelson Rockefeller had a reputation for attracting good people, and he did not relish being proved wrong. Anyone he had chosen must have had talent. "There has to be a place we can find for someone with that much ability," he would say of someone whose head he had just placed on the block.

At college I had an old German professor who preached *"Krankheit ist Dummheit"*—sickness is stupidity. Nelson, rarely ill himself, would have preferred, "Sickness is weakness." A faith in fundamentalist, unstylish health care appears to have been a family quirk. John D. Rockefeller, while donating millions for the advancement of modern medical science, believed in homeopathy, an outdated therapeutic philosophy in vogue in the nineteenth century. When sick, he relied on "medicasters" and smoked mullein leaves in a clay pipe. John D.

had apparently swallowed some of the preachments of his father, William Avery Rockefeller, Nelson's great-grandfather, who, among his several careers, had been a peddler of patent medicines and cure-all elixirs. Nelson described his great-grandfather as a "botanic physician"; a cancer quack is more accurate.

Nelson Rockefeller largely entrusted his health not to conventional M.D.s but to a D.O., an osteopathic physician. Doctors trained in this school believe that most illness arises from "structural derangement," from a misalignment of bones, muscle, and cartilage. They treat by manipulating the musculoskeletal system. Nelson literally placed himself in the hands of the same osteopathic physician for nearly forty years, Doctor Kenneth Riland. He usually saw Riland twice a week, and Kenny was not only his physician, but one of his few intimates. He was, as well, a great favorite among the Rockefeller circle, appreciated for down-to-earth sense and ready humor. The doctor and his portable treatment table became a fixture of the Rockefeller road show, as much as advance men and reporters. It was always with a certain uneasiness that I entered the Governor's suite in some out-of-town hotel where Riland would be thumping, bending and wrenching his patient with alarming gusto.

Rockefeller passed Riland around as one does a good tip at the track. At Nelson's request, Riland manipulated the bodies of the Shah of Iran, Chief Justice Warren Burger and Henry Kissinger. President Richard Nixon took Riland with him on his historic trip to China in 1972. Given Nelson's confidence in him, the osteopath came in for some unusual consultations. In the midst of the 1968 New York City garbage strike, Riland was performing his ministrations on a tense and exhausted Rockefeller at the 55th Street office. I was waiting outside to clear a statement for the press on the latest status of strike negotiations. A rugged, broad-shouldered man emerged from Nelson's doorway. "Are you Persico?" He put out his hand with a smile. "Nelson wants me to look over the draft." Thus I first met the Governor's physician.

Nelson Rockefeller's controlled reverence for conventional medicine was evident in his willingness to practice without a license. One drawer of his desk was crammed with pills which he dispensed freely. Al Marshall had stretched out one day on a couch in the Governor's office in great and mysterious pain. A doctor was called. As soon as the doctor left, Rockefeller went to his desk apothecary, announcing, "I've got just the thing for you, Al." Marshall reluctantly swallowed several unidentified pills which did no noticeable harm.

He claimed to have lost only three days of work because of sickness in his life. But his health and vigor were a gift of his genes and not the product of discipline. "He's in better shape than he deserves to be," Kenny Riland observed. Rockefeller followed no exercise regimen beyond weekend golf, ate three full meals a day, and managed to keep his weight at a fairly even 185 pounds. Once, when he had finished one of his desktop Christmas speeches, I had grabbed him under the arm to help him down and was astonished to find that the square, solid-looking physique was, in truth, quite soft. He assumed longevity the way he accepted his inheritance. "My grandfather lived to be ninety-seven," he told us. "My father lasted to eighty-six. I expect to make it to a hundred."

We were expected to share his disdain for physical weakness. Chuck Lanigan, Republican state chairman in 1970, put off treatment of a near-crippling hernia for months while he helped Nelson navigate the nomination of Charles Goodell as U.S. senator through a resistant Republican Party. "I waited until we had it locked up. But I was in agony all the time. I finally put myself in the hospital and told him I'd be out of action for a while. The flowers and cards came. But afterward, there was a coolness. I'd let him down."

Mike Whiteman, Nelson's last Counsel to the Governor, went to the doctor with a urinary infection. Explaining that the ailment was often induced by pressure, tension and exhaustion, the physician said, "I get a lot of you Rockefeller people over here with this condition."

As secretary to the Governor, Al Marshall was for five years the man most continuously under Nelson Rockefeller's thumb. "The tension started the minute he opened the door. He carried a certain weight wherever he went. You didn't saunter into a transaction with Nelson Rockefeller. You geared up. Your palms got a little damp. He was not a soothing man." This from a tough ex-Marine captain with his own capacity to dampen palms. In his second year as Nelson's chief lieutenant, Marshall began to experience severe stomach cramps, nausea and loss of appetite. He was routinely working an eighteen-hour weekday and ten-hour days on weekends. Rockefeller was not blind to the toll he was exacting from his deputy. "He'd say to me, 'Al, you're working too hard. You've got to let up.' And he'd mean it. But Jesus, if he wouldn't be on the phone calling me at home that same night with some grand new scheme he wanted started right away."

Marshall was hospitalized and tested and retested without result. He returned to the job, and the symptoms recurred. Taking stock, he saw that he was burning out, perhaps endangering his life. "The Governor had a professional detachment about people as staff," Marshall noted. "As soon as he saw you stumble, he already had his eye on somebody new to move into the harness. He wouldn't say anything. But you had a sense that you were used up."

Earlier, Marshall had received an offer to become president of an upstate utility company, and the prospect began to look tempting to a man who had never earned more than a civil servant's salary. He went to Rockefeller and told him that he wanted to leave. Rockefeller recognized that Marshall was too great a talent to lose, especially when there were equally important but less irksome Rockefeller vineyards to be worked. He made his counteroffer. If Marshall would agree to remain as secretary through the 1970 re-election campaign, Rockefeller would arrange for him to talk to the chairman of Rockefeller Center about possibly becoming the Center's president when the current president retired that year. Marshall did eventually become president of Rockefeller Center, at more than triple his government salary, plus the perquisites due the agent of the premier landlord in the country. The utility company's offer had been dwarfed.

Rockefeller's fatalism toward illness and death was especially evident to those who flew with him. If not actually fearless, he was able to repress his fears convincingly. Carl Spad was once flying with Nelson when smoke began belching from the cockpit. Spad went to the pilot. "He doesn't know what it is, Governor," he reported back. "Relax, Carl," Nelson advised, leaning back with arms folded. "There's nothing we can do about it." He had already survived three plane crashes of varying severity.

His passivity in the face of danger was a learned reflex. In his early thirties, Nelson had been rushed by a grizzly bear during an Alaskan hunting trip. His Indian guide had dropped the bear just feet from him with a single shot. Nelson was trembling as they left the site. Later, the party tracked two mountain goats up a mountainside. The animals crossed a narrow ledge skirting a sheer drop. Nelson got out on the ledge and froze there. He was unable to move and had to be coaxed back down slowly, which broke off the chase. Thereafter, he refused to display his fears before other men.

The later fearlessness had a self-centered quality. One afternoon as we approached the Albany airport, the winds were tossing the plane about like a kite. The pilot wanted to divert to another field. But, as Nelson ordered him to land, he sat back and smiled. "I'm not afraid. I'm sixty years old and it's been a terrific life." At the time, I was thirty-nine. He adopted the fatalism of a battlefield commander. Separation from family, sickness, exhaustion, risk, death, were the soldier's lot. If people got sick or burned themselves out in Nelson Rockefeller's service, they had spent themselves, he believed, in a worthy cause.

The arrogance, the arbitrariness, his obliviousness to the crushing nature of his demands, were usually sugarcoated. He could, when it suited him, make you believe that you were the most important single figure in his life, that he was overcome by gratitude for what you were doing for him. "You're my friend," he would exclaim with a warm handclasp and melting smile when you came through on an outrageous assignment. You were not simply a subordinate, an employee. You were Nelson Rockefeller's friend. The glow could last for days.

Sometimes the friends became hazy in his mind. Joe Canzeri, while still an advance man, was sent to the Gotham Hotel, near our 55th Street offices, to set up a particularly sensitive private meeting. Nelson wanted to court Mario Procaccino, a former New York City Democratic mayoral candidate, as a supporter of the latest Nelsonian multibillion-dollar bond issue. To keep the hotel staff away, Canzeri took the luncheon order, phoned it to the kitchen, and served the two men himself. The following day Nelson flew to Washington to speak at the Hotel Shoreham. His speech was inadvertently left behind in

New York, and Canzeri was immediately dispatched with it on the next shuttle flight. He delivered the text to the Shoreham just as Rockefeller was being introduced. On the return home, a puzzled Rockefeller turned to ask Mrs. Whitman, "What was that waiter from the Gotham doing in Washington with my speech?" At that point, Canzeri had been a Rockefeller advance man for a year.

Canzeri later experienced the lifting effect of Rockefeller's genuine confidence. He was parked with the Governor near a speaker's platform in Queens during the 1970 campaign. Arthur Goldberg had just spoken at the same site, and he and Rockefeller exchanged passing pleasantries through the car window as Goldberg left. Rockefeller turned to Canzeri. "Who's the young guy with the beard with Arthur?"

"He's a gofer," Canzeri answered.

"A gofer?"

"Like me. Go for coffee. Go for sandwiches."

Rockefeller spoke feelingly. "Listen to me, Joe. Never put yourself down like that. Don't demean yourself because you're pouring coffee or going for sandwiches. When you are sensitive toward people on little things, it makes them sensitive toward you on the big issues."

Louis Lefkowitz, who rose from a cold-water flat on the Lower East Side to become New York's attorney general, remembered his first private meeting with the man. "I was alone with him, and there was Nelson Rockefeller spreading caviar on crackers for me!"

Nelson rarely turned down his staff's request for personal favors. When I needed references to rent an apartment in Manhattan, I brought a letter of recommendation from the governor of New York. When I applied to join a club in Washington, Vice-President Rockefeller vouched for me.

For him, charm had become a conditioned reflex. I sat in his office while he put through a phone call to Dr. John Hannah, then director of the Agency for International Development. He began the conversation: "I want to tell you, John, you're doing a terrific job down there. The whole country is grateful to you. Yes, sir. You've taken on a tough, thankless assignment." As the conversation progressed, his eyes narrowed in puzzlement. He realized he had the wrong John Hannah. One imagines the equal confusion of the civil servant at the other end of the line, stirred from his routine by a call from Nelson Rockefeller. Nelson went on without missing a stroke. "I want you to know, you're doing a hell of a job, too."

He was highly sensitive toward people. No, "sensitized" is a better word, since he could be insensitive when that suited him. Rather, he had a sharp sense of how other people feel and react. During one campaign, Carl Spad picked up Rockefeller at the Fifth Avenue apartment regularly over a period of several weeks. Whenever he left, Spad said, "Goodbye, handsome," to an ivory carving in the foyer of the Hindu god Vishnu. The statue had been presented to Nelson and his first wife in India during their honeymoon.

"You like it, don't you, Carl?" Rockefeller said. "Here. Take it."

"He said it," Spad recalled, "the way you'd say, 'Here, Carl, have a mint.' "

Leaving for a dinner in New Jersey with the then Republican state chairman, Dick Rosenbaum, Rockefeller asked, "Have you got a tux?" Rosenbaum answered, "Not with me." "Let's go up to the apartment and you can wear one of mine." There, Rockefeller helped Rosenbaum dress, tying his tie as a father does for a young son off to his first formal.

When Jim Carberry, who wrote speeches in the 1970 campaign, had to work late one night at Pocantico, Nelson took him to a spare bedroom and brought a pair of his pajamas for Carberry to wear.

His art, his pajamas, his spare tux, his homes at Pocantico and Venezuela—he offered them so casually. Were these acts calculated? Or were they the impulses of a genuinely generous man? He was generous, but he also knew the effect that these gestures had. They helped charge the gravitational field that held people faithfully in his orbit.

The sensitivity and insensitivity were like alternating currents. In the heat of the 1970 campaign, he had berated me for omitting a point from a speech. I said nothing as he leveled me with cold rage. My only defense would have required implicating colleagues whose advice I had taken on the text. The staff ethic was to wait and parcel out blame later, away from him. But the tongue-lashing was not pleasant, and my face must have registered my bitterness, because he said, "You look as if I'd stabbed you." One evening, six months later, we were having a party for a departing staff member. At the end, as I was about to leave, he took me aside and said, "I was too hard on you. It wasn't your fault." We both knew what moment he meant.

His praise, when it came, was given exuberantly in front of spouses and peers to maximize the effect. It is difficult to resist a boss who tells your wife, "You've got a fantastic husband there. I couldn't make it without him." I was leaving his office one day as a *Time* reporter was entering. He introduced us and identified me as "the greatest speech writer in the country." Of course the hyperbole could be interpreted to his advantage. Would Nelson Rockefeller have anyone less than the best? Still, it fell pleasantly on the ear. Nelson knew all the devices of ego nourishment. On the phone with the President, he would say, "I'm here with Bobby, and Al, and Harry, Mr. President, and we've got this idea."

A squandering of superlatives is the upper class's contribution to the debasement of English. "Absolutely *fabulous* party, my dear." "Aren't you wonderful to say so. I'm just thrilled you could make it." Nelson Rockefeller was a prime offender, a man incapable of understatement. His "fantastics," "terrifics," and "aren't you marvelous's" rained down with all the value of the dimes his grandfather used to hand out to the public. He could say of a plan to extract oil from shale rock, "This is the most exciting thing I've ever heard in my life." On announcing a new plan to save the thirty-five-cent subway fare, he exulted: "I want to tell you, these are *terrific* times." Across the most innocuous memo sent into him, he would scrawl, "Great!" The staff learned to discount this verbal inflation and adjust it to the real market value of his praises. "You're fantastic"—B-plus. "You're the greatest" —C. "Thanks loads"—start considering new employment.

If he made a promise, his word was bankable. He might never mention the matter again, but someone out there in the Rockefeller empire was working on it. Still, he maintained an important distinction in dispensing his benefactions. He was once arranging a new post much desired by one of his lieutenants and discussed the man with Charles Lanigan. Lanigan began, "Now, Governor, I know you feel you owe this fellow . . ." Rockefeller stopped him. "No. Not owe, Chuck. I *want* to do it for him. I don't *owe* these people anything."

Sharing the Rockefeller power, even indirectly, gave one an illusion of immunity from the rude shocks of the world. Dick Rosenbaum, while state chairman, once accompanied the Governor on a goodwill mission among western state Republicans. On his return, I asked how the trip had gone. Rosenbaum shook his head dazedly. "We were coming back from the Dakotas in the F-27. I was looking out the window, and in the dusk I could make out these familiar shapes. The Governor asked me if I knew what I was looking at. He said it was Mount Rushmore. Did I want to see it? I told him I didn't want the plane to return on my account. He just smiled and picked up a phone. I have no idea whom he talked to. But we circled for a couple of minutes, and all of a sudden, the lights went on. And there's Mount Rushmore clear as high noon." Then Rosenbaum added, "When I'm flying with him, I always feel safe, you know, as though nothing would be permitted to go wrong with the plane."

A bolder entrepreneur than myself might have converted the knowledge gained from being in his court to profit. Shortly after my return from Nelson's ranch in Venezuela, we were alone in his office. He took a phone call, and while he talked, I continued to make last-minute changes in a speech. But it was impossible to ignore his half of the conversation. Someone in Brazil was alerting Nelson that the coffee plantations were undergoing some sort of calamity. I heard him reply, "You're kidding. The harvest's off forty percent?" Even a C student in economics could not fail to grasp the law of supply and demand at work here. If Brazilian coffee production was going down, coffee prices were going up. I left his office knowing that the most intelligent thing I could do was to call a broker and place an order for coffee futures. I did not. I suffered a moral paralysis. I should not, I thought, make money from information picked up coincidentally as a Rockefeller insider. This attitude was doubtless naïve, and Rockefeller himself probably alerted the 5600 investment staff instantly of this development. I followed the prices of coffee futures over the next months and watched them rise like a rocket.

The reflected power of working for him could be applied to sublime and ridiculous causes, as in the case of my family doctor, John V. Skiff, Jr. Dr. Skiff, as well as a fine physician, was a devout small "d" democrat. No crisis in which I found myself, no plea from the Governor's office ever moved him. When sick, I waited my turn in his anteroom with measled four-year-olds and octogenarian rheumat-ics. Until the matter of the falcons.

Dr. Skiff was an enthusiastic falconer, but the state had a law outlawing falconry. One day as he was treating me, it seemed that his mind was clearly elsewhere. He confessed that his favorite hawk was overdue and missing (since New York had few falcons, he and his fellow falconers used hawks). He then told me how unhappy they were to have to practice their passion illegally, a situation, Dr. Skiff pointed out, that bred disrespect for the law overall. The tiny lobby of falconers had enjoyed no success in its efforts to have the sport legalized. I volunteered to enlist the Governor's office behind this neglected cause. He gave me the number of the current falconry bill then languishing in committee in the state legislature. Back at the office, I called the Governor's counsel and asked if we could not give the bill the blessing of the Rockefeller Administration. The health of my family, I explained, might hang on this issue. "Christ, have you flipped?" was his response, but my request was granted. I then called the counsels to the State Senate majority leader and the speaker of the Assembly, who determined which bills did or did not reach the floor. I asked each counsel to meet with a delegation of falconers. "This is some kind of joke, isn't it?" the harried counsel to the Assembly speaker asked. Still, both men agreed to hear the falconers.

Now, it was Dr. Skiff who called me. Was my wife's cut finger mending? Had my hives returned? And, by the way, what was the status of the falconry bill? I was tempted to tell him to give his birds two worms and call me in the morning.

The falconry bill passed one house but was defeated in the other. Dr. Skiff was instantly on the phone, upset by the news. Fearing that my children's chicken pox would go untreated, my wife's stitches unremoved, I told him that I would see what I could do. I called the counsel to the speaker again. The legislative session was in its dying hours and the mountain of bills before him was crushing. He heard me out impatiently and hung up with a barked goodbye. Then a rare event in the legislative process occurred—a defeated bill was recalled and passed. The word had gone out. Governor Rockefeller, inexpli-cably, wanted this one. Days later, the legislation was on Nelson's desk for signature. Thus was New York State made safe for falconers.

Chapter XVII

NEW YORK'S LEGACY

Had Nelson Rockefeller been a less effective governor of New York, he might have been a more successful aspirant for President. George Hinman, long Rockefeller's chief link to the national Republican Party, observed: "Tom Dewey [a governor of New York who was twice nominated for President by the Republicans] would have one big state issue a year, maybe compulsory automobile insurance. That left plenty of time to run for the nomination. But Nelson was always juggling five or six big state programs at once, any one of which would have been enough for Dewey."

Rockefeller was the best governor in New York's history. Yet his administrative style was often wasteful, not simply of money but of people and human energies. He flung his divisions against virtually every social enemy in sight. He made the costly compromises and concessions, deals and trade-offs to get what he wanted. Like the salmon spawning millions of its young, of which a handful survive, Rockefeller launched so many programs that the best of them were destined to transform the face of his state and point the way for the rest of the country, while others never got off the ground.

Nelson liked being governor. He actually enjoyed wrestling with the unglamorous ills besetting a major industrial state. His idea of a stimulating lunch was a seminar on the causes of housing decay in the South Bronx. He might not read much else, but he would devour a report on switching-equipment failures and on-time performance on the Long Island Railroad. He once told an audience, "You could plop me down in a town of two hundred people, and the first thing I'd do is try to start solving their problems." A few days later we received a letter stating, "Thank God our town is too small for your plopping."

Concrete excited him most. He wanted to leave behind tangible evidence of his leadership, buildings that proclaimed he had been there. He became New York's Cheops and the Hudson his Nile. He regarded the construction of the State University of New York as his crowning achievement as governor. His Administration had inherited a string of small teachers colleges. Fifteen years later, he left New York with a university of 235,000 full-time students on seventy-two campuses, the largest system of higher education in the world. When student radicals heckled him at state campuses, which they usually did, his jaw shot forward and he said, with the smugness that comes of being right, "You wouldn't even be here today if it wasn't for me."

The Nelson A. Rockefeller Empire State Plaza, the most controversial and costly state government complex in America, best reveals his penchant for the visible and tangible. The Plaza is the ultimate example of his compulsion to construct. In this passion Nelson was his father's son. The proofs of Junior's worth endure in Colonial Williamsburg, The Cloisters in Manhattan, a reconstructed Versailles, and Rockefeller Center. It was Nelson who persuaded his father that the largest private development in the country ought to carry the name of its creator unapologetically; not simply Radio City, the original designation, but Rockefeller Center.

When questioned about the wisdom of his construction mania, Nelson harked back to the mother lode. "No less a sage than my very great friend Walter Lippmann wrote a most scathing piece about Rockefeller Center being completely out of tune with the times and a disaster for the future. I think you could say it has worked out reasonably well."

In 1960 Queen Juliana of the Netherlands visited Albany to celebrate the anniversary of the city's founding (as Fort Orange) by the

Dutch in 1624. Albany is not without its charms, though they may not be immediately apparent to the first-time visitor. Nelson described his discomfort on the day of the queen's visit: "The queen was riding with Mayor Corning and myself. I thought, 'Well, it's his city so I'll ride up there with the security guys,' so I had plenty of time to observe the scene. I could see the way the city was running down and what this lady might think. Here was a great Dutch city built in the New World, and then she comes to look at it, never having seen it before. My God!" At that moment, the Nelson A. Rockefeller Empire State Plaza was conceived. New York simply must have a capital worthy of its destiny, not to mention its governor.

The state was then spending heavily for rented offices. One department, Motor Vehicles, had offices scattered over sixteen addresses in the Albany area. Nelson could thus make a strong practical case for a new government complex, but what Rockefeller wanted went well beyond the resolution of a space shortage. Rather he envisioned an epic event of architecture, one that would humble other state capitals and rival, if not surpass, Rockefeller Center itself in originality, concept, and scope.

In a stratagem that he employed to a fare-thee-well as governor, Nelson named an eighteen-member Commission on the State Capital and installed Lieutenant Governor Malcolm Wilson as chairman. The commission, not surprisingly, recommended that a new capital complex be built in downtown Albany. The site chosen was "The Gut," nearly one hundred acres of run-down housing, barrooms, and brothels to the south of the State Capitol. Thus the project was known originally as the South Mall. And its architect was to be the designer of Rockefeller Center, Nelson's friend Wallace K. Harrison.

The cost of what Nelson wanted was originally projected at $250 million, then raised to $450 million. He recognized that he could never get the voters to approve a bond issue for so costly and seemingly vainglorious an enterprise, and so the mayor of Albany, the aristocratic Erastus Corning II, a man whose talents soared well above the modest city he served, came to his rescue. Corning devised a sinuous plan whereby Albany County would own the South Mall and sell the bonds to build it. The state, under a lease-purchase arrangement, would pay rent to the county to cover the bond financing and to compensate for the loss of property taxes on the buildings torn down to make way for the project. When the scheme was announced, Nelson embraced the Democrat Corning on the steps of the old state Capitol and pronounced the mayor "a genius of creative financing."

During construction of the South Mall, as completion deadlines fell and costs rose, the project was underplayed by Rockefeller and ignored in campaigns, except when it was absolutely essential to rebut critics, of whom there was no lack. The architectural writer Wolf Von Eckardt eyed Albany and found the Mall "a battleship floating on a lily pond." The urban planner Jane Jacobs described the South Mall as "planning insanity." A *New York Times* architecture critic said it was "foolish, silly and impractical." During the critical siege, Nelson mischievously credited Malcolm Wilson as the "far-seeing chairman of the State Commission who recommended construction of the project." Privately, Nelson remained undaunted. His office in the State Capitol overlooked the South Mall construction site, and he measured the progress with a proud eye, remembering the naysayers who had disparaged Rockefeller Center long ago. A satisfied smile crossed his face the morning he spotted the words "Rocky's Pyramid," which workmen had painted in huge, crude letters on the unfinished shaft of the main tower.

One afternoon, returning by plane to the capital, Nelson gazed down on the sprouting structures and said, "You know, this *is* the best thing since the pyramids." Chuck Lanigan, overhearing the Governor, whispered to his seatmate, "There's one difference. In the pyramids, they know where the bodies are buried."

Critics might argue with Nelson's appraisal of the Mall, but few would question that it is stupendous. A forty-four-story tower, visible from a distance of fifteen miles, clings gracefully to a steel core. Behind it stand four 23-story towers, identical children of the parent structure. Behind them a low building runs unbroken for a quarter of a mile, a modern temple of Karnak, where drivers' licenses are processed. In front of the main tower, poised delicately on a shaft, is an enormous ovoid, inevitably called "the Egg." Within this space are two of the most boldly conceived theaters in the country. The Mall also contains the largest state library and museum in America. One

would have to travel to Brasilia in this hemisphere to find more striking architecture. In the end, bond borrowing for the South Mall
reached $985 million, and the total cost of Rockefeller's new capital
complex was estimated at more than $1.5 billion.

In the fall of 1973, he directed me to start work on a speech
dedicating the South Mall as the Empire State Plaza. The project was
yet unfinished, but this haste to christen was occasioned by a tightly
held secret—Nelson intended to resign as governor. The dedication
ceremony was held on a blustery November day. Elected officials and
legislative leaders stood shivering before the audience as Rockefeller
proclaimed his construction credo: "Mean structures breed small vision. But great architecture reflects mankind at its true worth."

Still, the new name of the grand design did not have quite the
right ring. There was little that Nelson Rockefeller himself could do,
within the bounds of modesty, to correct the failing. His wife, however, could. In 1978, Governor Hugh Carey was running for re-election. Carey's Republican opponent was Perry Duryea, Minority
Leader of the State Assembly. There was bad blood between Nelson
and Perry, caused principally by Duryea's unsubstantiated belief that
the hand of Nelson Rockefeller lay behind Duryea's earlier indictment on a minor election violation charge. Happy Rockefeller feared
that should Duryea be elected governor, justice might never triumph.
The Empire State Plaza might never properly honor the man whom
it should rightfully immortalize, her husband. Hugh Morrow had
once joked, "Someday we might all be visiting the Senator Herbert
Lehman Memorial Plaza." The Rockefellers were not amused.

As strained as were Rockefeller's relationships with the Republican Duryea, they were warm with the Democratic Governor Carey.
Thus a felicitous convergence of events gave Happy the leverage she
needed. Ray Corbett, president of the state AFL-CIO, was devoted
to Rockefeller. Rockefeller's building boom had brought about a
golden age for his union, and Corbett had publicly stated that the
capital complex ought to bear its creator's name. Happy talked to
Corbett who talked to Carey. Meanwhile, Bob Douglass lobbied the
state's other Democratic power ministers. All the pieces fit and
pointed toward a logical solution. It was an election year, and with

one move, Carey could please both a kingpin of labor and the state's famous former governor. Carey saw the light. Why not the "Nelson A. Rockefeller Empire State Plaza"?

Thus, on October 6, 1978, one month before election day, Nelson stood before dignitaries gathered on the speakers' platform in the Empire State Plaza and lavished his praises on Carey. "I think that New Yorkers can be proud that they have a governor with the vision and sensitivity to recognize people's needs for the uplifting force of beautiful art and monumental architecture. And I'm proud that we have a governor who then has the courage to stop in the midst of the pressures and look back to recognize the efforts of a former governor while he's still alive."

Assemblyman Duryea, whom Nelson had patted lightly as "distinguished and extremely able and devoted," listened to this tribute to his opponent with a frozen smile suggesting that he suddenly felt cold steel between his shoulder blades. Then Governor Hugh Carey proclaimed the Nelson A. Rockefeller Empire State Plaza. Nelson had succeeded on his terms. History may choose to remember or ignore the abstract ideals that move public figures, but the towering complex in Albany stands there unignorable and all but permanent. In time, the present cumbersome name will inevitably be shortened, and Rockefeller Center in the state's premier city will be balanced by Rockefeller Plaza in the state's capital.

From 1972 until the end of his public career, Nelson Rockefeller rarely appeared at a public function without them. In Bronx shopping plazas or Nebraska prairie towns, the Right-to-Life picketers were there with placards proclaiming him a murderer. He had been chosen as their prime target because of his unequivocal support of legalized abortion. On this issue, he showed none of the expedient tacking and trimming by which politicians, including himself, ride out storms of controversy. In 1968, Rockefeller named a panel to review New York state's abortion law, which had remained virtually unchanged since the nineteenth century. "I knew he was for abortion the minute he appointed the committee," his counsel, Mike Whiteman, recalled. Armed with the committee's recommendations, Nelson unsuccessfully proposed liberalized abortion over the next two years. Then, in 1970, to his astonishment, the legislature passed a bill that virtually legalized abortion on demand.

Nelson made a rare Saturday visit to Albany to sign the bill into law. His first act after doing so was to call an elated Happy. The next call was to Terence Cardinal Cooke, the head of the New York archdiocese. Consideration for the Cardinal was politically wise, but there was more to it. Cooke's predecessor had been that wily ecclesiastic Tory, Francis Cardinal Spellman, and Spellman was one of the few major clerics in America who had shown sympathy toward Nelson and Happy at the time of their marriage in 1963. Soon thereafter he had invited both of them to his premier annual political event, the Al Smith Dinner. Cardinal Cooke, upon succeeding Spellman, became the beneficiary of this relationship, thus Nelson's delicate but politic courtesy call to Cooke on signing the abortion bill.

Over the next two years, deaths from childbirth plummeted by 50 percent in New York, and infant mortality dropped sharply along with illegitimate births. The champions of reason appeared to have triumphed. The Right-to-Lifers, however, soon picked themselves up, doggedly re-entered the ring and began throwing the fear of God into the state legislature. In 1972, the legislature reversed itself and repealed the law legalizing abortion. As soon as word reached the Governor's office, Nelson asked me to prepare a veto message. I leaped to the assignment perhaps too eagerly. After making the case that repeal of the law would not end abortions, but only those performed under safe, medically supervised conditions, I went an extra, unrequired mile, suggesting that he say, "I do not believe it right for one group to impose its vision of morality on an entire society." I took the message in, the Governor gave his approval and we issued it to the press. His veto was sure to arouse the wrath of the Catholic Church, but the gratuitous swipe I had added was salt to the wound. The words were seized upon by Catholic clerics and commentators, and Nelson became the target of their vilification.

To the end, his position on abortion remained uncompromising. He took the demonstrators and the abuse without complaint or retreat. His mentor and conscience throughout had been someone in whom he placed implicit faith where the rights of women were at issue. Happy Rockefeller had urged him to take his initial stand supporting abortion reform and saw to it thereafter that he never wavered.

Politically, Nelson Rockefeller was hanged for the wrong crime. Three times his party denied him its presidential nomination largely because of his perceived liberalism. It was a bum rap. Liberals have been defined as those who believe in the efficacy of government action, and conservatives as those who do not. By this simplistic measure, Nelson Rockefeller, as New York's governor, would qualify as liberal, indeed. He could not keep his hands off anything. Was the privately owned Long Island Railroad collapsing? Have the state buy it. Were private colleges having financial difficulties? Give them state aid. Did businessmen shun ghettos? Create a Job Incentives Board to attract them. Are cars dangerous? Build a model safety automobile. But he was an activist not an ideologue. If a problem exists, you attack it. If you lack the authority, pass a law. If you lack the machinery, create an agency. If you lack the resources, raise taxes, sell bonds. But, do something. He directed this compulsion to act, however, almost as easily toward conservative as well as liberal objectives.

In March 1971, he proposed a sweeping overhaul of the state's welfare system. Years before, in his first term as governor, he had rejected a residency requirement for welfare recipients: "The time a person has lived among us is no measure of his needs." But by 1971, he was saying: "For persons unable to provide for themselves to come to New York State from throughout the nation is . . . unfair." He now favored a year's residence before allowing anyone to collect welfare in New York.

Southerners who a few years before had suggested giving free one-way bus tickets to their poor had been branded as social troglodytes. Now they had a northern sympathizer. "I am asking federal authority," Rockefeller said, "for a voluntary resettlement program by which persons already receiving public assistance in New York State could be assisted in relocating elsewhere."

His program included what was immediately dubbed the "Brownie Point Plan." Under it, a welfare family could get a larger grant by performing neighborhood chores. Other able-bodied welfare recipients were to "work off" their grants by laboring for local governments. He unveiled his plan to the full staff at the regular Sunday-night meeting at the Governor's Mansion. As he described the reforms: "These people are going to have to earn their welfare. We'll have the kids sweep the streets after school to earn points toward the family's benefit."

A key political adviser listened uncomfortably, then spoke. "Governor, this could touch off riots in Harlem. It will hurt you and your humanitarian image." Rockefeller's gaze hardened, but the man pressed on. "Can't you see those mothers handing out brooms after . . ."

"One thing I can't stand is a goddamned bleeding heart!" Rockefeller shot back.

New York City Democrats called the program "horrendous." Minorities demonstrated against it. But Rockefeller had the votes, and the welfare reforms became law (the "neighborhood chores" provision, however, was not enforced). He did not believe that his humanitarian convictions had failed. To Nelson, too many beneficiaries, by going into the second and third generation of dependency, resisting work and even cheating, had failed him.

Nelson Rockefeller was indisputably liberal on one issue, health care. The closest America has yet come to socialized medicine occurred briefly in New York State during his tenure as governor. In 1966 the federal government passed legislation providing medical assistance for the poor. Rockefeller seized upon the federal plan and set a then generous standard so that one in every four New Yorkers was eligible for free medical care. A headline writer called the New York program "Medicaid," and Washington lawmakers began to wonder what they had wrought. Rockefeller never tired of telling of a frantic call from Senator Jacob Javits. "My God, Nelson, at the rate you're going, New York State will use up all the Medicaid money that Congress appropriated for the whole country."

Later, reluctantly, Nelson was forced to back down. With federal aid reduced, he had to drop more than a million New Yorkers formerly eligible for free medical care. He then tried for five years in a row to promote a state system of Universal Health Insurance, but state business interests, fearing the cost of such a program, killed the bill every year. He was one of the few major American politicians, and a rare Republican, to declare, "Access to good health care ought to be regarded as a basic human right."

The watchwords of the public administrator—efficiency and economy—were not often found in Rockefeller's vocabulary. "He was a political more than a public administrator," Al Marshall concluded. Nelson had studied political administration under a master, Franklin D. Roosevelt. During his wartime service as Coordinator of Inter-American Affairs, he absorbed for life Roosevelt's canons of leadership. One night, flying back from Washington, he gazed out at the illuminated White House and reflected on his first mentor. "Coming from a business background, I was shocked at first by Roosevelt's methods. I thought it was inefficient and wasteful the way he would set up a new agency if other agencies weren't doing what he wanted. If he tried to get the existing ones to do what he wanted and they didn't, he didn't fire people. He just set up another department. There was a competition, and the old one would slowly wither away. It had a lot of merit, because a President can't be spending all of his time arguing with cabinet officers and assistants."

In his own Administration, the clean lines drawn on organization charts were, in practice, tangled or ignored. He would fling parts of an assignment across the staff and state agencies, guaranteeing duplication, conflict, and confusion. Nevertheless, he was generally regarded as a good administrator, an image fostered by the press, Hugh Morrow held, "because Joe Canzeri never lost a reporter's bags."

Nelson created Potemkin villages of objectivity. He appointed committees, commissions, boards, panels, and task forces, heavy with respected names and recognized authorities. By his eleventh year in office he had appointed eighty-one such bodies. Their purpose was not to advise him, but rather to give the appearance of detached judgment to what he had already decided to do. "I am a great believer," he once said, "if you have a meeting, in knowing where you want to come out before you start the meeting. Excuse me if that doesn't sound very democratic." FDR would have been proud.

"He would," Marshall observed, "throw anything into a deal to get what he wanted, or to get as much of it as he could." In 1969, Rockefeller was short two Republican votes to put over a tax increase. Two wavering Democrats were invited to the Governor's office to meet with a top aide. The pitch was remarkably free of ambiguity: "If we get your votes, here's what you get." And voting "right," the two Democrats found themselves, after a decent interval, appointed to high posts in the Rockefeller Administration. When the Governor's aide was asked later if he had cut the deal on Rockefeller's authority, he answered, "Of course."

Rockefeller could be indiscriminate, pursuing half-baked and worthy schemes with equal fervor. During a period in which the state was hard pressed to find space to treat drug addicts, Al Marshall was abruptly summoned to Nelson's office. "I see the *Queen Mary* is for sale," Rockefeller said. "I want the state to buy it. We'll turn it into a drug rehabilitation center."

"Governor," Marshall demurred, "I'm just a little guy from Fenton, Michigan. To people like us, the *Queen Mary* seems a bit splendid. People might not understand why we're using a luxury liner to treat junkies."

Rockefeller was unfazed. "It's already built. And we can't find space. It's a good idea." Marshall left wondering how one went about buying an ocean liner.

Nelson was not the only official with his eye on the *Queen*. John Lindsay, the mayor of New York City, beat him to the media with a story that the city was considering purchasing the ocean liner for use as a high school. Marshall's buzzer sounded, and he reported to a furious Rockefeller. The charge flung at him was not incompetence or slowness, but disloyalty. "You didn't carry out my orders because you didn't like them."

Marshall stepped up to the abyss. "I can't stay on your staff if I can't tell you what I think. I'll have to quit." With that he went back to his own office. Within fifteen minutes Nelson was on the phone. There was no apology, merely a terse, "I want you to stay."

Nelson would, on occasion, stick stubbornly by certain plans beyond all seeming hope of success. The reason was usually a secret commitment, which he regarded as an obligation of honor. The plan for a bridge across Long Island Sound is illustrative. In gradually stripping Robert Moses of his extraordinary authority over transportation, parks, and electric production in New York, Nelson Rockefeller had shown himself a master power player. Moses had first come to prominence working for Governor Alfred E. Smith in the 1920s. He had grown as a force through successive Administrations, and at his peak, he held twelve state and city posts simultaneously. By 1967, Rockefeller had whittled Moses down to a single job, the chairmanship of the Triborough Bridge and Tunnel Authority, which ran toll facilities in and out of New York City. That year, Nelson launched a $2.5 billion scheme for financing transportation and for pulling all New York City area commuter systems under one administrative roof, the Metropolitan Transportation Authority. The proposed consolidation would absorb the Triborough Bridge and Tunnel Authority, and with it, Robert Moses' last base of power.

Moses had no love for the bond issue, and certainly none for its absorption of his sole remaining bastion of authority. He enjoyed a towering prestige in the transportation field, and if Robert Moses publicly opposed the Governor's bond issue, he might well cause its defeat.

Rockefeller, however, had his own cards to play. Moses long had nourished the dream of a bridge across Long Island Sound, a span that would eliminate the costliest bottleneck in America—the necessity for all traffic moving in or out of Long Island to pass through New York City. Nelson Rockefeller was the one man who could realize Moses' dream for a bridge over the Sound. The original bill creating the Metropolitan Transportation Authority had no provision for such a bridge. Then Moses journeyed to Albany to see the Governor and Ronan. Thereafter, Bob Douglass, the Governor's counsel, was instructed, without explanation, to add the Long Island span to the legislation, and Robert Moses suddenly became an apostle of Nelson's Transportation Bond Issue. The bonds were approved by the voters in the fall of 1967. Robert Moses lost his chairmanship of the Authority in the merger with the MTA, but he was given a consultantship to coordinate Triborough projects, with "primary responsibility" for the Long Island Sound crossing.

Uncharacteristically, Nelson ignored family interests in pressing for the bridge across the Sound. The Long Island end would infringe on the estate of his sister, Abby Mauze, who was furious about the development. "She won't speak to me," he announced, grinning all the while. He began encountering a different class of demonstrators on Long Island. At an appearance in Nassau County, he found his way obstructed by the local gentry, including a niece. He commented later, "I've been picketed many times. But they don't usually wear mink."

Charles Lanigan, at this time chief of state planning, pointed out to Nelson that scant thought had been given to the impact on ecology, housing, and roads at the proposed Westchester and Long Island terminals of the bridge. "Nothing," Lanigan noted, "beyond dumping cars off at each end."

"That's why we have our state planner here, Chuck," said Rockefeller, with a withering smile, "to show us the problems that we've all missed." Besides, Nelson noted, he could look out from his home at Pocantico to the Tappan Zee Bridge spanning the Hudson River and, "At night, with all those lights, it's quite beautiful." Vehicles coming off the Tappan Zee, however, were miles from Pocantico.

Rockefeller managed to enlist the support of industry and labor on Long Island, but local residents in Rye and Oyster Bay remained adamant in their opposition. Environmentalists closed ranks against the proposal. Faced with voter opposition, the state legislature, in 1971, stripped the MTA of authority to build the bridge. Nelson vetoed the bill. The next year the lawmakers repeated the action, and again Nelson vetoed. In March 1973, the Department of the Interior in Washington blocked the bridge, contending that it would violate a wildlife sanctuary in Oyster Bay. Rockefeller was asked if he still intended to proceed and, if so, how. "Yep," he answered. "That's up to me. You'll find out as the scene unfolds." But the legislature again struck down the MTA's authority to build the bridge, and at last, the Governor conceded defeat.

Robert Moses, stripped of his last vestige of power by Rockefeller, received almost nothing in return. A man who well knew how to hold and avenge a grudge, he nevertheless continued to sing Nelson's praises throughout the years of the bridge debate. In sticking so faithfully by the proposal, Rockefeller had gone the limit to deliver on his word, and Moses knew that he had.

Chapter XVIII

CRITICAL CHOICES

ON A SEPTEMBER EVENING in 1973, three men sat around the dining-room table of an elegant Victorian mansion. One was the most powerful man in the state and one of its richest. From the window, he looked out on his neighbors across the street, some of the state's poorest, least powerful people, for the Governor's Mansion in Albany was the sole intact survivor of a grander past in a now decayed neighborhood. The men with the governor were Malcolm Wilson, the lieutenant governor, and Louis Lefkowitz, the attorney general. The latter two began to excuse themselves, but the governor asked Wilson to stay. When they were alone, he announced to the startled Wilson, "Malcolm, you'll be governor soon."

It had been a long vigil. Malcolm Wilson had set a modern record for patience in a supporting role. He had been Nelson Rockefeller's understudy for fifteen years, or, as he liked to put it, "I've been number two longer than Avis." Only Pierre Van Cortlandt, in the late eighteenth century, had served longer as lieutenant governor of New York. "Whatever they called him," Wilson once said morosely, "it certainly wasn't Lucky Pierre." Nelson explained that he intended to resign three months later, in December, and he wanted Wilson in office then, so that he could run as an incumbent in 1974. As for himself, Nelson explained that he was deeply worried about the future of the United States, a concern that he could not satisfactorily address from the narrow stage of Albany, New York. He was going to resign, he said, to devote himself wholly to this concern.

Thus, on December 11, 1973, Nelson Rockefeller rose in the crowded Red Room at the Capitol and announced that he would leave office within the week in order "to render a greater public service to the people of New York and the nation." He was then in his 5,459th day in office, the only twentieth-century governor to serve so long. He left a New York transformed in those areas where state government reaches. What had been a modest chain of teachers colleges was now the world's largest state university system. Where rivers and lakes had become polluted, hundreds of treatment plants were being built to clean the waters. The state government, for the first time, had moved in to try to stem the collapse of mass transportation. New York had a new Department of Environmental Conservation, a no-fault insurance law, more than fifty additional state parks, and the record home-building Urban Development Corporation. Rockefeller's impatient leadership had reaped a harvest of firsts: the country's first council to support the arts, first state minimum wage law, first auto safety legislation, and a dozen more initiatives.

And New Yorkers paid for it. The first Rockefeller budget had been $2 billion. The last was $8.7 billion. Taxes were raised eight times while Nelson Rockefeller governed, and New Yorkers bore the heaviest tax burden in the nation. On his last day in office, the state's public debt totaled $11.8 billion. One dollar in five of state government indebtedness in the United States was owed by New York. When Hugh Carey became governor in 1975, Nelson remarked to Harry Albright, "Poor Hugh. I spent all the money. And it's no fun being governor of New York if you haven't got the money."

Did New Yorkers get fair value? In 1970, public administrators from across the country were polled to evaluate state governments in eight areas of public service. New York ranked among the leaders in all categories. Neal Peirce, in *The Megastates of America*, believed that Nelson Rockefeller had built "the most complex, fascinating and socially advanced state government in U.S. history." Robert H. Connery and Gerald Benjamin, in *Rockefeller of New York,* a thorough and objective study of his fifteen-year tenure, arrived at a judgment that would have delighted Nelson Rockefeller: "He tried to do too much too fast."

As Nelson Rockefeller was vacating the statehouse, John Vliet Lindsay was leaving City Hall in New York, his second term as mayor completed. Lindsay's inauguration eight years before should have signaled a new era for New York Republicans. The party then had a young, attractive mayor presiding over the nation's greatest city and an older, attractive leader governing the Empire State. Maybe that was the problem.

Rockefeller had helped launch Lindsay's ascent from Congress to Gracie Mansion, and the Rockefeller family, at Nelson's prodding, contributed $450,000 to the Lindsay campaign. But on the campaign's opening day, when a reporter asked Lindsay if he was running with Rockefeller's money, he denied it. Why, the very suggestion, Lindsay said, was offensive. This was a new experience for Nelson Rockefeller; he had expected gratitude, or at least deference, from Lindsay. But the younger man's outright denial of his patron was insufferable.

In 1968, New York City's sanitationmen staged an illegal strike, and the head of the sanitationmen's union was clapped into jail. Lindsay asked Governor Rockefeller to call out the National Guard to pick up the garbage and break the strike. By now, Rockefeller had endured what he regarded as two years of government-by-dilettante in New York City. When he spoke Lindsay's name, his lips compressed, his brow furrowed, and his voice lowered to a contemptuous rasp. His manner suggested an aging suitor forced, resentfully, to compete for Lady Destiny's hand with an effete Prince Charming.

Nelson seized upon Lindsay's appeal for the National Guard to demonstrate real leadership to this coxcomb. Refusing to call out the Guard, he had the union leader sprung from jail and negotiated a strike settlement. Politically, the solution was a disaster. Rockefeller was portrayed in the press, particularly by *The New York Times,* as the politician who had caved in to insatiable union bosses, while Lindsay had had the courage to stand up to their greed.

During the course of these negotiations, I sat in Nelson's office as he told Mrs. Whitman to get Mayor Lindsay for him. He ordered it in the manner of a general summoning his batman. He opened the telephone conversation with artificial clubbiness, then his face grew ashen. "Let me understand this, John. The governor of the state is asking you to come to his office and you're saying you won't come?" The voice had a steel edge.

John Lindsay could get under Nelson Rockefeller's skin as no other politician, Republican or Democrat. Lindsay drove him to reckless excesses. During the sanitation strike, Nelson even tried to take Lindsay's garbage away from him. He called his counsel, Bob Douglass, in Albany on a Friday evening. "I'll be up Sunday night, and I want a bill ready authorizing the state to take over sanitation in New York City. Use the Public Health Law. Use anything. Just get it done."

Douglass did not tell Nelson that his wife was in the hospital about to have a baby. He was a man of reflexive loyalty. He was also a lawyer of exceptional talent, but in this situation, the constitutional obstacles that he had to circumvent were formidable. Still, Douglass worked around the clock and had a bill ready by Sunday night. The next day, felled by exhaustion, he was carted off to the same hospital from which one of his assistants was bringing home his wife and new baby. After Nelson's fury cooled, the garbage bill was not pressed further.

The year after the garbage strike, Nelson savored a delicious moment as John Lindsay was defeated in the Republican mayoral primary by State Senator John J. Marchi. Rockefeller thus could withhold his support from Lindsay as the mayor went on to run as a Liberal-Independent. Chuck Lanigan, then Republican state chairman, told the press that the party now backed Marchi. Lindsay, outraged, called Lanigan. How dare he say such a thing?

"What else could I do?" Lanigan protested. "He won our primary."

"Don't you understand," Lindsay argued, "Rockefeller and I run the party." He had it at least half right.

To Rockefeller's chagrin, Lindsay went on to win re-election on his own. Thus both men were still in their corners waiting for the next bell, with Lindsay now totally free of obligation to the old Pasha.

He demonstrated that independence by his endorsement, in 1970, of Arthur Goldberg for governor over Rockefeller. But it was never an even contest between the governor and the mayor. New York City, as the law had it, was "a creature of the State," and Nelson Rockefeller was the chief of state. Thus, every year, Lindsay had to journey, hat in hand, to Albany to plead for state funds to make up the city's chronic deficit. He handled his supplicant role, in Rockefeller's estimation, with a want of humility. The sessions took place around a table at the Executive Mansion, staff facing staff. Lindsay, whenever he disagreed, gave a theatrical toss of his head, followed by a snide retort. The gesture enraged Rockefeller. Indeed, Lindsay's penchant for stagy effects was proof to Rockefeller of the mayor's feathery substance. For several years, Lindsay did a passable song-and-dance routine at the New York City Press Corps' satirical Inner Circle show. Nelson would watch with studied indifference, once remarking, "Why doesn't he stick to show biz."

In 1971, Nelson vacationed in London and came back with an idea that he hoped to use to cut off John Lindsay at the knees. While he and Happy danced at Raffles by night, Nelson studied London's government by day. He learned that the city was divided into hundreds of self-governing districts. Thus Londoners were not dependent on or beholden to a central executive such as a mayor, a John Lindsay. Rockefeller liked that. He came home and appointed a Study Commission of the Governmental Operation of the City of New York. He named the president of the city's bar association, Stuart N. Scott, to head the body, and gave it a push in the direction of the London form of decentralized authority. He was asked by a reporter if the Scott Commission's purpose was not to destroy Lindsay. "You have already said that the mayor is incompetent at running the city," the reporter noted.

ROCKEFELLER: "That wasn't the word I used."

REPORTER: "What was the word you used?"

ROCKEFELLER: "Inept."

Then it was Lindsay's turn for puerility. He threatened to create a commission to investigate the performance of state government under Nelson Rockefeller. The following year was the last in office in New York for both of them, which may have prompted Nelson to a

brief mellowing. He told Harry Albright: "After I got re-elected in
'70, I really wanted to do something in the one place where I felt I'd
failed. I sincerely wanted to work with John in New York. But Lindsay never trusted me. And every time I tried to do something for the
city, Johnny Oakes at the *Times* would say I was just out to knife
Lindsay."

In private moments, however, he revealed an incurable dislike of
the man. We had flown into the private terminal at La Guardia Airport, where Nelson's daughter Mary was waiting in a car to tell her
father that she intended to remarry. Her fiancé was Tom Morgan, a
former magazine writer and now John Lindsay's press secretary. In
both roles, Morgan had done his share of Nelson baiting. Back in his
own car, Nelson shook his head and wondered aloud, "Why on earth
would she want to marry that fellow?"

"Do you know him?" I asked.

"I know who he works for. I don't need to know anything else."

It was the old buck versus the young buck, aging star and rising
idol. Had Lindsay chosen to subordinate himself, had he played
Nelson's grateful protégé, all might have gone well. Rockefeller
could be magnanimous as a godfather, but not as a rival. At bottom,
Lindsay was, in Al Marshall's observation, "a charismatic threat
to Nelson Rockefeller." Even New York was too small a stage for
both men.

During his fifteen years as governor, Nelson Rockefeller gave
New York the most comprehensive antidiscrimination laws, covering
race, age, and sex, in America. Still, his attitudes toward women as
colleagues and professional equals remained ambiguous. He had no
difficulty in appointing women to high government posts. His record,
including seven women named as state agency heads, would likely
have earned at least an A— from NOW. Occasionally, women entered his inner councils. Ann Whitman, his executive assistant, was
a valued confidante. Another insider was Mary Kresky, young, attractive, enormously well liked, and professionally as tough as a rivet.
Kresky was involved in his key policy decisions and enjoyed an
unusual rapport with Rockefeller—when she talked, he listened.
Still, he was a man who had been shaped in a world in which

women experienced both the elevation and constraints of life on a pedestal. When he became Vice-President, he named Mrs. Whitman as his chief of staff, but confessed an odd motivation: "Men don't see women as a threat. So they won't mind taking orders from a woman."

My brother, Richard, while director of the state's Adirondack Park Agency, had hired a summer employee, a young woman fervently committed to the environmental cause. She was also Nelson's niece, and she agreed to try to enlist her uncle's support to stave off legislation to abolish that controversial agency. She explained that she would need to have her case perfectly rehearsed and pared to no more than thirty seconds. She would have to choose a propitious moment, state her position succinctly, and withdraw. Uncle Nelson, she said, did not suffer prattling female Rockefellers overly long. He was to her, she confessed, an intimidating figure.

His attitudes toward women were illuminated in an exchange with Bella Abzug, when she was a congresswoman from New York City. Rockefeller, as governor, opposed a federal bill which would have required that all pollution be eliminated from navigable waters by 1985. He went to Washington and testified against the bill with a vehemence suggesting that its authors were attempting to overturn the Republic. Congresswoman Abzug, her trademark hat pulled low over her eyes, formidable in presence and delivery, began to question the Governor's figures in her sandpaper style. Rockefeller heard her with a bemused lack of reverence. He broke in, "Bella, may I just make one suggestion."

The congresswoman counterpunched with surprising speed. "Yes . . . *Nelson* . . ."

Rockefeller, smiling, went on. "The distinguished representative from New York has questioned my figures. My concern is that in challenging my figures, she has none to substitute except for the beautiful figure of her own."

A brittle silence followed, and then the audience burst out laughing. Bella Abzug flushed darkly. The hat and head lowered. "That is one demerit, Governor. We left a serious discussion on that level. We have to finish our serious discussion. You got a demerit for that." He still had a long way to go, baby.

Nelson Rockefeller left the governor's office with a heady goal. Few Americans would have the audacity to appoint themselves chairman of a commission to divine humanity's future, and fewer still would ask Congress for $20 million to finance the project. Nelson Rockefeller did both. In 1972, while still governor, he had created a body called the Commission on the Role of a Modern State in a Changing World. A typical Nelsonian improvisation, no legislation was passed, no budget developed, the commission's existence was simply declared. It needed a roof, a staff, money; thus Nelson had the State University concoct something called the Institute for Policy Alternatives, in effect, the staff arm of the Commission on the Modern State and its sugar daddy.

For all the influence he expected to wield over his commission, Nelson realized that it must have a quasi-public appearance. Study groups on the scale that he favored were expensive, and he wanted to keep the cost as much as possible off the family's back. Thus, soon after Richard Nixon's 1972 re-election, Nelson went to see the President at Camp David where he made his pitch for a national commission on America's future. All went well until John Ehrlichman noted slyly that if the idea was so good, maybe it ought to be done by the federal government. Nelson quickly counterattacked, arguing the superiority of a panel independent of government. Four months later, Nelson was flashing a letter from Nixon asking him to head "a national commission which would be bipartisan and broadly representative of all Americans." Nelson unhesitatingly agreed to serve as chairman. The letter from Nixon had, of course, been drafted by Nelson.

Among Nelson's recruits for the budding national commission was a Harvard-trained lawyer named Peter Wallison, from the politically connected, prestigious New York firm of Rogers and Wells. As a newcomer, Wallison was astonished by the unblinking acceptance among the Rockefeller circle of the leader's every word. "It seemed the wilder his idea, the more it was greeted as revealed truth." Wallison listened with a sense that the patients had taken over the asylum as Nelson explained how he intended to finance his commission: "I'll go down and talk to Bob Byrd in the Senate. We'll get about twenty million dollars from Congress." Wallison waited for the sobering counsel of Rockefeller's advisers. How, he wondered, did they go about returning him to reality? They did not. They all agreed it was a splendid idea. Wallison soon found himself swept along on the tide of fantasy as Nelson instructed him to draft a federal bill to appropriate the money.

In May, Nelson went to Washington to lobby the congressional leadership. Dreams of $20 million had by then fluttered earthward. On the advice of friendly congressmen, his goal was now a mere $1 million. He saw the majority and minority leaders of the Senate, Mike Mansfield and Hugh Scott. He talked to Speaker of the House Carl Albert and House Minority Leader Gerald Ford. All looked promising, and it was agreed that a rider for his $1 million would be tacked onto an unrelated piece of legislation. His expectation of public funding in no way diminished Nelson's intention to own the national commission. He was admirably blunt on that score. "Who will appoint the commission members?" a Washington reporter asked.

ROCKEFELLER: "I will."

REPORTER: "Who will finance it, Governor? New York State?"

ROCKEFELLER: "At the present time, New York State has financed it. But I hope that there will be funds from the executive branch, the congressional branch, and private groups."

REPORTER: "But are you going to appoint *all* the members?"

ROCKEFELLER: "Yes, sir."

REPORTER: "What would be your role, Governor?"

ROCKEFELLER: "Chairman."

Not only would he take the ball home with him if he could not have his way, but the taxpayers had to buy the ball.

The Rockefeller million-dollar rider was, in the end, sidetracked by the Senate. In the meantime, his panel had received a crisp, new name, coined by Bill Ronan: the Commission on Critical Choices for Americans. Its funds came largely out of family coffers, but Nelson managed to raise a surprising $1.6 million from foundations and individuals. Dwayne Andreas, the "soybean king" and longtime Hubert Humphrey backer, came through with a major contribution. Wallison was asked how Nelson was able to solicit these people. "If you've got it," he answered, "it's rather flattering to have a Rockefeller ask you for money."

On December 11, 1973, Nelson left the state capital for the last time as governor. He had already announced the "leading Americans" whom he had enlisted for the Commission on Critical Choices for Americans: former ambassador and playwright Clare Boothe Luce; Clarence Jones, publisher of New York's biggest black newspaper; Norman Borlaug, the agronomist and Nobel Peace Prize laureate; Lane Kirkland, AFL-CIO leader; Edward H. Teller, H-bomb developer; Bess Myerson, consumer champion; Daniel Patrick Moynihan, then ambassador to India; Bill Paley, board chairman of CBS; Brooke Astor, philanthropist; Belton Kleberg Johnson of the fabled King Ranch in Texas; and twenty-eight more. Nelson also persuaded most of the congressional leaders, including Thomas "Tip" O'Neill, Jr., the majority leader of the House, to become "ex-officio" members of the commission; Gerald R. Ford stayed on after he became Vice-President.

At the commission's first meeting I ran into Pat Moynihan. "I'm not sure what I'm doing here," he said unconvincingly. Of course he knew; Nelson Rockefeller had asked him, and no trader in political negotiables was going to let that one get by. Later, popping peanuts and sipping white wine aboard the F-27, Nelson exclaimed his ambitions for the new commission. "I'd like to get Mao Tse-tung or one of his guys to do a paper for us on the nature of man. I'd like to poll the world!"

Chapter XIX

HIDDEN HANDICAP

ON A SUNDAY in August 1916, a chunky eight-year-old stood up in a small chapel in Maine and began to read a passage of Scripture at a vespers service. He stumbled over the simplest phrases, halted repeatedly, blushed in embarrassment, and finally fled to his seat. The boy was Nelson Rockefeller, and he suffered from a disability that would not be commonly diagnosed yet for decades. Nearly sixty years later, the memory of those early humiliations still rankled.

I found in our files an interview with Nelson that Hugh Morrow had conducted to provide information to a magazine writer doing an article on dyslexia, Nelson's reading impediment. In part it read:

MORROW: "How old were you when you first realized that you had a problem?"

ROCKEFELLER: "I just had trouble reading."

MORROW: "Was it just as long as you could remember that you had trouble?"

ROCKEFELLER: "Always. But I didn't know what it was."

MORROW: "Did you find that this made a problem for you with other kids in the family?"

ROCKEFELLER: "No."

MORROW: "This was simply your problem."

ROCKEFELLER: "My problem. Nobody else had anything to do with it."

MORROW: "You used to walk to school from Fifty-fourth Street and . . ."

ROCKEFELLER: "What's that got to do with dyslexia?"

Eventually he loosened and described the agony of his school years. "I saw words backwards. Or I repeated them backwards. Even today, if I just glance at something, I still get mixed up. . . . I have no confidence in reading. . . . I can't see a whole word. I have to go through it syllable by syllable."

When the reading problem threatened to bar him from college, Rockefeller drew on a fierce will and stubborn pride. "I had to be determined and I had to discipline myself in order to overcome it . . . to be an achiever. . . . You have to have a strong sense of courage to overcome something like this."

As he grew older, Nelson came to believe that his determination had turned his handicap to advantage, just as a bone grows back strongest where it has been broken. He described his mind as now having the concentration of a flashlight. "I can fix a beam of attention on a subject, snap it off and instantly focus it on something new. My mind is disciplined. I can read on an infinite variety of subjects without any problem, making a decision and going immediately on to the next. It's a challenge when you overcome that condition. In the process, you so discipline yourself that you are way ahead of everyone else. Run circles around them. I concentrate on everything, which is a bad habit, because few people concentrate. If you do, it's hard on everyone else . . . spoils everybody else's fun. They're waiting to talk themselves. As a result, I have a kind of a grasshopper mind. You see what people are going to say before they've said it. My trouble is that I concentrate on it. And after I find out what they're going to say, well, I'm bored. Then I just go off and think of something else." The accuracy of this self-appraisal was borne out by those who worked with him. He listened with the suction power of a vacuum cleaner, impatient with needlessly reiterated points and diffuse argument. "I hear what you're saying," he would mutter, his eyes glazing over.

He opposed special training for children with dyslexia. When he learned from a fellow governor that the man's dyslexic children had been placed in special schools, he thought it unwise. "I think people pamper them too much. They're just taken out of the mainstream. It's got to be done by self-discipline."

His struggle with a learning disability prompted a rather startling self-appraisal for a Rockefeller. "People are too prone to find escapes or reasons for their lack of success. I have never felt sorry for myself." Nelson Rockefeller never felt sorry for himself? One may be tempted to scoff. Still, there is a comforting lesson here in our common humanity. Something in the neuro-muscular coordination between Nelson Rockefeller's mind and eye prevented him from seeing words as others do. He overcame, or at least learned to deal with his handicap. And it was important to him, in facing adversity, to believe that he had never felt sorry for himself. That someone of his advantages ever even considered himself a candidate for self-pity makes one's own occasional temptation to slip into that futile refuge somehow more forgivable.

For eleven years I wrote speeches for a man with dyslexia and a tin ear. The music of language bored him. He had no great respect for the writer's craft, which he rated about on a par with applying frosting to a cake after others had done the serious baking.

Ivy Lee, a public-relations genius, had long ago counseled Nelson's father and grandfather: "Crowds are led by symbols and phrases." Nelson either never learned or never believed this truth. In his speeches, he favored precision over poetry, literalness over imagery, the worn and comfortable over the fresh and striking. If Nelson Rockefeller, and not Franklin Roosevelt, had delivered that immortal 1933 Inaugural Address, instead of "One-third of a nation ill-housed, ill-clad, ill-nourished," we might have had "32.2 percent in substandard housing, 29.9 percent inadequately clothed . . ." He had absolute faith that if he could just pile the facts high enough, then the rightness of his case must prevail. He never accepted that most people are stirred emotionally rather than persuaded intellectually, that for every rationalist there are ten sentimentalists.

I heard him deliver the first speech that I had written for him in 1966, before the Albany Chamber of Commerce. He was introduced, went to the podium and spent the first five minutes recognizing everyone in sight who possessed the remotest political value. When he finally turned to the subject, I realized that he was not using the text. He went on, hitting essentially the same points I had covered, extemporizing in a style of patrician folksiness: "I wanna tell ya, this is some problem."

He had already covered what was in the prepared text when I saw him reach for his glasses. He adjusted them and abandoned all further eye contact with the audience. He riveted his gaze to the speech, which he now held as though it were a hostile object. The voice went lifeless and tentative as he began to read. Words became twisted and emphasis misplaced. "Conservation" emerged as "conversation," "reserve" as "reverse," "1965" as "1956." At that point, I had never heard of dyslexia. He stumbled on to the end, like an unhappy child forced to eat spinach, a man clearly miserable with the task before him. It is difficult to say for which of us the experience was more painful.

He struggled hopelessly with anything in writing which was at all unfamiliar. Once, after a particularly harrowing evening, he came to me the next day, rolling his eyes and wrinkling his eyebrows. In the future, he asked, would I please leave people's names out of speeches.

Clichés held no terror for him precisely because they were comfortably familiar. Joe Shannon, a reporter for the Westchester Rockland Group of newspapers, coined an acronym for Nelson's platitudinizing talks—BOMFOG. It caught on, and whenever Nelson began extolling "the brotherhood of man under the fatherhood of God," reporters scribbled BOMFOG in their notebooks and sat back for another eye-closer. During my years as speech writer, I never used the phrase, fearing it might touch off guffaws from the press corps. Although the words had gone unused for more than a decade, they were, however, almost always cited whenever any journalist wrote a Rockefeller profile.

In Nelson's final year in public life, a mood of mischief seized me. Was he so immune to language, I wondered, as to be unaware of the seriocomic history of BOMFOG? The occasion was the Bicentennial Bishops' Banquet in Philadelphia honoring Richard Allen, founder of the African Methodist Episcopal Church. One part of the text that I submitted read: "The motive force of Richard Allen's life was the brotherhood of man under the fatherhood of God." Nelson delivered the line with a warmth suggesting that he had coined it on the spot.

Only rarely could a writer slip eloquence past him. During his 1970 re-election campaign, when he was running against Arthur Goldberg, it was enormously important for Nelson to "out-Israel" his opponent in an address before the Zionists of America. I assigned the speech to Jim Carberry, a former writer for Mayor Lindsay, who had joined us for the campaign. Carberry turned in a splendid draft, just the tenor that succeeds with this wing of the New York Jewish community, a style describable as Manhattan Biblical, ringing with Jehovist righteousness.

Carberry and I were called over from campaign headquarters on Madison Avenue to the Governor's 55th Street office where we were to clear the speech. It was Carberry's first working exposure to Rockefeller. On this day, the Governor was unusually testy and impatient, worried about the election's outcome. He also showed his customary uneasiness at having a new face in the inner circle. Or perhaps it was simply that Carberry had been a Lindsay man. Whatever the reason, it was a charmless session, with Nelson, his expression set like plaster, snapping the pages, grunting his grudging approval.

Then he stopped. "What about the missiles?" Carberry and I eyed each other blankly. "Where's my position on the missiles?" He asked it as though he were dealing with imbeciles. How could we have omitted the stand of the governor of New York on the disposition of strategic weaponry in the Middle East? He buzzed his secretary. "Get me Henry."

Kissinger was on the line instantly, though at the time he was deeply enmeshed in tense Arab-Israeli cease-fire negotiations. Nelson explained his upcoming speech, and as he and Kissinger talked, he relayed phrases that he motioned for us to take down. Clause piled on top of clause, correction over correction. He and Kissinger finally exchanged warm farewells, with Nelson offering fatherly encouragement to him for the hard days ahead. He hung up and said with satisfaction, "Okay. That ought to do it."

Carberry is a wry Gael, and on the walk back to headquarters, he looked his wriest as he asked, "How the hell am I supposed to handle that business about the missiles?"

"You'll figure it out," I responded, helpful and leaderlike.

Later that afternoon, Carberry turned in his latest version. He had done what a professional speech writer does. He had taken the technical, clause-ridden word heap of our notes, and he had recast it into readable English, while preserving Nelson's and Kissinger's ideas. Still, an antenna somewhere inside me quivered a warning.

The next morning we met again with Nelson. He moved quickly through the pages. "Where is it?" His jaw protruded, and his eyes became narrow pits. "The stuff about the missiles. It's not here!"

"Well, you see, Governor, it's still all there, but for ease of reading . . ."

He angrily cut off my explanation. "We had it all worked out perfectly. With Henry. Exactly what I wanted." He exhaled the exasperation of a man put upon by idiots. Then he called Kissinger and we repeated the performance of the day before. That night Nelson's speech to the Zionists of America shone with this jewel: "In view of the recent general agreement on intelligence reports confirming Egyptian violations of the cease-fire agreement, the United States must—in conjunction with the Soviet Union, our cosponsors of the cease-fire and peace talk proposals—see to it that the Egyptian government immediately withdraws the Soviet missiles and other military equipment moved into the thirty-two-mile cease-fire zone in violation of the agreement." A sixty-three-word sentence.

Not perhaps in a class with "blood, toil, tears and sweat." But did Winston Churchill possess Nelson Rockefeller's precision?

His usually cryptic manner of instruction became even more obscure when he was communicating his wishes on speeches. I once received a call from the press secretary who was on the road with the Governor reporting that Nelson was unhappy with his text for an address at the State Fair.

"He's mad that you left out the moths."

"Moths?"

"Moths. That's all I can tell you. And he muttered something about Cornell."

By six o'clock the next morning, I had tracked down Dean Palm, of the Cornell School of Agriculture, in a Washington, D.C., hotel.

Yes, Dean Palm remembered, the Governor had been fascinated by the leaf-roller moth during a recent visit to the college. After this conversation I was able to telephone an addition to the text, which the Governor gleefully delivered to the fairgoers: "They put a synthetic attractant in a little plastic capsule inside an open box. The lining of the box is sticky, like flypaper. The box is hung in the apple tree, and the male moth senses this attractant—as far as a mile away —and makes a beeline for it—or should we say a mothline. Anyway, he gets stuck in the box, which ends the mating game for him. So the female moth doesn't get fertilized, no larvae are produced, and the apple crop is saved." The sex life and death of the leaf-roller moth became a staple of his 1970 stump speeches.

Nelson's hypersensitivity to appearing indifferent to the hardships of others occasionally produced odd results in his speeches. He was plugging no-fault auto insurance before the League of Women Voters, and the draft I submitted read, "Suppose a member of your family was injured in an automobile accident." In the middle of the speech, Nelson decided that rather than impose this hypothetical misfortune on his listeners, he would assume the burden himself. And so he improvised: "Suppose I was injured in an automobile accident." He went on, gamely adapting the text to the first person. "And suppose my family had nothing to live on while I was out of work." The laughter was clocked at three minutes.

After delivery, the speeches were returned to me in large blue envelopes for my files. One envelope was unusually hefty, and when I opened it, out rolled the most handsome fountain pen I had ever seen, a gold Parker 75. A wonderful souvenir, I thought, for the time when these days were over. But anything so elegant would surely be missed, so I returned it to Mrs. Whitman. "Thanks," she said offhandedly. "He goes through these things like ball-points."

Writing speeches for Nelson Rockefeller provided useful insight into ethnic groups. No state has the cultural diversity of New York, and Nelson Rockefeller spoke before Greeks and Haitians, Scandinavians and Ukrainians, along with the more commonly found ores in the melting pot. Before he spoke to ethnic audiences, I called their leaders for guidance. One group was so much better organized and so much more helpful as to make the others appear mute. One proof of their energy: of all speeches delivered by Nelson Rockefeller before ethnic organizations in a typical year, 40 percent were to Jewish audiences, while Jews made up only 12 percent of the state's population. The Jews were the only ethnic group who would contact me before I could call them. I became the object of a barrage of phone calls and personal visits. Complete texts were sent, and more follow-up phone calls were made, "to make sure everything is going all right. And, Mr. Persico, just let us know if there is *anything* else we can do." The only danger was to succumb to the policy overkill included in their suggested speeches, which tended to place Nelson Rockefeller somewhat to the right of Israel's Likud Party on Middle East issues. Once the hard line rhetoric was defused, these drafts were eminently usable.

Black organizations ran a trailing second in effective speech lobbying. In a last-place tie were virtually all others. The Poles, Hispanics, and Italians all seemed oblivious of the opportunity to put their words in the mouth of an important public figure. When they received a call from the Rockefeller offices, they seemed paralyzed with exaggerated deference. Most galling were my contacts with Italian-American organizations.

PERSICO: "The Governor is speaking to your group on March nineteenth. It would sure help us, and you too, probably, if you could suggest what he might talk about."

ITALIAN-AMERICAN REPRESENTATIVE: "Listen, kid, we all love him down here. Anything Rocky says is okay by us."

I concluded that Jews and blacks have a clearer cultural cohesion and common objectives that they want advanced. The others either have no similarly unambiguous self-interest or are insufficiently skilled at pursuing it.

Occasionally, while writing for Nelson, I wrote material for his wife, Happy, his daughter, Mary, former Governor Thomas E. Dewey, once even for Jackie Robinson. Robinson believed deeply in Nelson and always played a prominent role in directing our Blacks for Rockefeller campaign committees. His participation was not, however, wholly a labor of love. During the months of the campaign,

Robinson was paid at a rate equivalent to approximately $60,000 per year.

During the 1968 presidential campaign, we were working out of Rockefeller headquarters across from the Algonquin Hotel in Manhattan. Robinson came into my office with his tigerlike grace, poised on the balls of his feet, as though ready to pounce twenty feet from a standing start. He glared at me and shook the papers in his hand. Some days before, at a meeting of black publishers, Robinson had said that if the Republicans chose Richard Nixon over Nelson Rockefeller, he would bolt the party. William F. Buckley, Jr., thereupon, had skewered Robinson with Buckleyan logic in his column. Robinson had supported Nixon for President in 1960. What, Buckley asked, had Nixon done to earn Robinson's disdain in 1968, except to stand in the way of Nelson Rockefeller's ambitions.

Robinson handed me a rebuttal to Buckley's column which he had written. "Hugh Morrow said I ought to let you take a look at this." His tone invited no small talk. I asked him to sit down while I went over Buckley's piece and his response. He leaned close, his eyes fixed on me. I was uncomfortable because I knew immediately why Morrow had sent him to me. His counterblast was ranting and fuming. Buckley was called a bigot in every other paragraph. Robinson was an intelligent man, but rage had made him incoherent. I told him that his letter made all the right arguments but needed some changes to sharpen his point. I rewrote the letter, hoping to moderate his fury into a usable rebuttal. The draft was printed in several papers that had carried the original Buckley column, and Robinson returned to thank me. Later, when Nixon was nominated, Robinson did indeed move over to support Hubert Humphrey.

On the subject of William F. Buckley. I began to suspect that the rich all follow the same code, if not the same political philosophy. Bill Buckley had written few kind words about Nelson Rockefeller and many that were scathing. His publicly expressed scorn did not, however, prevent Buckley from writing privately to ask Nelson to sponsor one of Buckley's friends for membership in the Century Club. Nelson sent the letter to me with instructions to draft a highly favorable reply. Class was evidently thicker than political water.

Another of my writing odd jobs involved Happy Rockefeller. A man whose wife was about to undergo a mastectomy wrote to her in the hope that someone who had already faced this ordeal with courage could send some words of comfort to his wife. The letter was passed on to me to prepare Happy's answer. I tried to imagine what one woman would say to another at such a time. Happy had spoken simply and movingly of her ordeal to reporters, and I wondered why this letter had been "staffed out," as the phrase had it. Force of habit, I concluded. Rockefellers were accustomed to having things done for them. The habit dies hard.

On the whole, Nelson Rockefeller was a stimulating man to work for, but impossible to write for. The dyslexia, his disdain for "that fancy stuff," his instinct for the banal, made speech writing perhaps the least satisfying function in his service. He took no pleasure in language, lacked delight in the well-crafted phrase and the satisfaction of moving people through the power of speech. Quite literally, he and writers did not speak the same language.

Ambivalence may also be built into the speech writer's job. If he achieves the highest level of performance—functioning as a writer-conceptualizer-confidant—he feels a vague unfairness at forever having his inventions credited to another. He becomes cynical, knowing that behind the moving expression and persuasive argument of most public figures there labors a performer as faceless as himself. The client, on the other hand, quite naturally resents the inference that someone else is putting words in his mouth, doing his thinking for him. Thus the alliance between speech writer and speech giver remains uneasy.

Probably the most substantial work I ever produced in Nelson Rockefeller's name was an article entitled "A Conception of the Presidency." It was written in 1968 for *Saturday Review* magazine, which lost interest after it became probable that Richard Nixon would be the Republican nominee. In 1973, the essay appeared in full in Emmet Hughes's book, *The Living Presidency*. Other hands had tinkered with it along the way, but it was essentially the same document I had written four years before. Reading it, I felt faintly flattered, but mostly depressed. I would like to have known Nelson Rockefeller's own deep feelings about the Presidency.

I rarely wrote a speech for Nelson Rockefeller of which I was not reasonably proud when it went in to him, and rather chagrined at the way it came out. Words were not his weapons. His most remembered speech occurred at the Cow Palace in San Francisco when he refused to let the yahoos of the Republican right drive him off the stage during the 1964 convention. And that was largely a triumph of silence.

His unreverential attitude toward writers included the news media as well. His Commission on Critical Choices for Americans had brought together some of the most original minds in America to focus their wisdom on the country in its third century. His mind virtually danced with the ideas they had stirred in him. And what did reporters perpetually ask? Was he a candidate for the Presidency in 1976? How about 1980? 1984? He managed, on the whole, to conceal his disappointment in the press with unfailing charm. Most reporters would have been surprised to learn that they thought much better of him than he did of their profession. Nelson Rockefeller was good copy, and, on the whole, reporters liked him and respected his motives and abilities.

During a 1970 campaign swing, a reporter called out to him as he boarded his plane, "Hey, Governor, there's more than your image showing." Indeed, the seat of his trousers had split along the seam. He grinned confidently. "Get me the sewing kit." Sitting unselfconsciously in his shorts, he sewed up the seam with confident jabs of the needle, while reporters and staff first gaped, then cheered as he completed the rescue. He looked up with the smile of one who knows he has pleasantly startled. "See. I went to a progressive school."

When he wanted to brief reporters on the need for another multi-billion-dollar bond issue, he did so at Pocantico at a lunch, for 150 of them. On a few occasions, he moved to their court, dropping by the press room in the State Capitol. He would have a beer with the press corps, the only time I ever saw this drink pass his lips.

He accepted that he had to respect the power of the press if not its performance. But, in his private opinion, the investigative journalism of the Vietnam-Watergate era fell somewhat short of a holy crusade. He had a less exalted explanation for its vogue. "Television is hot stuff, you know, with thirty-second and one-minute spots. How do these poor newspapers compete with them? They have learned they can do these in-depth investigations and that brings a lot of readers. I think frankly that sometimes it gets overdone."

His reverence for the journalist's craft remained under firm control to the end. In part, it was the dyslexia. Since childhood, the written word had been his enemy. He had always had to work around it, to learn by being a listener. Still, he had emerged the intellectual superior, he believed, of facile scribblers. His scant esteem for practitioners of the word went even deeper. Truly first-rate people, in his view, strive to move the world, not to record its movements. They plunge into the arena, in Teddy Roosevelt's image, "marred by dust and sweat and blood." The choice was *doing* versus *observing*, firsthand experience compared to secondhand recounting. There could be no doubt which Nelson prized more.

We once talked about the possible influence of news stories in stimulating imitative violence. "There is no question," he said. "The psychiatrists say that prominent attention given to individuals who have attempted to assassinate, for example, does stimulate those who may not have been thinking about it . . . so you have this problem of balancing society and a free press. They are in conflict." I asked how he would resolve that conflict. And to his credit, he did not hesitate. "I come down on the side of the free press."

Chapter XX

DOUBTFUL PRIZE

NELSON ROCKEFELLER BEGAN 1974 as a private citizen for the first time in fifteen years. He immediately immersed himself in the Commission on Critical Choices for Americans, which served him just as he had intended. The ferment of ideas from the people he had drawn around him stimulated his imagination. Irving Kristol was doing a paper on the nature of man. His old friend Edward Teller advised the commission on the oil potential of shale rock out west. Lester Brown became a commission consultant on world hunger; Walter Levy, on energy. More than 125 of the nation's authorities were part of Nelson's personal brain trust. And since his work with the commission was not demanding, he could do the Party Track bridge building that he had so long neglected. He was now able to move between the high road of the mind and the two-laners leading to Republican dinners, clambakes, and picnics all across America.

In May 1974, we flew to Arkansas. Nelson was going out to visit Winrock Farm and Win Paul Rockefeller, his brother Winthrop's only child. While there, he also planned to look over some of the *objets d'art* that Win had left and to do some politicking among Arkansas Republicans. For Nelson, it was a sentimental journey. He was now doing what Win had always urged on the family while he was alive. He was going to Win's spread to see what his brother had made of his life, after a disastrous first act as a Rockefeller.

We were flying in the Grumman Gulfstream jet, a two-engine plane accommodating twelve passengers; it was the middle-sized aircraft in the family fleet of three planes and a helicopter. Nelson, Laurance and David shared the aircraft on a first-come, first-serve basis, and they paid according to an hourly rate set for each plane. John III traveled by commercial airlines. The favorite of Nelson's staff was the F-27, a red-and-white Fairchild Wayfarer, which seated twenty-six and resembled a lounge in the Hotel Pierre transported aloft. The smaller Grumman was just as lush but less congenial than the F-27. The atmosphere airborne with Rockefeller was marked by overcivilized banter and was never entirely relaxed. It was the same climate that he generated on the ground, but the guardedness was more concentrated in the plane.

On the trip to Arkansas, Nelson sat at a collapsible conference table plowing through the clichéd "bulging briefcase," signing papers and making notations. (He had a peculiar style of writing—he held a pen between the index and middle finger with the shaft pointed outward.) A dingy fleece of clouds rolled past the window limiting visibility, and I wondered by how much we were clearing the Ozark Mountains. The copilot came down the aisle and spoke to Rockefeller. Something in the pilot's voice betrayed the casualness he affected. "We won't be able to make the Winrock airstrip, sir. Petit Jean Mountain is socked in." The cement-gray chin thrust forward; the mouth became a drooping curve. Nelson grunted something unintelligible. The pilot pressed on manfully. "We'll have to land at Little Rock and hope things clear up."

I, whose life could be measured in missed planes, wrong turns, and botched plans, was about to witness what happened when it rained on Nelson's parade, for the journey to Winrock had been long planned and meant much to him. A few minutes later, the Grumman touched down on the Little Rock runway. As we taxied toward the terminal, a Mercedes bore down on the plane. The driver stopped, leaped out, and, in a whirlwind of arms and legs, appeared to fling open all four doors of the automobile at once. Two other cars pulled up behind him and the drivers performed similarly. The man driving the Mercedes was up the plane's staircase just as it touched the ground. He was young, deferential, but confident, and introduced himself as a staff member from Winrock Farm. "We were advised that you couldn't make Petit John Mountain, Governor. I've taken the liberty to set up some alternative arrangements. They are ready for you for lunch at either the Hilton Inn, it's the best in the city, or the Little Rock Club, which was Mr. Winthrop's club. In the meantime, I'll be getting weather reports from the Petit John airstrip every fifteen minutes. As soon as the weather breaks, the cars will be standing by to take you and the party back to the airport. We can be at Winrock five minutes later." The Governor barely glanced up. "We'll go to Winnie's club."

During lunch the young man appeared at intervals, whispering into Nelson's ear. At the third report, a small smile crossed Nelson's face, and we were out of the Little Rock Club with the usual vacuum that he created whenever Nelson Rockefeller decided to move. We piled out of the plane at Winrock some fifteen minutes later and were driven across fields and grazing lands populated by Win's prize Santa Gertrudis cattle, handsome beasts with slow, regal movements. We arrived at the main house, a great rustic lodge of glass, stone, and timber offering a sweeping view. Around the house, Winthrop had had quotations from the Bible carved into stones.

The chief of the welcoming party at Winrock asked Nelson if he wanted to see Win's car collection. He did, and we were then driven to what resembled an indoor sports complex. Inside, more than fifty antique cars, each in showroom condition, were set within paths of white crushed stone. One of our party remarked to the Governor, "It's done with perfect taste, just as your family does everything." She dropped back a few steps and said softly to me, "Who couldn't with their money?" We learned that Win, with Rockefeller practicality, had made the collection pay by charging admission to visitors.

We stayed for a down-home barbecue given for a few hundred of Win's old friends and neighbors, then returned to Little Rock, where Nelson hosted a cocktail party for Arkansas Republicans and delivered a speech in tribute to his late brother at a high-school auditorium. As the jet lifted off for the return to New York City, I had my answer; I now knew what happened when rain threatened a Nelson Rockefeller parade.

By the time Nelson had returned to private life, Watergate was becoming for Richard Nixon the wound that would not heal. A matter rating a footnote to a footnote throws some light on Nelson's attitude toward the issue. John Ehrlichman, as a Watergate defendant, twice asked Nelson Rockefeller for money to aid his legal defense. "I am embarrassed to say that I did not answer the letters," Rockefeller later confessed. His inaction here mirrored his stance throughout Watergate. He resisted getting ahead of the most middle-of-the-road Republican on the matter. He had gone hard after Nixon in 1960 and 1968, but all that this behavior had earned him in the party was an almost ineradicable reputation as a spoiler. Nixon had gone on to be elected President twice, while Nelson Rockefeller remained a governor.

As support for Nixon began to crumble away in great chunks, particularly after he fired the Watergate special prosecutor, Archibald Cox, Rockefeller was still saying, "I have to think that the President's position on law and order has been one of genuine concern for this country. I also have to think that the President must be, of all the people in this country, the most distressed about Watergate and that it's got to be as tough a situation as any President ever faced. So I feel for him."

In the fall of 1973, there had occurred a major test as to whether his loyalty was cutting any ice with Nixon. On October 10, Spiro Agnew was forced to resign as Vice-President for presumably taking envelopes stuffed with cash, in the shadow of the White House, for favors rendered while he had been governor of Maryland. Nixon was to announce his choice for Agnew's successor two days later. On that day Rockefeller was restless; he went distractedly through his schedule, a hospital dedication in Westchester County, a political dinner that evening at a nearby country club. There a reporter cornered him and asked, "A lot of people are hoping that the nod will go to you. Are you hoping it will?" He answered warily: "Anyone who is interested in public service, as I have been all my life, wants to be of service where he can. I leave it right there."

He was on the phone much of the day with Republican Party leaders. He had been particularly heartened by a call from Murray Chotiner, a charter Nixon loyalist. Chotiner told Rockefeller that he had urged Nixon to name him as Agnew's replacement. But the besieged President was not about to put his old nemesis in line for his job, no matter Rockefeller's present fidelity. The poor kid on the block with the patched pants and hand-me-downs would give nothing to the rich kid up the street who had long scorned him. Nixon picked Gerald Ford. Thus Nelson went back to the tag ends of his remaining months in office and then on to his Commission on Critical Choices.

Rockefeller reacted with curious distinctions toward the Watergate cast. He had worked with Attorney General John Mitchell for years and admired him. After all, Mitchell had invented the "moral obligation bonds" that financed Nelson's construction dreams in New York State. Yet when Mitchell was indicted, Rockefeller responded mechanically when a reporter asked, "Don't you have some feelings about what has happened to him?" "Yes," Nelson answered, "but I think this goes beyond the personal question. This is now in the hands of the courts."

Nelson was also one of those favored by the marathon telephone calls that won a fleeting celebrity for Mitchell's wife, Martha. I walked into the press office late one afternoon to find one of the secretaries, Maxine Paul, hand clapped over her phone's mouthpiece, smiling incredulously. "It's *Martha Mitchell!*" The call had been transferred to the press office by a switchboard operator who thought Mitchell was a crank caller. The treatment did not deter Martha from baring her soul for a half hour to the stranger at the other end of the line.

Nelson responded unpredictably to Spiro Agnew's plight. On the day Agnew was forced from office, Nelson did something rare. He drafted his own statement, a short, curious pronouncement: "The resignation of Vice-President Agnew is the culmination of a tragedy both for the country and for him personally. He's my friend." When he read the statement to the press, a reporter asked, "Is that it, Governor?" Rockefeller replied, "Yes, sir." Perhaps it was his way of atoning for leaving Agnew high, dry, and embarrassed when he dropped out of the '68 campaign. Privately, Nelson said, "Nobody ever got to the top climbing over the dead bodies of his friends," an expression he savored from his Latin-American days.

If Nixon eventually had to go, Nelson favored impeachment over resignation. Resignation meant the immediate elevation of Ford, another Republican, to the Presidency. Ford would then have over two years in office and become automatically the party's front-runner for 1976. In May 1974, we were on the road and having lunch in a hotel suite. The noon television news reported another sordid disclosure from the Watergate tapes, this time Nixon's crude characterization of certain ethnic groups.

"When it gets bad enough, he'll resign," I offered. "He'll never allow himself to be impeached."

Nelson glared. "He'll never resign."

A fellow staffer smiled triumphantly. "So much for your opinion, Joe." That's the way they behaved around the sovereign.

What did Nelson really believe? Was his fidelity toward a man for whom he had not the slightest affection explained solely by political expediency? Was it an attempt to eclipse his old liberal, maverick image by a belated show of party fidelity? Hugh Morrow, at this point, was invited to come aboard the Nixon ship to try to salvage the public relations of the Watergate disaster. He reported the offer to Rockefeller and said, "I can't very well avoid at least going to talk to them. They're sending a plane up to bring me to Key Biscayne. Besides, I'm dying of curiosity." Rockefeller eyed Hugh carefully. "I hope you're not seriously thinking of going to work for *him*."

He disdained Nixon to the end, but at the same time, he had a grudging respect for the man. He had been impressed by Nixon's toughness on Vietnam. The President's extension of the war into Cambodia may have outraged millions of Americans by its questionable moral and military wisdom. But Rockefeller remarked to us after the attack, "You can say what you want about Dick Nixon. But the man sure is a patriot." The Nixon-Kissinger rapprochement with China and the pursuit of détente with Russia also won his authentic admiration. They were just the bold acts that a Rockefeller-Kissinger foreign policy would have initiated. Nixon had made great achievements in areas that Nelson regarded as historic and significant. Thus Nelson's attitude toward Watergate suggested an unspoken, "What's all the fuss about?" He could sympathize with Nixon because he could imagine himself subjected to the same extraordinary pressures in the Oval Office. In fact, he was supposed to be there!

For his part, Nixon knew that he could use Rockefeller for his fortune, for his connections, and for his stature in the liberal wing of the Republican Party. He also admired the fact that while Rockefeller may have inherited power, he had mastered its use superbly. But there was little reason for him to *like* Nelson Rockefeller. People like the Rockefellers had made the Richard Nixons of this world feel uncomfortable all their lives, made them resentful of unearned privilege.

In the early years of their rivalry, Nixon had tried friendly overtures, swallowing his pride and Nelson's fourteen points in 1960, only to be rebuffed when he asked Nelson to run with him as Vice-President. In 1968, after Nixon had won the Republican nomination, Nelson had to rethink his position. First, to Republicans, he had been the spoilsport, the man who had selfishly hurt his own party's candidates, Nixon in 1960 and Goldwater in 1964. Secondly, he had to face the possibility, as a state governor, of dealing with and depending on a Nixon White House. He was not going to cut off New York's nose to spite Nixon's face. He pocketed his pride and his prejudices and decided to campaign enthusiastically for Nixon that fall.

On election night, Leslie Slote, then Nelson's press secretary, sat alone before a television set in the library at 812 Fifth Avenue as Nelson and Happy dined with friends. From time to time, Nelson popped his head in to ask Slote the latest returns. At about 11:30 P.M., Slote told him, "It looks as if Richard Nixon's the next President." Nelson was silent for a moment, then spoke with tired resignation. "I guess we'd better pay our respects to the President-elect." He directed Slote to have the driver bring the car around.

At the Waldorf Astoria, New York City police parted the barricade to allow the Governor's Lincoln to burrow below ground to the well of the hotel. There, Secret Service agents whisked Rockefeller and his press secretary to the Nixon penthouse suite. The two men passed down a corridor and into an anteroom. "There they all were," Slote recalled, "Haldeman, Ehrlichman, John Mitchell, Ron Ziegler, toasting their moment with champagne." While Slote waited uncomfortably among his recent adversaries, Rockefeller was ushered to the Nixons' quarters. Much to Slote's astonishment, Rockefeller re-emerged almost immediately. He marched, grim visaged, to the elevator. Slote fell in beside him. In the elevator, the press secretary broke the stiff silence. "How's the President-elect," he asked?

"I wouldn't know," Nelson answered acidly. "I never saw him. I was informed the President-elect was resting."

When Nixon named Henry Kissinger as his national security adviser, it was like rival ruling families joined by a marriage of convenience. Although, with Kissinger going to the Nixon White House and Nelson offered nothing in the new administration, it was also rather like big sister answering the doorbell only to find that the football captain had come courting little sister. Still, the alliance worked well for all parties. Nixon got a brilliant adviser. Kissinger obtained power beyond an academic's dreams. And Nelson had his private line into the White House.

In 1972, when Nixon was running for re-election, Nelson told us that he was taking personal control over the Nixon campaign in New York State. His action was not intended to slight Nixon's CREEP, the Committee to Re-elect the President, but rather to outdo it. We were expected to work eagerly for Nixon's re-election. That fall, Nelson Rockefeller delivered forty-four speeches in thirty-five cities in the course of 30,455 miles of campaigning for a man he never could learn to like.

Nelson even consented to place Nixon's name in nomination as the Republican presidential candidate at the 1972 Republican Convention, a performance referred to by some on the staff as the "Mmm, good! hemlock speech." And, he and his brothers contributed $260,700 to the Nixon campaign. Thereafter, Nixon and Rockefeller managed to maintain a friendship with the inherent warmth of Styrofoam. Nixon supported Rockefeller's quelling of the prison insurrection at Attica, and Rockefeller supported Nixon's invasion of Cambodia. Nixon supported Rockefeller's Commission on Critical Choices for Americans, and the most fevered Nixonite could not fault Rockefeller's cautious pronouncements on Watergate. Nelson, in fact, strained mightily for whatever excuse to make amiable contact. He called the White House to congratulate Nixon when the Dow Jones average broke 1,000. Yet when Nixon could have given Rockefeller what he wanted above all else, in effect, the Presidency in August of 1974 by first giving him the Vice-Presidency in the fall of 1973, he had turned instead to Gerald R. Ford. Nelson was stoically mute about it, but Happy said privately, "Weakness doesn't go to strength."

On a sunny August day in 1974, Mom, the kids, and the dogs waited in the car, impatient to start their summer vacation, while Dad was still in the house, on the phone, tied up with last-minute business. A scene of Rockwellian America, with small differences. The car was a chauffeured limousine. The destination was a private jet waiting to whisk them off to the home at Seal Harbor. And the business on the phone involved Nelson Rockefeller becoming Vice-President.

The day before, Hugh Morrow had been called by Godfrey Sperling of the *Christian Science Monitor*. Melvin Laird, the former secretary of defense, Sperling said, was planting stories around Washington that Gerald Ford intended to name Nelson as his Vice-President. Morrow passed the story on to Rockefeller just before the departure for the Maine vacation. Nelson told Morrow, "I don't know what to make of this. You know Mel, he's so devious. He's usually in business for himself." Then, just as Nelson was about to join the family, Laird had caught him at home and confirmed that Ford wanted him as Vice-President. Nelson tried to outfence his caller. "You know what I think, Mel? Jerry ought to name you as Vice-President. You're the ideal person. Why are you talking to me?"

"No," Laird demurred. "It's time for me to go out and start earning some money." Rockefeller remained skeptical and went ahead with his vacation, after taking an odd step. "I had all my phone numbers changed and waited. I figured if the White House wanted to get me, they could find me. I didn't want to discuss the thing or do anything about it." Ford did call Seal Harbor on Saturday morning to sound out Rockefeller. Nelson did not agree immediately, saying that he would call back the next day after he had talked it over "with Happy and the kids."

Few men except those who had actually served in the office had a clearer picture of the Vice-Presidency. As a young man in the Roosevelt Administration, Nelson had played tennis regularly with Vice-President Henry Agard Wallace. Wallace would show up at seven o'clock in the morning to play at Foxhall Road, Nelson's home in Washington. "You have to be pretty frustrated to do that," Nelson recalled.

Rockefeller had known them all, from the quixotic Wallace to the tainted Agnew. Relaxing one afternoon, he said, "They were all really . . . well . . . frustrated is the only way to describe it. When I worked for President Eisenhower, I was chairman of his committee on government organization. He said, 'Make a study of what might be given to Dick Nixon as a job.' We studied for about three months and came to the conclusion there was nothing in the Constitution for the Vice-President except presiding over the Senate. I had the opportunity before to run for Vice-President, as a matter of fact on both tickets. I always said I am just not built for standby equipment." Now he was being offered the job for the third time.

Rockefeller and Ford were not close, but each had observed the other in action. Nelson had witnessed Ford's performance in Congress during the successful revenue-sharing campaign that Nelson had led. He had later recruited Ford, then minority leader of the House, as a member of the Commission on Critical Choices for Americans, a coup in light of Nelson's desire to give the commission a semipublic aura. He had been impressed by Ford's diligence.

Nelson Rockefeller was an unabashed patriot of the self-proclaiming breed who tend to make sophisticates uncomfortable. The country then stood at a fragile nexus, with constitutional power passing over a divide never before crossed. Nelson saw Ford's appeal as a call to duty. If Ford wanted him, he did not see how he could say no. Equally important, the Vice-Presidency was the only game in town left for him. Watergate had destroyed his latest presidential timetable. Ford, now the incumbent, had an apparent lock on the 1976 presidential nomination. The novelty of the Commission on Critical Choices was wearing thin, and Nelson was getting restless. He confided to Kurt Waldheim, the U.N. Secretary-General, "The Vice-Presidency is not much of a job. But at least Washington is where the action is."

And, as the staff pointed out to him, nine Vice-Presidents had succeeded to the Presidency. For all his awareness of the fate of every predecessor in the Vice-Presidency, he convinced himself that it could be different for Nelson Rockefeller. He would agree to accept the job if he could have from Ford a grant of genuine authority. On Sunday they talked again, and Ford agreed that Nelson would be a working Vice-President.

On Tuesday morning, August 20, Nelson was ushered into the Oval Office. Not until that moment did Ford formally make the offer to him. As soon as Rockefeller accepted, Ford put through a call to San Clemente, California. He gestured to an astonished Nelson, telling him to listen in on an extension. Soon Ford was eagerly reporting his choice, seeming almost to court the approval of the man who had been driven out of the White House in disgrace twelve days before. Richard Nixon praised Ford for picking a "big man for a big job." Then Ford was off the line and on to another call, leaving Rockefeller to one of the clumsier moments in his always uncomfortable association with Richard Nixon.

Since Ford had been so solicitous of Nixon's opinions, a curious senator later asked Rockefeller if Nixon had "promoted your selection as Vice-President." Rockefeller responded dryly, "I cannot believe that."

Shortly after Ford designated Nelson as Vice-President, I was filling in as press secretary for Hugh Morrow, who was ill. Tom Poster, who had long covered Nelson for the New York *Daily News*, called. "I've got a story here that Rockefeller didn't pay any federal income taxes in 1970. My editors want to go with it. But I want to check it out with you people first."

The confirmation hearings for Nelson's Vice-Presidency were about to get under way. The issue Poster was raising could prove disastrous. It had been part of our litany for years that Nelson Rockefeller paid his taxes; "in seven figures" was the standard press-office response. "If you go with that, Tom, you'll be wrong," I said with utter confidence.

"Then I'll kill it," he answered. "On your word."

Nevertheless, I thought I had better inform Rockefeller of Poster's call. His voice was coolly guarded. He neither confirmed nor denied, but told me, "I think you'd better talk to Bobby in Washington." He was referring to a team that he had set up in the capital to prepare for the confirmation process. Bob Douglass, the former counsel to the Governor, had been called up from private practice to head the operation. With Douglass was Jim Cannon, Nelson's longtime liaison to Congress. At the peak, eighteen staff members, mostly lawyers, were working a twelve-hour day readying Rockefeller to win congressional approval for a job that he had always found beneath his interests. In Washington, the confirmation team worked in the L'Enfant Plaza, the capital's newest luxury hotel, owned 40 percent by the Rockefeller family. I discussed Poster's inquiry with Douglass, who answered with cheery fatalism, "That's nothing. Wait till you hear what you'll be getting next." With deep embarrassment I realized that I had unwittingly misled a reporter and later apologized. But Douglass was right—worse was yet to come.

While others on the staff were immersed in preparing the Vice-President-designate for the confirmation hearings, I was lightly employed drafting the few speeches that he consented to give during this delicate period. My marginal role in the confirmation was to frame questions to feed to Republican senators on the committee that would review Nelson. Since journalists had taken a beating during the Nixon-Agnew heyday, my first suggested question was "What responsibility do you believe that public officials have to the press?" A softball toss for Rockefeller, since it would allow him to describe his pioneering espousal of shield laws, which enable journalists to protect their confidential sources. Another cream puff: "How would you relate to organized labor?" This to a man who had been George Meany's friend for nearly forty years and who, as a candidate for governor, had attracted labor endorsements like water running downhill. After I had submitted these and other rubber bullets, I received a refreshingly offbeat assignment for a speech writer. I was to deliver to the White House staff advance copies of Nelson's opening statement. Then I was to proceed to an anonymous address in a Washington suburb with an envelope containing the questions I had drafted and other background material to arm Nelson's friends on the Senate committee. I was not told to whom I would be delivering the envelope, only to drop it into a mail slot. What intimations of adventure for one who had lived for years deskbound, scratching out speeches. Accompanied by Bill Tekwerk, one of Nelson's security men, I caught the shuttle to Washington. We took the statements to the marvelously rococo Old Executive Office Building next door to the White House, where most of the presidential staff is housed.

It was a Saturday morning, barely five weeks since Nixon had been driven from office. The building appeared deserted, and as I walked down dimly lit corridors, I had a sense of passing through the recent scene of awful crimes. Was that doorway where Nixon had his hideaway office? Was that the office where Chuck Colson drew up the "enemies list"? Was that where E. Howard Hunt, Jr., plotted the Watergate break-in? Was it here that Donald Segretti faked the letters smearing Hubert Humphrey? I found the man to whom I was to deliver the statements, and in a brief conversation, I learned that he was a Nixon holdover. Blameless, no doubt, yet I felt an unreasoning resentment at his continued presence there.

I next gave a cabdriver the address where we were to make the drop. He took enough sinuously confusing turns to create the desired air of intrigue. I shoved the envelope through the mail slot of a re- morselessly unmysterious suburban house. Mission accomplished.

On September 23 the hearings opened in Room 318 of the Russell Senate Office Building. Nelson Rockefeller was tense and unsmiling as he faced the senators. He had released the details of his personal fortune in detail—Exxon Corporation, 14,338 shares; Newsweek, Inc., 4 shares . . .—giving unprecedented public exposure to the Rockefeller fortune. He might be rejected, a humiliating prospect. He had, he knew, taken a huge risk for a doubtful prize. His skin showed its pink-white mottling more vividly than usual, and he began in arid, cracking tones. "Before my opening statement, I would like to express my very deep appreciation . . ."

"Would you pull the microphone in a little closer, please," Senator Howard Cannon interrupted.

There was a faint, nervous tremor in Nelson's voice, but his unease proved short-lived. He began to detect the familiar deference paid to Rockefellers, even by U.S. senators passing judgment on them. As he answered the questions with breadth and knowledge, he knew too that he was impressing them. He began to enjoy his performance, as a good batter does, believing that he can hit anything thrown at him. He gulped down the Gatorade that he kept at his side and waited for the next pitch. I perked up at familiar phrases. An accommodating Republican senator was reading my questions verbatim, even in the order in which I had written them. And Nelson Rockefeller was knocking them out of the park.

He was also able to explain his failure to pay federal income taxes in 1970. He did not want the impression left, he said, that he had paid nothing to the federal government that year. Transactions in one of his trusts had legally spared him merely any income tax payment. But he had paid $6,250,000 in capital gains taxes, plus $814,701 in other federal imposts. Later, after an audit, he wound up paying federal income tax on his 1970 earnings as well.

The Senate hearings closed on an optimistic note, leaving little doubt that even after the anticipated tougher House hearings, Rockefeller would be confirmed. Then on October 4, when I was again filling in for Hugh Morrow, Spencer Rich, a *Washington Post* reporter, called. "We have information that Nelson Rockefeller gave fifty thousand dollars to Henry Kissinger. We are not asking for confirmation. We know he did. We just want to give you people an opportunity to respond." The disclosure immediately had the feel of a serious wound. I called Morrow at home, and he heard me with more than professional concern. The tale only began with Kissinger's $50,000. Reports followed, day by day, of Rockefeller's several gifts to Bill Ronan, eventually totaling $625,000. Other amounts reported were: Al Marshall, $306,867; Hugh Morrow, $135,000; Henry Diamond, $100,000; Ed Logue, $31,389; and lesser sums to other present and former members of Nelson's staff. His largess had usually taken the form of loans, later canceled, rather than outright gifts.

A pained cry went up, particularly from the liberal Democratic quarter of Congress. Had Nelson Rockefeller bought off his own public officials, purchased their obedience? Were the recipients possibly guilty of violating state bribery statutes? Here was a novel situation in American public life. Countless politicians had been destroyed for being on the take—Nelson Rockefeller was in trouble for being on the give.

At the same time, Nelson stepped on another land mine planted long before. Four years earlier, he had approved John Wells's idea for a book by Victor Lasky deflating his gubernatorial opponent, Arthur Goldberg. Nelson then had turned to his brother Laurance to find a means of funding the project. Congressional researchers had traced the book's circuitous back-door financing, which certainly looked suspicious, if not illegal. Because of the gifts and the Goldberg book, Rockefeller was called back to the Senate committee to face fresh questioning, and his investigation by the House, already expected to be rough, now loomed even less inviting.

A curious point about the Rockefeller gifts. Among the staff they were not common knowledge. Those who did not receive knew nothing of those who did. Those who received knew little or nothing of others who had. Nelson's gift giving was handled with hermetic discretion. As one recipient after another became known, we on the staff looked at one another with renewed curiosity. How much might the fellow in the next office have been given, and were we the only fools who got nothing?

I had always regarded Rockefeller's wealth as impersonal and impervious. The fortune seemed about as accessible as the Federal Reserve, and the idea of tapping the boss for real money had never occurred to me or most of my colleagues. I felt not envy so much as amazement to learn otherwise. The fraternity who knew that he was touchable was small but surprising in its diversity. Along with his highest associates, one of his drivers had hit him for $8,000 for a new car.

Al Marshall described what it was like to get almost a third of a million dollars from Nelson Rockefeller. During 1966, he had done, for the first time, what he was to do often in Rockefeller's service—take over the reins of state government to allow Nelson to devote himself to his gubernatorial and presidential races. That fall, basking in the warmth of his recent re-election, Nelson was feeling particularly grateful for the job Marshall had done. At the time, Marshall's personal finances were a stereotype of the middle-class squeeze as he strove to raise a family of five children on a state bureaucrat's pay.

Nelson believed implicitly in the significance of what he was doing, and thus, by extension, in what his staff did for him. Niggardly government salaries tended to demean that significance. As he told Al Marshall, "I know you're worth a hell of a lot more on the outside. And I understand that you're with me at great personal sacrifice."

Marshall sometimes found himself alone with Rockefeller in the limousine as they returned late at night from one last appearance or meeting. "How are things going?" Nelson asked on one of those occasions. Marshall unburdened himself of worries he had suppressed during grueling weeks on the job. He told Nelson about children getting ready for college, the mortgage, the heavy expenses for the care of a retarded son. "Can I offer a loan? Would a hundred thousand dollars help?" Nelson said gently. Thus eventually he gave Marshall more than $300,000, mostly in loans, forgiven at Christmastime with a cheerful handwritten note.

As the Governor's longtime right hand, in effect the state's general manager, did this money influence Marshall in his job performance? "Of course it could have been intended to buy my loyalty, if you want to put it that way. But it never bought my mind or judgment. We fought as hard over state business after I got the loans as before. And when I finally told him I wanted to leave for financial reasons, he could have pulled the rug on me easily. Just call in the loans. They were never mentioned, not once, after I got them."

Nelson's horn of plenty could open unexpectedly. Jim Cannon, a survivor of Rockefeller freezes and thaws, was in good grace at the time Nelson resigned as governor. Rockefeller was well aware of his debt to Cannon for helping to lobby the passage of revenue sharing, and he also wanted Cannon to have a role in the Commission on Critical Choices. Cannon seized a timely opportunity to explain his financial situation. Shortly thereafter, Cannon attended a staff luncheon at Rockefeller's West 54th Street town house. Nelson drew Cannon aside. "Stock or cash?" The message was cryptic, but not so much so that it addled Cannon's wits. "Cash," he answered. "Room 5600 will be in touch," Nelson said and moved off. Within days, Cannon had a check for $40,000, given "out of friendship and respect," according to Nelson's accompanying note.

The nineteenth-century town house where this transaction took place gave one a sense of stepping into a time machine. Nelson's family was living there when he was born, and the lower floors, in their decor and furnishings, appeared to have been unchanged since. On the fourth floor, Nelson's friend Wally Harrison had designed a small jewel of an apartment also suggesting another epoch with its deep-red walls and Toulouse-Lautrecs. The 54th Street town house offered something available in none of Nelson's other five homes, privacy for himself alone. It was back-to-back with his offices on 55th Street, and the passageway connecting the two buildings was always locked. There was only one key, and Nelson kept it.

Jim Cannon was happy to accept Nelson's generosity. So were most beneficiaries. Occasionally, though, his offers were turned down. One staff member who had told the Governor that he would have to leave his service recalled Rockefeller's reaction. "We were on the plane flying to Rochester, and he waved me into the seat next to him. He looked me straight in the eye and said, 'I don't want you to leave. I need you!' Then he leaned into my ear and whispered kind of shyly, 'I can help, you know. I'm very wealthy.' "

Was there a pattern to his bounty? Some claimed it had fallen from heaven, with no effort on their part. Others had gone to him in need. In either case, certain similarities emerged. Virtually all the beneficiaries met three criteria—they were close to him; he had a personal affection for them; and all had future utility to him.

As for his own financial situation, early in the confirmation hearing Nelson had tried to pass himself off as a garden-variety multimillionaire, net worth $62 million, of which his art collection represented at least half. Everything else—his homes, other property, stocks, bonds, and cash—totaled an unremarkable $31 million. This initial accounting omitted the two trust funds set up for him by his father. Their value totaled $116.5 million, and the funds generated an annual income of $4.6 million per year if he did nothing more than open his mail. In the course of handling press queries about Nelson's money, I learned that he could invade the principal of his trusts only after receiving approval of the trustees. It seemed odd that so powerful a man at his age had to go to others—McGeorge Bundy, then president of the Ford Foundation, for example, was one of Nelson's trustees—to get his own money.

The other fresh obstacle to his confirmation, Victor Lasky's dull-edged hatchet job on Arthur Goldberg, proved more painful to Nelson than to Goldberg. The book's financing had been obscured through a looping arrangement with a Philadelphia law firm. The lines were traced by congressional investigators back to Room 5600, exposing Laurance Rockefeller in an embarrassing service for his beloved older brother. Nelson was mortified. "I've done Laurance in. I didn't intend to. I've got to do something about it." Thus he apologized publicly to Laurance before the Senate committee.

Arthur Goldberg was called to testify before the Senate about the Lasky book. On his arrival in the hearing room, a smiling Rockefeller put out his hand, but Goldberg refused to take it. The former Supreme Court justice was unforgiving, and he told the committee, "I could not believe that Governor Rockefeller, who said to this committee that he is my friend, would be a party to publishing a book about me. . . . Such a person should not be confirmed."

Some time afterward, Arthur Goldberg explained his vehemence to me during a chance meeting. When he learned that I was on Vice-President Rockefeller's staff, Goldberg said, "I will judge you independent of my judgment of Nelson Rockefeller." He said it with that characteristic pomposity which unfortunately concealed an open and generous nature. "Do you want to know why I refused to shake your boss's hand that day? And why I spoke out against him?" Indeed, I did. "Because he and his brother and their people had the gall to testify, under oath, that the purpose of that Lasky book was not to defame me but to make money! The Rockefellers said it was purely an investment!" His chin still quivered with indignation two years after the event.

After completing the Senate hearings, Nelson had to go before the House Judiciary Committee, which only weeks before had voted impeachment articles against Richard Nixon and was still burning with a righteous flame. The majority Democrats on this committee pressed for details on every root and tendril of the Rockefeller fortune. The committee already had an unremitting X ray of Nelson's wealth from every Picasso to the $21,803 he had contributed as governor to the New York State Retirement Fund. Now some committee Democrats were demanding a complete breakdown of the assets of his brothers, his sister, and all their children. Douglass and Cannon met with Nelson one evening at his Foxhall Road home to consider the committee's demand. He was silent while the two aides analyzed alternative responses. Nelson had sacrificed privacy and secrecy, Rockefeller virtues practiced for nearly ninety years. He had made the sacrifice for an office that one of its occupants had described as "not worth a bucket of warm spit." Finally he spoke. "I won't give them that. What they want is an unwarranted invasion of privacy. There's no way I will provide that information. If they insist, I'll have to withdraw." Bob Douglass, who had navigated the nomination through all previous shoals—the money gifts to subordinates, which were not found improper, the Goldberg book, the tax questions—suggested a compromise. Rockefeller heard it with an appreciative murmur.

Douglass and Cannon believed that the committee's pivotal member on the issue of total disclosure was Jack Brooks, a Texas Democrat described by some as "the meanest son of a bitch in the House." The two Rockefeller men met with Brooks and explained Rockefeller's adamant opposition to the disclosures that the committee's Democrats demand. The Democratic congressman respected the Republican nominee and did not want to see Rockefeller's nomination founder. Douglass then offered his compromise. The committee would be given anything it wanted on the family's wealth and holdings, but the figures had to be in the aggregate, with no breakdown by individuals, except for Nelson. Brooks bought the plan and was able to swing enough support in the Judiciary Committee to win its acceptance. The proposal had satisfied Nelson Rockefeller's gravest concern. As he explained it, "Some of our children have gotten more than others. We can't let that out. It would destroy the family."

Nelson's confirmation hearings allowed the country, after decades of speculation, to have its curiosity satisfied at last: how much money did the Rockefellers have? Estimates had run as high as $10 billion. J. Richardson Dilworth, the family's chief financial adviser, testified before the Judiciary Committee that the assets of the Rockefellers, eighty-four persons including the four surviving brothers, sister Babs, their children, spouses, and grandchildren, totaled not quite $1.3 billion. Taxes, philanthropy, and division among numerous heirs had made the remaining fortune seem rather disappointing for a name synonymous with wealth.

Nelson was in Washington, between hearings, attending a meeting of the President's Foreign Intelligence Advisory Board, when Mrs. Whitman called him from the room to take an urgent call from his wife. Happy Rockefeller was then forty-eight, physically active, a sailor and golfer who described herself as someone "who loved being in touch with nature." She had nursed all her six children. Yet something had been wrong the past few years. As she later recalled, something "had been dampening my natural enthusiasm for the adventure of living. I simply wasn't up to my normal zest."

During August, while the family was in Maine, she had told Nelson: "My left side just doesn't seem to feel right. I don't know what it is, but my left side feels different. It feels funny." In the fall, she went to her gynecologist for a regular checkup. She was told that she was a healthy woman. Two weeks later, she discovered a small, hard spot, about the size of a quarter, near her left armpit. Her gynecologist ordered a mammogram and referred her to a cancer specialist, Dr. Jerome Urban, at the Sloan-Kettering Memorial Hospital in New York. Urban examined her and read the mammogram. "I think," he said, "we'll be lucky with this one." When Happy began to express her relief that the problem appeared not to be serious, Urban told her not to kid herself; she was not that lucky. She would have to enter the hospital the next day. At that point, she had called her husband in Washington. After the call, Nelson confided to Mrs. Whitman, "Happy's going to have to go into the hospital for breast surgery." He said it with a matter-of-factness that amazed her.

Happy underwent a radical mastectomy, and Nelson returned to complete his second round of questioning before the Senate. Then he faced the House. As he fielded the far stiffer interrogations of the Judiciary Committee, the cameras occasionally fixed on Happy. Barely a month after her operation, she was spending every day with Nelson at the hearings. Unknown to the public or the committee, she was not merely recuperating, but merely awaiting her next ordeal.

During the course of the first operation, Dr. Urban had performed a biopsy on her right breast. Urban had immediately informed Nelson that Happy would have to undergo a second mastectomy. "We can't let her know that," Nelson answered, "not right away. There is no point in her agonizing needlessly." Happy thus went home to Pocantico after the first operation, as she recalled, "blissfully ignorant" of what lay ahead. During the next weeks Dr. Urban examined her regularly. One evening in her bedroom, as he checked the wound and while Nelson sat waiting outside, she asked him, "How's everything going?"

"Before I answer," Urban began, "don't you want your husband in here with you?" In that instant she knew that she would have to undergo a second operation. She refused to return immediately to the hospital. "I decided to wait because I wanted to be with Nelson while he appeared before the House Judiciary Committee." During this anxious hiatus, Nelson called a meeting of a half-dozen aides at the 55th Street office. The meeting's sole purpose was to discuss whether or not Happy should undergo the second mastectomy. Each person present was asked to comment. "We were stunned, not quite sure what was expected of us," Mrs. Whitman remembered. "But he just seemed to need our psychological support."

As the hearings dragged on, a worried Rockefeller went to see Chairman Peter Rodino and explained to him that Happy would not leave his side for the needed operation until the House had finished with him. Rodino made a rare accommodation in House procedures. He scheduled day and night sessions to complete the hearings by the end of the week. That weekend, Happy re-entered the hospital.

On the morning that Happy had her second operation, I received word from Mrs. Whitman that the Governor was calling a staff conference. The meeting was already under way by the time I arrived, and its subject was not immediately evident from the discussion. If Nelson was feeling the anxiety natural to the moment, no trace was visible in his face or manner. He seemed, if anything, jaunty. His aplomb may simply have been that flashlight mind focused on the matter at hand to the exclusion of all else. It was impossible to know what he felt. We had come up against the sealed wall of his private self. He thanked me for my words of encouragement, then plunged back, undistracted, into the meeting, which it turned out was to develop a State of the Union message for Gerald Ford. At this point, Nelson was still in the confirmation process and had not yet been approved as Ford's Vice-President.

"The President can't go before the country without a program," he said earnestly. Someone remarked, "Especially since we're not exactly dealing with a heavyweight." Nelson glared at the speaker. "He's an able man. I've watched him in the Critical Choices meetings." There were no more disparagements of Gerald Ford's capacities that morning.

It became evident, as we worked, that this meeting was not in response to any request by Ford for Nelson's help with his State of the Union address. Rather, it was Rockefeller's assumption that he should show Ford the way. One imagines with difficulty another Vice-President, even one as overweening as Lyndon Johnson, submitting an unsolicited State of the Union program to President John F. Kennedy. Nelson Rockefeller never hesitated. He was never overawed by someone's position, expertise, or intelligence alone, but only if these qualities were encased in a powerful ego, especially one rivaling his own. Thus he had no reservations about attempting to mold so modest a man as Jerry Ford to his will.

Since he prized the combination of brains and brass so highly, his own circle was rich with outsized egos, of which William J. Ronan was my favorite for Himalayan self-assurance. When a reporter asked Ronan how he had responded to Nelson Rockefeller's giving him $625,000, he gave a complacent grin and answered that he had said, "Thank you." Bob Douglass found that "if it was transportation or government organization, Bill Ronan could tell Nelson the moon was made of green cheese. If it was foreign affairs, and Henry Kissinger said it, then Nelson believed it."

The staff learned to live with a double standard. Toward most of us he could be abrupt, impatient, and intellectually arrogant, but toward the small, charmed circle of egotists, he was curiously uncritical. "Both his parents were authority figures, particularly his mother," Hugh Morrow observed. "He hungered for those who projected authority." Mrs. Whitman concurred. "People who took strong, clear positions made him feel secure."

After one such peacock had sailed into Nelson's office, sold him an outrageous idea, and then sailed out, one of the staff commented, "The fellow's a bit aggressive, isn't he?" Nelson looked pained. "But I *like* aggressive people."

On December 19, 1974, four months after President Ford had selected him, Nelson Rockefeller was confirmed as the nation's Vice-President. During the hearings, opposition to his confirmation had made strange bedfellows. The Marxist, Angela Davis, representing the National Alliance Against Racist and Political Repression, testified: "The Rockefeller dynasty has plundered the world." Curtis B. Dall, chairman of the right-wing Liberty Lobby, called Nelson "an agent for the Soviet Union." The head of the wildly leftist U.S. Labor Party, Lyndon H. LaRouche, testified: "If the Rockefellers are not stopped, the future survival of the human race is unsure." Back on the right, the anti-abortion Coalition for Life found Nelson Rockefeller "the incarnate symbol of the anti-life movement in the United States." These were admittedly voices from the fringes. Yet they reflected in caricature the opposing ends of the political spectrum that historically united against the Rockefellers. The vote for confirmation in the House was 287 to 128. As Nelson read the results, he commented, "There were about a hundred and twenty conservatives and liberals, so identified. I got the opposition of both. Those in the middle voted for me. And that is about where I stand."

On the night he was confirmed, he sat alone with Ann Whitman and Harry Albright at his West 55th Street office. He had just come off the phone, telling Happy to get ready to travel to Washington for the swearing-in ceremony. Albright asked Nelson to come to the window and pointed out the crush of reporters on the sidewalk below. Spotting Rockefeller, the press gave him a rousing cheer. He smiled and waved, but the smile was rueful. "You know, when this appointment first came, I thought, 'Terrific.' Maybe I can really be of some help. But after all these months, it's lost much of the meaning."

Still, there was the commitment he had extracted from Ford for a working Vice-Presidency. Intellectually, he had accepted his own verdict—the Vice-President was a title without a job—but his activist soul rebelled at being locked in a powerless, ceremonial niche. He was determined to be the first to make something of that peculiar office.

Chapter XXI

THE VICE-PRESIDENTIAL YEARS

PERHAPS THE MOST SPLENDID OFFICES in America are to be found in a relatively anonymous structure on Pennsylvania Avenue next door to the White House, the Old Executive Office Building. A corner of its gray stone bulk is occasionally glimpsed in tourists' snapshots of its illustrious neighbor. The Old EOB, with its buffet of architectural styles piled tier upon tier, its pillars, porticoes, ironwork sculpture, peaks, and mansard rooftops, suggests a bejeweled Victorian dowager, imposing yet a little ridiculous. For much of its century of life, the Old EOB housed the State, War and Navy departments. Dozens of historic figures have occupied it, from William Tecumseh Sherman to Franklin D. Roosevelt. With the growth of the President's personal bureaucracy, it now houses most of the White House staff. In size and splendor, its offices dwarf those in the White House. The smallest offices are charming, and the largest, opulent, with thirteen-foot ceilings, marble fireplaces, molded ceilings, polished woods, and stylish furniture. Nelson Rockefeller, in his various Washington incarnations, had occupied a half dozen different offices in the Old EOB. Now, as Vice-President, he had the most resplendent.

As he wandered through his suite, he turned to Mrs. Whitman, his chief of staff, who had spent eight years as President Eisenhower's personal assistant. "Annie, you've had more White House experience than any of us down here. When I do something wrong, I want you to tell me about it." "Then he proceeded to do everything wrong," Mrs. Whitman observed. "And he got annoyed if I pointed it out."

What Rockefeller expected to achieve as Vice-President was extraordinary, given his foreknowledge of the job. His protégé, Henry Kissinger, had effectively taken control of U.S. foreign policy in the Ford Administration. Why should Nelson not handle domestic policy? Who was better prepared? Political commentators encouraged the idea, writing of Rockefeller and his staff arriving at the Ford White House as though the New York Yankees were taking over a high-school locker room. One began to wonder, between Nelson and Henry, what was left for Jerry Ford.

The Ford staff, however, refused to roll over and play dead. Nelson found himself negotiating for power with Ford's chief of staff, Donald Rumsfeld, a tough forty-two-year-old former congressman. At first, Rockefeller emerged from these bargaining sessions elated. "He acted as if he were President," Mrs. Whitman remembered. "He'd come back from a meeting announcing that he was going to run the White House." But in the end, Rumsfeld outboxed him. Nelson moved like an aging heavyweight, dazzled by a fast, young puncher. As his capture of the machinery of domestic policy making became less certain, Nelson muttered darkly about "people only out to serve themselves and who don't give a damn about the country." With Rumsfeld, it was the Rockefeller-Lindsay rivalry all over again, youth and age in collision.

Ultimately, he found himself in an ambiguous position. The Ford people agreed to appoint Nelson's man Jim Cannon as executive director of the White House Domestic Council. Cannon, in turn, appointed as key deputies three Rockefeller aides from Albany, George Humphreys, Arthur Quern and Richard Parsons. Thus Nelson and his people appeared to have gained control over the domestic-policy machinery. For Nelson, it was only an appearance. His post was largely ceremonial. Cannon had difficulty getting it through Nelson's head that his primary duty now lay with the President. To Nelson Rockefeller, this shift of allegiance smacked of disloyalty. Although the two men continued to work together, Cannon once more felt the killing frost of Rockefeller's disfavor.

In October 1975, Cannon learned that the President intended to announce a huge tax cut to be achieved by an equal reduction in federal spending. At four o'clock the next morning, he boarded *Air Force II*, the Vice-President's plane, which was headed for the Westchester airport to bring Rockefeller back to Washington after his weekend at Pocantico. Cannon, trying to perform his job for the President yet do right by his old chief, wanted to alert Rockefeller to the Ford proposal before Nelson arrived in Washington.

Nelson Rockefeller had considerable capacity for self-deception, but it was not limitless. "This is the most important move the President has made," he sighed wearily, "and I wasn't even consulted." He accepted a painful truth. His Vice-Presidency was to be little different from all those that had gone before. At this time, Philip Shabecoff, a *New York Times* reporter covering the White House, remarked to me, "Rockefeller sure gave up a lot of power to become Vice-President." Aptly put. No computer gone haywire could have made a worse match of a man and a job.

Outwardly, he accepted his semi-impotence with self-effacing humor. "I go to funerals. I go to earthquakes," Nelson answered when asked what he did as Vice-President. In that first year in office, he represented the United States at the final rites for the assassinated King Faisal of Saudi Arabia and two generalissimos, Chiang Kai-shek and Francisco Franco. He was sent on a mission of mercy when earthquakes struck northern Italy.

Nelson was the first to live in the new official residence for the Vice-President, the Navy's former Admiral's House on Embassy Row. He and Happy gave nine separate housewarming parties over four weeks for three thousand guests. Senators, congressmen, diplomats, and distinguished figures dined under a great green-and-white-striped tent on the Vice-Presidential grounds. Guests toured the turreted Gothic mansion, now furnished with Nelson's art and a $35,000 bed created by Max Ernst. The bed had mirrors attached to the bedposts which could be turned in any direction. The surfaces of the mirrors, however, had been painted over. I drafted Happy's remarks on the house for a women's magazine—"I think of the Vice-President's residence as warm and embracing. It may be a house of history. But, to me, it's a real home too. It's livable." In two years, however, the Rockefellers spent only one night in this livable official residence. Happy was in New York most of the time, and with his house on Foxhall Road, the last thing Nelson Rockefeller needed was another Washington address.

The Foxhall Road house managed to achieve hunt-country rusticity in the middle of a Washington residential neighborhood. The driveway was marked by a simple plaque bearing the house number "2500." The drive wound through a forest for a quarter of a mile and emerged upon a vista that would have pleased the eye of a Revolutionary-era squire. Indeed, it once had. One of the ten highest-assessed homes in the capital, the house, built in 1790, stood on twenty-six acres of the costliest real estate in the District of Columbia. A Revolutionary War colonel had built the place. Nelson had acquired it when he first came to Washington to work for President Roosevelt in the 1940s. Like the ranch in Venezuela, Foxhall Road was fully staffed at all times for his possible arrival. In 1977, when he left Washington for good, Nelson sold the Foxhall Road property to an entrepreneur who planned to subdivide the estate and build $300,000 houses there on one-acre lots. Nelson's old Washington neighbors were furious with him for pulling out and selling his land to a "ticky-tacky developer."

During his first six months as Vice-President, Nelson carried out a reasonably well received investigation of the Central Intelligence Agency's domestic sins. He was also chairman of a National Commission on Productivity, the Federal Compensation Committee, the Committee on the Right to Privacy, and the Water Quality Commission, with duties as stultifying as the titles. Nelson also became the champion of *Status*, a new statistical magazine produced by the Bureau of the Census, and gave a press party in his office to launch its first issue. He declared *Status* the "most important achievement of the Ford Administration." Any irony in the remark escaped him utterly. His ego was such that if Nelson was doing something it was, *ergo*, important.

Time now hung heavily on his hands, and he began to display a pleasure in the pomp and ceremony of high office, which had never interested him as governor. We were riding into Chicago one night for a speaking engagement. All along the route from O'Hare International Airport, cars were pulled off the roadway. Police sirens wailed and lights flashed. "There must have been an accident," someone commented. "No," Nelson said, beaming with a boyish grin. "That's for me."

The unaccustomed leisure aggravated one of his less attractive qualities. Nelson Rockefeller's enthusiasms were never scaled to the importance of the business at hand. À la Professor Parkinson, his energy expanded to fill the time available. As governor, he would invest furious effort in a program to rescue mass transportation for 5.5 million New York commuters. In Washington, he would attack a one-page preface to *Status* magazine with the same zeal. If he had two free hours for a task that required ten minutes, he would have a coterie of aides tied up redoing it twelve times in the two hours. He compulsively hatched projects, invented deadlines, imposed pressure where none existed. He rattled around in his undemanding office like an animal in a cage. His underoccupied mind occasionally produced bizarre conceits. He sent his counsel, Peter Wallison, an article from the op-ed page of *The New York Times* describing the economic strain that Greenland had become to its parent, Denmark. To the clipping, Rockefeller had attached a note: "Peter, why don't we look into buying it?" Wallison left the suggestion to wither of neglect.

During one of these lulls, I was summoned into Nelson's office, where he sat tense and tight-lipped, looking very much the leader who has just made a fateful decision. He motioned me to a chair. "I want you to take this down. It's a speech I'm going to give. I want you to put it into final shape. What I have to say may seem unorthodox, even extreme." He went on to explain how the free world was utterly dependent on open sea-lanes to import oil. He traced in impressive detail the buildup of the Soviet Navy over the previous twenty years and described a parallel decline of American naval power. In the Atlantic, the Pacific, and the Mediterranean, he concluded, the United States had become so weak that we were easy prey to blackmail by the Soviet Navy. The Soviets could rupture our oil lifelines at will.

He had a solution. I looked up from my note-taking to see his expression shifting to a beatific glow. His answer was a $200 billion, ten-year Freedom of the Seas Bond Issue. The money would be spent to restore the U.S. Navy to a strength that the Soviet Union would never dare contest, and the sea-lanes serving the free world would then be secure. The bond issue was to be raised by subscription, apart from the regular defense budget. Dilapidated housing, derelict subways, crowded parks, and now, threatened shipping lanes. No matter what the problem, the solution to Nelson was always the same —float a bond issue.

"The first one hundred billion dollars would be purchased by the American people," Nelson continued. Fair enough, I thought. World War II War Bond drives. Defense stamps saved by kids in school. It had worked before.

"The Japanese would also invest twenty-five billion dollars," he went on. My incredulity must have shown, since he added, "Sure. Don't they depend totally on oil imports?" Europeans were to buy another $25 billion share. The final $50 billion would be supplied by the OPEC countries. "Freedom of the seas is absolutely indispensable to them," he concluded, with pleased emphasis.

Here my pen did stop. "Emperor, aren't you chilly, sitting there in nothing but your delusions?" I thought it, but did not say it. I tried to imagine Freedom of the Seas bond drives held across France to raise billions for the U.S. Navy; the Japanese financing a new U.S.S. *Arizona*; the Venezuelans kicking in for an American nuclear sub or two.

He stood up, looking satisfied, a leader who had broken through the prison of conventional thinking to arrive at a brave new solution. "Joe, you fix it up. You know. All the right words." A squeeze of the arm, a smile. "I'm always grateful."

On the way out, I ran into his assistant for national security affairs, a bright young Navy captain, Jonathan Howe. "I see you got to him, Jon," I said. Howe looked at me blankly as I described my recent encounter. He shook his head. "I can't imagine where he got such an idea. It certainly wasn't from me." Nor did anyone else seem to know. I completed the draft and sent it in to the Vice-President. Thereafter it disappeared, never mentioned again, its fate as mysterious as its origin.

I was with Nelson Rockefeller the moment he came closest to becoming President of the United States. It involved no primary, convention, or election. On September 5, 1975, we had flown to Rochester, New York, where he was to speak at two hospital dedications and a savings-bond luncheon, a typical vice-presidential day. While he delivered one of the speeches, I was in a staff room in the same building phoning changes for the next day's speeches to Deborah McPherson, my secretary back in Washington. A Secret Service man rushed in and snatched the phone next to me. His staccato delivery had the quality of cool professionalism sorely tried. I could hear only his grim-faced "Who? When? Where? How? Why?" Other agents from our security detail began to gather in the room, speaking with tight-lipped confidentiality among themselves in a manner that excluded the rest of the staff.

I gathered just enough from the overheard telephone conversation to feel the dawning horror that those present must have experienced twelve years before in Dallas. I also had, frankly, a sense of wonder at the prospect of witnessing history. The Vice-President came in after finishing his speech. Another agent walked close beside him, whispering in his ear. Rockefeller moved with his usual confident stride. Only a paleness and the lines about his mouth betrayed any stress. An agent handed him a phone. His voice was subdued, rather more rasping than usual. He asked few questions. He hung up and walked away, giving no faint hint of what he had learned. Only then did the agents brief us quickly on what had happened in Sacramento. Lynette Alice "Squeaky" Fromme, a Manson gang moll, had been apprehended two feet from President Ford wielding a loaded Colt .45 semiautomatic pistol with which she intended to assassinate the President. Ford was on the gang's hit list as a "polluter of water and air."

On the motorcade back to the airport and aboard the plane, Rockefeller remained maddeningly uninvolved, responding to comments on the assassination attempt with shrugs and conversational dead-enders: "Crazy," said with a shake of the head. "Imagine that."

He remained unreflective, absorbed in his paper work throughout the return trip to Washington. The only question he did raise revealed more of his disconnection from the popular culture than his state of mind. "What," he wanted to know, "is the Manson gang?"

During his Vice-Presidency, Nelson was called upon for one of the tasks that he understood least, being funny. He was invited to speak at the Washington press corps' annual Gridiron Club Dinner, an evening of satire, song, and irreverent speeches. As I prepared a text, my mind went back to a campaign rally in San Francisco a few years before:

MAN IN AUDIENCE: "Governor Rockefeller, I represent a national organization of homosexuals, and I would like to know, sir, where you stand on discrimination against us in jobs and promotion?"

ROCKEFELLER: "I understand your problem. I used to work in the State Department."

This exchange raised a question: Was his ingenuousness contrived or authentic? He had a sense of humor, but no particular wit. He did not tell jokes spontaneously or well. He could adopt a light manner before an audience, but essentially he lacked a light side. Writing humor for him was complicated by his prohibitions. One subject was forbidden, no jokes about the money. Easier to write humor for Mae West and ignore sex. As a Rockefeller, Nelson also felt, perhaps unconsciously, but quite unmistakably, that most targets of humor were out of bounds for a person of his advantages. The scruffy kid knocking off a swell's top hat with a snowball is funny. The swell tripping the scruffy kid is despicable. A Rockefeller had no right to poke fun at people. The most good-natured ethnic or religious reference was also forbidden. He spoke one evening to the United Jewish Appeal. After the speech he was scheduled to depart on a trip to Florida, and I had given him the line: "As soon as I leave all of you tonight, I will engage in an ancient ritual of the Jewish people. I'm heading for Miami Beach." His revised version left his audience mystified—"As soon as this evening is over, I am flying directly to Miami Beach. Unfortunately, I won't be staying at the Fontainebleau."

He also resisted any remarks that mocked a political rival, however gently. Virtually all that remained were jokes about himself, but

Nelson Rockefeller did not enjoy being the butt of his own humor. Among jokes he killed and why: "Head Start programs do work. I am living proof." Rejected: the money rule.

"If I didn't live in New York, I'd love to live here in Montana. Imagine, twenty-five hundred miles from Mayor Lindsay." Killed: the Lindsay nonperson rule.

"This year I've represented our nation at the funerals of Chiang Kai-shek, Franco, and King Faisal. I'm the only Vice-President ever awarded an honorary degree in mortuary science." Killed: He was not eager to advertise his ritualistic Vice-Presidency.

Part of the problem of writing humor for Nelson Rockefeller was his remoteness from everyday culture. The USO once gave a party at the Four Seasons in New York to honor Pearl Bailey as Woman of the Year. Rockefeller was to present the award. As we were going over the text, he looked up at me incredulously. " 'It takes two to tango'? What's that got to do with anything?" "Well, you see, Governor, Pearl Bailey recorded this song and . . . well . . . oh, never mind." He was particularly uncomfortable with prepared humor. And I would have to place a series of stars between the jokes so that he knew where the punch line ended and the next gag began.

Teasing utterly escaped him. At a meeting with his then state chairman, Richard Rosenbaum, Rockefeller announced that he wanted a man named Pirro appointed to a particular commission. Rosenbaum pretended to object vociferously. "Pirro. We can't accept. Now, *Sha*piro, I would support." Rosenbaum then broke into roaring laughter. Rockefeller eyed him as though he had inherited a madman.

For his remarks before the Washington Gridiron Dinner I had help from Robert Orben, a leading comedy writer and, at the time, a speech writer on President Ford's staff; Ray Siller, a Hollywood gag writer; Mark Russell, the political satirist; and Jim Carberry, who had a sharp comic ear. Given so much support, Nelson acquitted himself satisfactorily at the event: "My selection by the President proved one thing. The Ford White House is an equal opportunity employer." Speaking of his confirmation hearings and the trouble that the gifts to his staff had caused him: "I should have stuck by my grandfather's example. He only gave away dimes."

He was at heart a serious man. He would loosen and relax after arriving at an affair like the Gridiron Dinner, but he could not understand why grown men would put on white tie and tails to spend an evening telling jokes and singing funny songs. In eleven years of close association with him, I never once heard Nelson give a deep, unrestrained belly laugh.

Chapter XXII

THE LAST CAMPAIGN

"Anytime you're dissatisfied with what I'm doing, I'll write you a letter," Nelson had told Jerry Ford more than once. He was not fishing for approval; rather, as 1976, an election year, approached, anti-Rockefeller grumbling from the Republican right was sounding again, and Nelson wanted Ford to know that he heard it. Soon the conservatives' calls for Nelson's head began to break into the open. Howard "Bo" Callaway, whom Ford had chosen to head his campaign, was among the first to suggest that Rockefeller, at sixty-seven, was a mite old for the ticket.

In the wake of the Callaway sniping, Ford made a small but foolhardy gesture of support for Rockefeller. On a helicopter trip to Andrews Air Force Base, he insisted that Nelson ride with him, thus putting the President and the Vice-President together in the same aircraft. Ford did not, however, rebuke his campaign director, and Nelson needed more than supportive chopper rides. He believed that he had gone to the well for Jerry Ford. He had exposed his fortune and much of his life to the glare of public scrutiny to become Ford's Vice-President. He gamely toured the South, hardly his natural political habitat, hoping to show conservative skeptics that he "had no horns," and paying obeisance to Dixie Republicans: "Of course, I know your Strom Thurmond in Washington. I have always admired Strom and respected him and what he has done for our country." Was he annoyed over Bo Callaway's comments? Callaway, he said, "is a good friend of mine." A reporter reminded him that in 1968 Callaway had said that George Wallace should be a Republican. Nelson replied, "George Wallace is a good friend of mine." He was the friendliest fellow in Dixie.

He went after Ford's chief rival for the Republican nomination with undisguised glee, for Nelson was one of those who underestimated Ronald Reagan. A mediocre speaker himself, Nelson resented that Reagan's political successes seemed to be based wholly on the former actor's speaking skill. Told that Reagan had just electrified an audience, Nelson observed: "Yes, he's got a tremendous speech. Twenty-eight sure applause lines. How can you top that? But that doesn't deal with the tough issues." When a reporter asked the differences between him and Reagan, Nelson answered: "He can tell stories better than I can." Asked why he thought Reagan opposed the Panama Canal treaty, Nelson answered: "Mr. Reagan hasn't had a chance to get into this kind of thing before. He has been busy in California, and busy making movies, making money." Contrasting his views on the Soviet Union with Reagan's, he said: "My position is based on facts. My criticism of Mr. Reagan's position is that he bases it on slogans and demagoguery." Reagan might be "extremely amusing and clever," Nelson concluded, but he was "a lightweight."

He remained faithful to Gerald Ford but harbored no illusions about the man. One morning, riding from the White House, where he had just attended a meeting with the President, Nelson gazed into the distance and said to no one in particular, "He's sure no Roosevelt." Still, he had been loyal, helpful, even deferential, as few thought a Rockefeller could be. Surely the President would not feed him to the sharks of the right. But, in the end, he was not to be Ford's running mate in 1976. Did he jump or was he pushed off the Ford ticket?

On Monday morning, November 3, 1975, we were awaiting the Governor's arrival from Pocantico. Hugh Morrow, who had flown down with Nelson, hurried into the press office without his usual air of detached amusement. He was carrying a single sheet of paper that he slipped into a Xerox machine in a guarded manner which said that he welcomed neither witnesses nor questions. The letter was from Rockefeller to Ford. It had been drafted by Bill Ronan and edited during the plane ride. Nelson, on his arrival, had also shown it to Jim Cannon. The final paragraph read: "After much thought, I have decided further that I do not wish my name to enter into your consideration for the upcoming Republican vice-presidential nominee." Cannon told Rockefeller that he thought the move premature and precipitate, and asked, "Do you really have to do this?" Rockefeller nodded glumly. "The President called and told me at home yesterday." He had not jumped.

Ford's reason for easing him from the ticket was political, but not entirely. For all Nelson's hunger for power, he had slighted his job in a way wholly out of character—he had not worked at it hard enough. He had become a commuter Vice-President. He flew to Washington on Monday morning and back to Pocantico early Friday afternoon. Happy had balked at leaving New York because she did not want to uproot the two boys from school. Also, during the first months, she had felt uncomfortable in this world of movers and shakers. She later came to enjoy Washington's diplomatic round, the ceremony, the global junkets, but by then the pattern of Nelson's nine-to-five Vice-Presidency had been fixed. The White House was a seven-day-a-week operation, and he simply was not on the scene when much of the action took place.

On the afternoon of the day that Nelson submitted his letter of withdrawal, President Ford held a press conference and said the decent thing: "The decision by Vice-President Rockefeller was a decision on his own . . . under no circumstances was it a request by me. It was a decision by him." The truth, however, was inescapable. Nelson Rockefeller had undergone a galling four-month confirmation to become Ford's Vice-President. He had served less than a year when Ford buckled to the Republican right wing and turned away from him. At the Vice-President's offices on the second floor of the Old EOB, the staff was dispirited. "Relax everybody. We're good to January 20, 1977," someone joked. "How often do you get fifteen months' notice on a job?"

Nelson and Happy had been married for twelve years when he became Vice-President. The marriage had not curbed Nelson's meandering eye, yet, on most matters, such as Happy's recent surgery and Nelson's difficult confirmation, they remained close and drew strength from each other. Nelson's becoming Vice-President had produced something of a conjugal draw. Happy had set aside her own wishes and gave the move her blessing, just at a point when Nelson had finally left public office and had more time to be a husband and father. Yet she resisted moving to Washington, which would have been helpful to Nelson.

I had written occasionally for Happy, the assignments usually filtering through the office apparatus. We did not collaborate personally, consequently, I did not know her well. When she traveled with Nelson, she was approachable, without pretensions, eager to play up her novice standing among us, and flattering in her professed admiration for what we were doing for her husband. Her initial appeal for Nelson was evident. Happy Rockefeller was a man's woman, radiating an elemental warmth and unaffected physicality. She struck one as an attractive amalgam, a seductive girl-next-door.

Nelson made Happy a limited but useful partner in his political life. The Main Line pedigree and wealth had given her neither elitist sentiments or tastes, and she was an unlikely everywoman, a reliable predictor of public reaction to Nelson's proposals. In 1962, before their marriage, Hugh Morrow was discussing a possible re-election theme with Tom Losee, the campaign advertising director. "See the good-looking gal sitting over there," Losee said. "That's Happy Murphy. Check it out with her. You'll get a perfect woman-in-the-street reading." Over the years Morrow found "her gut-level reactions on issues were remarkably close to the public mood."

In the occasional councils in which she took part, she said little until Nelson asked, which he did when he wanted an intuitive judgment. Happy was compassionate and articulate, particularly on issues involving the poor, minorities, and women. What she once said about the women's movement, however, was revealing: "I don't think you are a liberated woman if you want to be a man. I think that women deserve to be treated equal in terms of equal opportunity and equal pay for equal work. But they've got to keep the whole thing in perspective. Personally, I don't think there's anything for today's woman to be liberated from, except to be recognized as a free and equal human being."

One evening I had gone out to Foxhall Road to work with the Vice-President on an Annapolis commencement address. It was late, the servants were gone, and Happy let me in, leading me to a sitting room where Nelson was poring over the speech. She seemed delighted to have a potential ally for a position she was arguing. "Joe, do you really think it's necessary for Nelson and me to go out to Andrews at this awful hour to meet the President?" Ford was flying in from abroad, and members of the Administration would be at the airport for the traditional welcome home. "We've both had a long day. Just this once it shouldn't make any difference." She smiled hopefully. "What do you think?" Nelson looked up from his text, his expression making it clear that a second opinion was not welcome. "I'm going out there to support the President." He gazed over the top of his glasses and resumed editing. "And so will you."

He dominated the marriage even in what are conventionally considered women's spheres. When the Rockefellers entertained, whether for ten or two hundred, Nelson decided on the menu, chose the wine, and selected the silver and china. One suspects that being Mrs. Nelson Rockefeller was not always an easy lot.

In August 1976, Gerald Ford was nominated for the Presidency, and in something of a ritual act of political hara-kiri, Nelson was asked to nominate Senator Robert Dole for the Vice-Presidency. He loyally complied. Though out of the game, he still could not resist second-guessing. When the microphones went dead for twenty-seven minutes during the first Ford-Carter debate, Rockefeller expressed amazement that Ford had remained woodenly at his microphone throughout the breakdown. "If I had been the President," Nelson told us the next morning, "I would have stood there maybe a minute. Then I would have gone over and shaken hands with Mr. Carter. Of course, the President is about four inches taller. That wouldn't have hurt him. I would have talked to the people, asked questions and gone out into the audience and said 'hello.' All this time, the television cameras would have been on me instead of Walter Cronkite. That is the advantage of having been a politician seventeen years."

But he criticized only in private. Before the world, he performed dutifully. He took Senator Dole across New York, introducing the vice-presidential candidate to the voters of his home state. Occasionally, however, the old Rockefeller hauteur broke through, and his introductions of Dole tended to condescending hyperbole. Nelson began to sound like an MC straining to inflate a second-rate act. At a rally in Binghamton, a reporter asked, "Mr. Vice-President, are you deliberately trying to upstage Senator Dole? Or do you do it because you can't help it?"

It was also in Binghamton that Nelson Rockefeller shocked, amused, outraged, or delighted, depending on one's sense of decorum, when he gave the finger to jeering radicals from the State University. The photographer for the Binghamton *Sun-Bulletin*, Don Black, recorded the moment. The photograph presents a remarkable portrait of long-suppressed belligerency unleashed at last. The tight ear-to-ear grin emits pure vengeance.

Afterward, Nelson was clearly pleased with himself, slapping people on the back as they joshed him or praised him for giving back the hecklers some of their own. When told that he had been photographed in the act, he was briefly chagrined but soon resumed his naughty-boy glee. For days thereafter, as visitors to the Vice-President's office reported reactions of outrage or delight from around the country, Nelson would raise his eyebrows in mock horror, while a slow smile played across his lips. For a time, he autographed copies of the picture. He had mailed out more than a hundred of them when Dick Rosenbaum suggested that the photograph "may not help the humanitarian reputation you've built up over a lifetime." He stopped the autographing immediately. In two years in office, the largest outpouring of mail to Vice-President Nelson Rockefeller was generated by a rude gesture. I checked with the mail room to see how public opinion was running. Those who cheered and those who deplored the finger had split virtually 50–50.

In the summer of 1976, Hugh Morrow came to my office looking uncomfortable and speaking with throat-clearing hesitation. Did I need any help? No, not really, I told him. The speech load was far lighter than it had been when Nelson was governor, and I was managing it easily. What about articles, congratulatory messages, any odd writing chores that I might want to farm out?

"What's up, Hughie?" I asked. "Have you got a contract?"

He nodded.

"Who's the contractor?"

"Nelson."

I shrugged my shoulders. "Then I guess I can find work for whomever it is."

He said that he would bring down a young lady who had just gone on the payroll, and half an hour later, I met Megan Marshack.

What struck me immediately was an outsized quality about her. Not just physically, though she was tall and well proportioned. *Zaftig* is the word. While no great beauty, she had the roseate appeal of a twentieth-century Rubens wearing aviator's glasses. It was her manner that was grand scale, projecting an irrepressible exuberance. Within days, everyone on the staff was aware of Megan Marshack. Brash and uninhibited, she took delight in a shocking frankness, and was not easily ignored. One had a sense of Megan's never having suppressed anything she had ever wanted to do or say in her life. Something in her manner put women off. Not so with men. I found her candor and high spirits a pleasure in those lifeless, final months of the Rockefeller Vice-Presidency. I liked Megan Marshack.

She was a willing worker and attacked the literary cats and dogs that I assigned her, congratulatory messages from the Vice-President to undefeated football teams and birthday greetings to centenarians, with uncomplaining zest. Occasionally after work, we chatted at length, and she told me of her early life in California and her work as an AP radio reporter. I found her an odd composite of precocious worldliness and girlish vulnerability.

She was soon promoted to assistant press secretary to the Vice-President, and another staff member was moved so that Megan could take the office adjoining Rockefeller's. She now began to appear at staff meetings and accompanied Nelson on speaking engagements and his other public appearances. He also brought Megan into what little decision making was left in the last weeks of his Vice-Presidency.

Through it all, she displayed a refreshing lack of awe before the great man. "Nelson Rockefeller, where have you been?" she would say, confronting him in the corridor, hands on her hips. "You're supposed to be at the National Press Club in ten minutes." She was, at the time, twenty-two years old.

Nelson's valedictory to the staff occurred just before election day. A dozen of us sat around a long conference table, while he remained standing. He expressed his gratitude for our services, and he spoke of the historic uniqueness of this Administration, with its appointed President and Vice-President. "I don't think there is any Vice-President in the history of the United States who has been given as many responsibilities and as great a latitude as I have."

He was particularly grateful, he said, that Ford had never used him shamelessly. "When Lyndon Johnson was Vice-President, he told me that Kennedy's people shoved speeches into his hands and practically pushed him in front of the microphone. Johnson was the bitterest man I ever knew in those days. I was never told to make a speech or to clear a speech with this President." He went on to say that he was sure the institution of the Vice-Presidency could be improved. He saw no sense in the sterile ritualism of the Vice-President presiding over the Senate. "That job could be made into a genuine responsibility." He turned, as he spoke, to Spofford Canfield, who had run the Vice-President's office on Capitol Hill. The need, Nelson observed, was to overcome resistance by Congress. As he warmed to this idea, his earlier civilized drone quickened and his eyes brightened. It was as though a terminal patient had suddenly sat up in his sickbed, charged with febrile energy. He began to think aloud about how the Vice-President could be made an authentic power in Congress, ignoring, with his customary dismissal of history, a central fact. Why would the legislative branch agree to surrender any real authority to a member of the executive branch, particularly a Vice-President who rides into office on a President's coattails?

He turned to another defect in the Vice-Presidency. "Think how badly Harry Truman was prepared. Truman had no idea what was happening in the executive branch when Roosevelt died." It was scarcely better today. He began to describe how a Vice-President ought to be used. "In fact, I'm getting an idea right now." He rolled on, infecting himself with his own enthusiasm. "We can start right away. We can write a manual on the conduct of the Vice-Presidency. It will help whoever wins the election." He gazed about, as though expecting his subordinates to snatch at the idea as they always had, but no one spoke. "Finally, there is the next State of the Union message. If the President wins, we'll have to start thinking about that right away." The lame duck still expected to make his contribution. I was by now surprised only that he limited his participation in preparing the next State of the Union message to a Ford victory.

After Ford lost the election, Nelson's schedule grew lighter, until one day the most pressing business on his calendar was an appointment with the White House barber. My final assignment was to draft his farewell letters to members of the Administration and Congress. These notes were gauged to the degree of intimacy—the "A List" letter for those "personally close or influential"; the "B List" letter for those "known, but not personally close"; and the "C List" letter "for all others." I also had to draft a letter of appreciation to be sent from Nelson to his own staff. Preferring to be spared this stock expression of gratitude by the boss, I drafted a separate and especially warm letter to myself, which Nelson unhesitatingly signed along with the standard edition.

In January 1977 Nelson gave a farewell party for the staff in his office just before the new Administration was to assume power. It was a strained affair. We sipped California champagne while a pickup chorus attempted to enliven the event with parodies on Nelson's Vice-Presidency sung to Christmas carol melodies. Nelson behaved with the determined good cheer of a high-school coach hosting a football banquet at the end of a best-forgotten season. Throughout the party, Megan Marshack remained at his side, which had become the custom in recent months. Observing the attachment, I could not help thinking of something a psychologist had told me. When a man reached Nelson Rockefeller's age—he was then sixty-eight—it was not enough that he enjoyed the attentions of a younger woman, the world had to know about it.

After the party, I said goodbye to him. My plan after eleven years at it was to leave speech writing and to hazard a living as an author. The Nelsonian charm did not fail. He knew about the book that I was going off to write on World War II espionage and made some comments about his old adversary, General Donovan of the wartime OSS, one of my subjects. He wished me success and apologized with disarming modesty for not having been a better speaker. I left him feeling the same conflicting mixture of emotions that I had experienced during all those years in his service.

As of noon, January 20, 1977, Nelson was again a private citizen as he boarded *Air Force II* for the last time. Gerald Ford was already on *Air Force I*, and the two planes circled Andrews Air Force Base, then separated, one headed west, and the other north, taking Nelson Rockefeller home to his beloved Pocantico. He had gone into the job, he claimed, with a clear eye, but evidently with a dreamer's heart. While in it, he had never been able to accept the essential truth of his condition, the difference between being Nelson, a Rockefeller, and being a subordinate to a President. Finally, there was the ultimate irony. For the only time in American history, a Vice-President's people controlled a large share of presidential power, domestic and foreign. Nelson Rockefeller's handpicked aides dominated the White House Domestic Council, and internationally, Gerald Ford's foreign policy was Henry Kissinger's foreign policy. And Nelson had, to an important degree, made Kissinger. Nelson Rockefeller, after years of questing, had won a strange, stale victory. Rockefeller people, to a remarkable extent, ran the country in another man's Presidency.

From his seventy-one-member vice-presidential staff, a handful returned to New York to continue in his service: Hugh Morrow, as his public-relations adviser; Joe Canzeri, who would still manage the Pocantico estate; and Nelson's personal secretary, Kathy Huldrum, a young woman possessing the cool competence necessary to survive under his unremitting pressure. Mrs. Whitman had returned earlier. And there was a relative newcomer. Nelson had already fixed on his next project—the commercial promotion of his art collection—and his chief assistant in this enterprise was to be Megan Marshack. He returned to New York and installed her in the office adjoining his at

Room 5600. Her move to New York had been eased by a loan-gift from Nelson that allowed her to buy an apartment in a building a few doors from his West 54th Street town house.

At the close of his public career it is understandable to ask how intelligent, how able a man was Nelson Rockefeller. He was subjected to a river of information and, over a period of thirty-five years, was probably the best-briefed man in America. He bathed in expertise. Witness the composition of the 1956 Rockefeller Brothers Fund Special Studies Project and the Commission on Critical Choices for Americans. The Rockefeller Foundation and Rockefeller University, deep mines of knowledge, were available to him. He had a curious mind, and when he called, experts came. The staff and the several circles in which he moved continuously poured information into that eager ear. If Edward Teller were on to something new in nuclear power, he alerted Nelson Rockefeller. When Rockefeller attended a performance of the musical comedy *1776*, we provided historic tidbits that he might use at a reception afterward. He was privy to the most rarefied gossip. "The Soviets, you know, have just taken over the biggest hotel in Lisbon," he would mention casually over lunch. This far-ranging knowledgeability seemed to suggest a high order of intelligence. But Mike Whiteman, his last counsel as governor, observed, "I doubt that he ever had an original idea in his life." Peter Wallison, his vice-presidential counsel, found that "he lacked an analytical, critical intelligence." He was forever reinventing the wheel and was drawn to intellectual fads. There was something mechanical and ephemeral in his embrace of ideas, in the way a magnet holds an object briefly without really incorporating it. One always had a sense that someone had told him something over dinner the night before, which now burned in his imagination like a quarter in a little boy's pocket.

I submitted a speech on the environment, and he complained, "You left out exponential." It was the vogue word that season. A member of the Critical Choices Commission had given Nelson an illustration of how certain problems grow: if, on the first day, a lily pad appears on a lake, and if that lily pad produces two lily pads the next day, and if this geometric progression continues, with each lily pad producing two more, then the whole lake goes from being half covered to being entirely covered from one day to the next. "Exponential" growth became a fetish. No matter what the speech was about, the word had to appear somewhere in it. Then, as rapidly as it had arrived, "exponential" faded from his vocabulary.

He was far more a creature of lunging enthusiasms than cool cerebration. He paid tribute to objectivity and rationality, but had the booster mentality of a sophisticated Rotarian. He deplored those who said, "Don't confuse me with facts," but his own charts, thick fact books, and slide shows were post-facto props to support what he had already believed.

While Nelson was still governor, Bob Douglass had faced him at the end of a legislative session with a stack of bills to sign or veto. One bill made it a crime to interfere with a religious service. Opponents of the Vietnam war had recently broken up a Mass at St. Patrick's Cathedral, and the state legislature had responded with the legislation now before the Governor. Douglass gave Rockefeller a thumbnail description and his recommendation. "This is exactly the kind of thing the courts are trying to get away from, these overspecialized offenses. There are already a half-dozen adequate laws on the books to cover situations like this, disturbing the peace, criminal trespass. This one doesn't add a thing. My recommendation is veto."

"Didn't this business at the cathedral bother you, Bobby?"

Douglass conceded that it had.

"And aren't you a Catholic?"

Douglass admitted to this too.

"And you want me to veto the bill?"

Douglass repeated the cool legal arguments.

"Well, I don't care," Nelson answered. "Cardinal Spellman is a friend of mine. So I'm going to sign it."

If he lacked deep intellect, he had an iron will, a powerful ego and the economic position to indulge both. George Bernard Shaw must have had people like Nelson Rockefeller in mind when he said: "The reasonable man adapts himself to the world; the unreasonable one persists in trying to adapt the world to himself. Therefore, all progress depends on the unreasonable man."

He was intelligent. He once confided that his IQ was a high if not overpowering 137. And he had earned a Phi Beta Kappa key at Dartmouth. But, in the final analysis, it did not matter if he was brilliant or intellectual. Nelson Rockefeller was an unreasonable, determined man, and rich to boot. Thus, he was able, as few men are, to make happen most of what he wanted. But not what he wanted most.

He possessed another power growing out of his ego and fortune, call it the power to summon. Figures who loomed large in their own spheres often appeared as spear carriers on the Rockefellers' stage. Of Zbigniew Brzezinski, Nelson said: "Oh, yes, my brother David hired him as a staff director of the Trilateral Commission. He's a bright enough fellow."

He once appeared on the Phil Donahue show, and Donahue asked him if it ever occurred to him that someone might not take his phone call. Nelson answered with innocent candor, "No," that had never occurred to him. No single figure, other than the President of the United States, demonstrated this power of Nelson Rockefeller's to summon people to his side. Many men were far richer than he—Jean Paul Getty, Howard Hughes, H. Ross Perot, Aristotle Onassis, even Pablo Picasso and John Lennon, for that matter. It was, however, not the size of the fortune that defined his power but the depth and breadth of the root structure that the money had nourished over three generations. The money represented, by now, only the original seed capital of his and the family's penetrating and pervasive influence.

Chapter XXIII

∾

RESTLESS IN REPOSE

NELSON ROCKEFELLER, out of public life, spun a web of contradictions around himself. Retreat and deceleration were alien to everything he had ever been or done. Thus, for every withdrawal from an old pursuit, he began a new one, as though resisting a tide pulling him toward some inevitable and dreaded end. He withdrew from politics with a thoroughness and suddenness that left the Republican Party initially disbelieving, until old comrades tried to get a contribution or an appearance out of him. This part of Nelson Rockefeller was now certifiably dead. He never made another speech of consequence or gave a dime to anyone's campaign. But he plunged into a new venture, investing nearly $4 million in a long-held dream. He had found an amazingly accurate process for reproducing his art. He could now make the collection pay rich dividends and provide a satisfying release for his underemployed energies. He created The Nelson Rockefeller Collection, Inc., to market the reproductions, and he created a second company to publish books on his art.

Contraction and growth. He sold the Foxhall Road estate in Washington for $5.5 million, and one floor of the Fifth Avenue triplex to Michael Cowles of the publishing empire, cutting the Rockefellers down to twenty-two rooms. He sold the Seal Harbor retreat for something under $1 million, and put the ranch in Venezuela on the market. Then he added another ten thousand to the six thousand acres he already owned adjoining the King Ranch in Texas. He wanted a place where his two young sons could master the manly pursuits, hunting, fishing, camping. He launched plans for a ranch house, sumptuous yet rustic, and was stocking his Texas spread like an exotic zoo. Besides giraffes and bison, he brought in the oryx, an African antelope, and the Indian nilgai, an animal with a romantic past. The nilgai had been set free by a bankrupt circus years before and had bred wild in Texas. Thus, with his expenses still on a royal scale, the art book and reproduction ventures had the serious long-term objective of balancing Nelson's cash flow, as well as allowing others "to share the joy of living with these beautiful objects," as he liked to put it.

In July 1978, when his brother John was killed in an automobile accident, Nelson became the *de jure* as well as the *de facto* head of the Rockefeller family. Win, John, and sister Abby had all died in less than six years, and the surviving brothers began to prepare the institutions they supported for the day when these beneficiaries could no longer count on Rockefeller largess. They began to make capital grants from the Rockefeller Brothers Fund to longtime philanthropic dependents—Rockefeller University, the Museum of Modern Art, Colonial Williamsburg, the Memorial Sloan-Kettering Cancer Center. These large gifts, $15 million to Rockefeller University, for instance, said, in effect, "We cannot last forever. We are cutting you loose. Prepare to make it on your own."

For every retrenchment, he made a new advance. When Arthur Taylor, the president of CBS, was fired by Nelson's friend and the corporation's founder, William Paley, Nelson's net was out to catch Taylor. With him, he launched a new venture, Sarabam, its objective to persuade the OPEC nations to invest their petrobillions in the West. When a visitor suggested that Nelson appeared to be making work, he answered, "I create things to do. If I don't have enough, I create more." He remained, even with his public life now behind him, a paradigm of the unreflective activist, a man for whom unfilled

284

hours had an almost terrifying quality and to whom movement equaled forward motion.

Two years after Nelson Rockefeller had left public life, I was startled, while watching the television news one morning, to see a former colleague appear on the screen in an unexpected pose. I had known Robert Armao well. While still in his twenties, Bob had become Nelson's labor adviser, succeeding the late Victor Borella. I admired not only Armao's mastery of the field, but his manner, unfailingly polite, yet direct and unapologetic. His advice to Rockefeller had the hard edge of authority. But what was Bob Armao doing there in April 1979 in the Bahamas, standing next to Mohammed Reza Pahlavi, the deposed Shah of Iran? In a way, it made an odd kind of sense. The Armao trademark had always been an aura of mystery. His seignorial style of life, for one so young, was the cause of much speculation among the Rockefeller staff. When the Rockefeller entourage flew into New York City, Nelson bounded out of the plane to his waiting chauffeured limousine, and Bob Armao went to his. The rest of the staff boarded government-issue automobiles. Bob owned a Manhattan town house near Gramercy Park and a place in the country and enjoyed insider connections to both Republicans and Democrats. Edward Koch, New York's Democratic mayor, had appointed Armao the city's Official Greeter. Thus his appearance alongside the Shah was surprising, but somehow of a piece with his enigmatic past.

The affairs of the Shah and the Rockefellers intersected at enough points to form a strong web of common interests, beginning with the Chase Manhattan Bank's involvements in Iran. Nelson also admired the heir to the Peacock Throne as his kind of foreign leader, autocratic, development-minded in the capitalist mode, insatiable in his consumption of military hardware, and reliably anti-Communist. On Nelson's around-the-world bicentennial tour as Vice-President, he had spent more time with the Shah than any other chief of state. In his last trip outside the United States, a few months before the Shah's fall, Nelson had again been the Iranian monarch's guest amid the splendors of Kish Island.

Robert Armao, bearing a letter of introduction from Nelson

Rockefeller, had thereafter gone to Tehran and succeeded in winning the confidence and the public-relations account of the Shah. His mission was to improve the Shah's image abroad, events in Iran then suggesting that abroad was precisely where the Shah would be spending his future. Armao also bought Nelson's bulletproof limousine. It seemed a sensible investment, considering the prospects of his new client. Nelson's former chauffeur eventually became Armao's chauffeur.

Henry Kissinger has said that in January 1979, with all signs pointing to the Shah's inevitable departure from Iran, he went first to David and then Nelson Rockefeller to try to find a home for the imperiled ruler in the United States. Joe Canzeri, then manager of the Pocantico estate, recalled his role in pursuit of this objective. Canzeri had by now performed a myriad range of assignments for Rockefeller, from pouring his coffee to moving his trees, catering his parties and advancing his political campaigns. During that last visit to Iran, while the Rockefellers dined with the Shah and the Shahbanou on Kish Island, Canzeri had been the dinner guest of the head of Savak, the Iranian secret police. On a Sunday afternoon that January Rockefeller summoned Canzeri and told him, "I want you to find a home for the Shah in America."

Canzeri decided to begin his search in the South, where he expected the Shah might find a more congenial political climate. During his travels as an advance man, he had come across an unusual property, Callaway Gardens, near Warm Springs, Georgia, an estate belonging to the family of Bo Callaway, the very Bo who had urged Nelson's departure from the Republican ticket in 1976. Callaway Gardens was no longer a private residence and was now used for conferences. Canzeri called a Callaway associate and arranged to inspect the property. Callaway Gardens was located off the main highway on a small country road. Fencing it off and guarding it would be relatively easy. The estate was spacious, with a great lodge crowning the top of a hill, surrounded by numerous smaller houses.

Canzeri reported back to Nelson that he had found a suitable residence for the Shah. He was then instructed to contact Ardeshir Zahedi, the Shah's ambassador in Washington. Zahedi, with State Department officials, visited Callaway Gardens and declared it satisfactory. The Shah had a home in America. And none too soon, for within a week he was forced out of Iran. He could then have come directly to the United States, but Zahedi argued, as a matter of principle, that his sovereign should not rush into the arms of that false friend, America, which had abandoned him. Thus the Shah and his entourage lost critical days in Morocco. Two weeks later, the Shah's staunch friend Nelson Rockefeller died, and by mid-March the government of the United States began to slam the gate on its fallen ally.

David Rockefeller then arranged temporary refuge for the Shah in the Bahamas, and it was at this point that my former colleague, Bob Armao, surfaced at the Shah's side. Thereafter, wherever the Shah was seen, in his Flying Dutchman odyssey, Mexico, New York, Panama, until his death in Egypt, Bob Armao was there, as coolly professional as befits a young man who had trained under Nelson, whom he described as "a far tougher man than the Shah."

Chapter XXIV

THE LAST DAYS

ON JANUARY 27, 1979, I WAS AWAKENED in the middle of the night by a telephone call from George Humphreys, a longtime friend and fellow Rockefeller colleague. It was 1:45 A.M. when Humphreys told me what the news services were reporting, that Nelson Rockefeller had died of a heart attack at 10:15 P.M. while working at his office at 30 Rockefeller Plaza.

I went through the conventional reactions of disbelief, partly from being awakened out of a sound sleep, but as much because of the effect the man had on those around him. The overpowering ego, the sheer demandingness, laid an invisible weight on his associates. It was difficult for me to accept, though I had by now been away from him for two years, that this forceful presence suddenly no longer existed. After the truth of his death had sunk in, my next reaction came from knowing so well the rhythms and patterns of another's life. As I tried to get back to sleep, I said to my wife, "There is no way that Nelson Rockefeller was working at ten o'clock on a Friday night at 5600."

Nelson had arrived at his office that morning in high spirits. Paul Anbinder, a highly regarded art editor, was scheduled to see him on a project close to Nelson's heart. Anbinder had entered into a partnership with Nelson and the art photographer Lee Boltin to publish books on Nelson's art collection. The first time that Anbinder had met Rockefeller, he had been both surprised and amused. Years before, Nelson told him, he had subsidized the publication of a book on the primitive art collected by his son Michael. Rockefeller's eyes widened like a child's as Anbinder explained that if he wanted books produced on his art, publishers would gladly pay *him* for the privilege.

Nelson may have been innocent of art publishing, but Anbinder was impressed from the start by his artistic grasp. "His eye was nearly impeccable. He relied heavily on advisers, of course, still he himself was an extraordinary judge of quality. Nelson Rockefeller collected in a dozen areas and did almost all of them well." Anbinder had been further surprised by another talent rare even among serious collectors. "He was his own installations adviser. And he was as good as any professional at hanging his collection." He also thought well of Nelson's assistant, Megan Marshack. With little formal background in art, she nevertheless handled the managerial details of the publishing project with brisk competency, he thought.

Several months after he had begun working with Nelson, Anbinder attended a meeting to discuss publicity for the first book to emerge on the Rockefeller collection. There he learned of Nelson's intention to announce jointly the other art enterprise on which Rockefeller had embarked—reproductions of his sculpture and paintings to be sold through retail outlets and a mail-order catalogue. For Anbinder, the situation presented an unfortunate convergence, and he advised against announcing the books and the reproductions simultaneously. The reproductions, he said, could harm the reception of the art books among purists who shuddered at the idea of commercial replications. Nelson professed to be astonished. He lived happily with copies of Matisses, Légers, and Mirós. If Nelson Rockefeller could, why couldn't other people? As he put it: "Happy and I have decided to share with others the joy of living with these beautiful objects and the thrill we have experienced in collecting them."

He had not invented the reproduction business. As he noted in the introduction to his catalogue: "The ancient Romans had their best sculptors create copies of outstanding pieces of Greek culture . . . the same was true in China." He was, however, mauled by *The New York Times* for the reproduction venture. He ascribed the criticism to the long-standing animus that he believed the paper bore him. This belief was hardly diminished when the *Times* rejected an advertisement for the reproductions on grounds that all ad space in the paper for the date requested was already sold. Still, with or without critical approval, he was enjoying his newfound enterprises. Over dinner with Bob and Linda Douglass, Nelson exulted, "How many guys can make money doing something they love?"

In September 1978, he came to Washington to open the Nelson Rockefeller Collection in the capital's new Neiman-Marcus branch. He held a private reception before the art was offered to the public, bringing together government officials, journalists, and other Washingtonians bound in one way or another by a Nelson Rockefeller tie in their past. Nelson greeted his guests in a salon set aside for spitting images of Lachaise's *Torso 1932*, bronze Degas figurines, Chinese temple jars, and Picasso sketches. He pumped hands in a reception line, exclaiming, "Aren't they beautiful. Absolutely beautiful!" He labored manfully to put his guests at ease, most of whom were having difficulty accepting their old mentor as salesman.

Bill Ronan, rehabilitator of mass-transportation systems, architect of a dozen major Rockefeller governmental enterprises, and now a marketer of art copies, smiled uncomfortably. "When I went with this man twenty years ago, I never thought I'd wind up in the mail-order business."

I had not seen Nelson Rockefeller for nearly a year and noticed that the physical momentum of his latter years had continued. The face appeared to be setting like concrete, getting harder and tougher all the time, yet beginning to crumble about the edges. It was the last time that I was to see him alive.

On that Friday morning, January 26, 1979, Nelson Rockefeller had arrived at his office at Room 5600 in buoyant anticipation. Paul Anbinder had recently returned from Colonial Williamsburg, which Nelson's father had restored fifty years before. The editor had gone to Virginia to survey the folk art collection assembled by Nelson's late mother, and he had arranged to have sent back to New York hundreds of photographs of the pieces comprising her Williamsburg collection. On this day they were to discuss publication of a book based on Abby's folk art. Anbinder came up to Nelson's office on the fifty-sixth floor for their 10:30 A.M. appointment. Nelson was exuberant as he pored over photographs that stirred long-dormant memories. What excited him most, he said, was the opportunity to make a small repayment, however inadequate, for the gift his mother had given him, her own love of art, which had become the one unfailing pleasure in his life.

Rockefeller seemed to Anbinder more fit, less tired this day than he had appeared of late. Maybe it was the diet. Nelson had, uncharacteristically, allowed himself to balloon to a lifetime high of more than 210 pounds. The staff surmised that the added weight reflected a general malaise, of a piece with his growing irritability and impatience, a certain barely sublimated frustration in the two years since he had become isolated from the arena of public events. Only the art ventures now genuinely engaged him. Bothered by chest pains, he had gone to see a physician, Dr. Ernest Esakof, in December and had been advised to lose weight. He had been dieting faithfully for more than a month and the results were beginning to tell.

Megan Marshack was in and out of the office frequently as Rockefeller and Anbinder discussed the book, and as Nelson tried to remember which of the hundreds of objects had meant most to his mother. The rapport between Rockefeller and the young woman, Anbinder recalled, was casual but correct, with a good-natured banter going on between them over the state of the art projects.

The two men broke off work at noon, and Nelson went to lunch with another colleague from the art world. Anbinder came in one last time in the afternoon to tie up loose ends. Rockefeller was still animated and expressed his delight to Anbinder over the folk art project. Rockefeller left his office late in the afternoon for the Buckley School, on East 73rd Street, which his sons, Nelson, Jr., and Mark, attended. There Nelson was to introduce Henry Kissinger, who had agreed to talk to the students. Afterward, he and the boys returned to the apartment on Fifth Avenue.

Hugh Morrow was asleep when his phone rang late in the evening of January 26. ABC News was calling to confirm a story just received from a police reporter that Nelson Rockefeller was in an ambulance on his way to Lenox Hill Hospital. Morrow told the man that he would check out the report and get back to him. He called the apartment at Fifth Avenue and was told by a security man that Rockefeller was indeed on his way to the hospital and that his condition appeared serious.

Morrow dressed quickly and sped into Manhattan from his Bronxville home. Entering the hospital emergency room, he found Happy Rockefeller, Nelson's brother Laurance, Laurance's wife, Mary, and members of the hospital staff. Reporters were gathering outside the hospital. Dr. Esakof had arrived shortly before and had pronounced Nelson Rockefeller dead at 12:20 A.M. Morrow assumed that Nelson had been stricken at home. No, said Happy Rockefeller, gesturing abruptly toward someone whom Morrow had not yet noticed in the emergency room, Megan Marshack. The young woman wore a long black caftan and still clutched the oxygen bottle that she had held during the ambulance ride to the hospital. She kept repeating tearfully that she had tried everything possible to save Nelson. Morrow marched her past the small crowd and out of sight. He returned to Happy and said quietly, "Don't worry. She's not here." Happy nodded.

Morrow now faced the most painful dilemma of his career. He was a public-relations professional who had earned, over long years of fair dealing and irrepressible wit, the respect and affection of the press corps. He had also been, for nearly two decades, the confidant, as well as the employee, of Nelson Rockefeller and his family. Prompted "solely by my intention to protect the widow and her children," Morrow made his decision. Gathering the reporters in the driveway leading to the hospital's emergency room, he spoke somberly. Nelson Rockefeller had died at his desk on the fifty-sixth floor of 30 Rockefeller Plaza at about 10:15 P.M. He had been working on a book on modern art when stricken by a heart attack. His bodyguard had tried to revive him but had been unsuccessful. Thereafter, paramedics arrived from St. Clare's Hospital. But all efforts to revive him had failed, and he was pronounced dead on arrival at the hospital. After the press left, Morrow dropped Megan Marshack off at her apartment at 25 West 54th Street. By 2:00 A.M. the last of the Rocke-fellers had left Lenox Hill Hospital.

Then it began to unravel. *The New York Times* went after the story with tabloidal ardor. For two days accounts of Nelson Rockefeller's final hours underwent continuous revision, and in the end, the facts were forced into the open. After dinner with his family on the evening of the twenty-sixth, Nelson had gone, at about 9:00 P.M., not to 30 Rockefeller Plaza, but to 13 West 54th Street, the town house con-nected to his offices on West 55th Street. He was not alone and discovered by a bodyguard as originally claimed, but with Megan Marshack, his assistant on the art project. The time of death was not 10:15 as initially reported. That was when the attack had occurred. A 911 emergency telephone call had been placed at 11:16. Two police officers arrived at 11:18. Two hospital attendants arrived from Roo-sevelt Hospital at 11:22, when Rockefeller already appeared dead, and a paramedic team arrived at 11:37. It was not Megan Marshack who placed the 911 call, but a friend, Ponchitta Pierce, the hostess of a weekend television show for NBC, whom Megan had summoned in her desperation. Miss Pierce later recounted her actions: "Between 10:50 and 11:00 P.M. I was alone in my apartment at 25 West 54th Street. I was awakened by a phone call from my friend and neighbor, Megan Marshack. She told me that Governor Rockefeller had suf-fered a heart attack and asked me to come to 13 West 54th Street. I hastily dressed, took the elevator to the lobby, where I met one of the employees of my building. I asked him to come with me to 13 West 54th Street, where I had never been. I did not ask anyone to call Governor Rockefeller's chauffeur. We walked to West 54th Street. I rang the doorbell and Megan let us in. My building employee waited in the hallway. I entered a room where I saw Governor Rockefeller lying on a couch. I saw no one other than Megan and Governor Rockefeller in that room. Megan was administering mouth-to-mouth resuscitation. It seemed to me that the best thing I could do was to call 911. I phoned 911 and asked for emergency medical assistance. Shortly after I made the 911 call, I left 13 West 54th Street and walked back to my apartment. On my way I saw a police car ap-proaching and I directed the policemen to 13 West 54th Street."

All the contradictions in the original story of Rockefeller's death, save one, were of value only to the extent that they fed an interest in gossip. The one significant discrepancy was the one-hour lapse between the onset of the attack and the summoning of aid, which raised the vital question: could Nelson Rockefeller's life have been saved by immediate medical attention? As to what went on at the town house in the hour before the attack and the hour after it occurred, only one person has the answer, Megan Marshack.

Nelson Rockefeller remained, to his last breath, a controversial and extravagant figure. His passing demonstrated once more the old wisdom that nothing ever happens to people that is not just like them.

When one's arrival in the world is announced on the front page of *The New York Times*, the world has a right to certain expectations. Were Nelson Rockefeller's life achievements commensurate with the immense advantages with which he began? Four times he was elected governor of a major state, and measured alongside other great men who filled that office, the two Roosevelts, Smith, Hughes, Dewey, Lehman, he ranks first. Was it enough? He became Vice-President of the United States, as had Hannibal Hamlin, Levi Morton, Thomas Riley Marshall, and Spiro Agnew. That was surely not enough. The Vice-Presidency was a trick mirror, a distortion of the authentic national leadership which he sought.

Years before, when Nelson was still governor, the majority leader of the New York State Senate, Warren Anderson, had come to 55th Street to discuss the upcoming legislative program. He entered the conference room and surveyed the clutter of filing cases. Picking up a folder, Anderson shook his head in amusement. "Pakistan? What in God's name is New York State supposed to do about Pakistan?" Nelson Rockefeller's eye never entirely left global center stage where he yearned to perform. "I always took it for granted I'd be President," he confessed one day. "It was always there, in the back of my mind." So convinced was he of his innate and acquired talent for leading the nation that he occasionally gave the impression that Nelson Rockefeller denied the Presidency was rather like Willie Mays denied baseball.

Shortly before he died, he gave us his explanation of why he had not succeeded. "I have a feeling that in a democracy you don't get a government that is much better than a reflection of the people. A dictatorship can get an unusual person." With a candor born of banished hopes, he went on: "Getting the nomination for the Presidency in this country has nothing to do with ability in terms of the person's capacity and so forth. So, if I really wanted to be President that bad, I should have done what Dick Nixon did, what President Kennedy did, or what Carter has done, and that is take two or three years and just concentrate on the science of how do you influence and get the contacts to get the votes. Frankly, my interest is more in doing things than it was in that." The Nixon path both fascinated and repelled him: "He took four years off. He was in a law firm, but he spent his time supporting senators, making speeches. I was governor and so I never really made a full-time occupation out of trying to get the nomination."

William Kennedy, a novelist and journalist writing a Rockefeller profile for *The New York Times Magazine*, asked him how he could have missed the Presidency. "I would say that I did not have a sufficient singleness of purpose and sufficient ambition to put everything else aside to do just that."

KENNEDY: "Where was the singleness of purpose dissipated?"

ROCKEFELLER: "I never had it."

Yet he did not disparage those who succeeded where he had failed. He served six of the seven Presidents between 1940 and 1977, in significant or minor roles. He had done nothing for John F. Kennedy only because he had never been asked, which puzzled and even hurt him. How, knowing his placement of country above all else, he wondered, could the Kennedys suspect his motives. He actively courted Presidents. Lyndon Johnson spent his last weekend in the Presidency at Camp David with Nelson and Happy. Coming from opposite ends of the economic spectrum, the two men were nevertheless drawn together by a shared philosophy of power, by a common belief in muscular internationalism and by their mutual assumption that the world could be molded to American values. Happy liked LBJ too. He was, she said, "a magnificent animal," and added with an amused laugh, "I guess it takes one to know one."

Richard Nixon had tested his veneration of the Presidency most severely. His scorn for Nixon the man and his unalloyed support for

Nixon the President is explained only by Nelson's near mystical reverence for the office. As he prepared to leave the Ford White House, someone had asked Nelson if he would be willing to serve in the Carter Administration. He did not hesitate. "Sure. I'd serve in something part time."

He had been introduced to the Presidency through Franklin D. Roosevelt, which, in a sense, was his misfortune. He was young then, thirty-two, and his first exposure had been to a giant, a President of social vision, a leader possessed simultaneously of uncanny political acumen and statesmanship, a President who towers above all others who have since followed him. A confidant who watched Nelson fail in his presidential bids, observed: "I think Roosevelt was too much for him. He had seen the Presidency first at this exalted level. And for all his apparent arrogance, he never felt quite sure that he had it in the same way. This paralyzed him in a sense. His sights were fixed upward, on that man instead of on mediocre people who also made it."

He was, to the end, always a better government man than a political man. He wanted to rise by example. Nelson Rockefeller wanted to be elected President because he had been an outstanding governor. Is it so wild a hope that the captain of the Western World be chosen for demonstrated capacity? he reasoned. He accepted slowly and reluctantly that the office was noble but that the way to it was largely the mad scramble of nomination politics. It does credit to his seriousness of purpose that he long resisted, even disbelieved, the idea that a President was born of a thousand chicken dinners and a hundred thousand small-town handshakes. But it suggests a naïveté that it took him so long to learn this lesson.

After he returned to New York and private life, we had a reunion of those who had served him during his seventeen years in elective politics. Jim Cannon scanned the faces gathered in a posh retreat, the studio apartment atop Radio City Music Hall. "I looked around at the damnedest collection of talent, people who could run banks, governments, newspapers. But there was nobody there who knew how to elect a President."

Nelson Rockefeller was never prepared to step outside the protective palisade of eastern Republican enlightened capitalist orthodoxy to take his stand. He never seriously exposed himself to that arch-Republican epithet flung at FDR, "a traitor to his class." Indeed he had never so much as voted for a Democrat. He also lacked Nixon's spit-in-my-eye-and-I'll-still-keep-running ambition. And he exhibited Adlai Stevenson's crippling indecision at those moments of truth that he faced during his presidential quests.

It is said of strong-willed men who ran aground in the Presidency, Lyndon Johnson and Richard Nixon in our century, that they began to confuse the nation's destiny with their own. Nelson Rockefeller exhibited that confusion without ever being elected President. The greatest legacy of the fortune and the rarefied environment in which he matured was his unshakable sense of self-importance. He believed that he had been freed by wealth to see things not only differently but better than other men. He was in a sense the freest man in America, free not simply from want, but free to think grandly, free to move into or draw from every circle of authority, power, and wealth, free to pursue his designs unfettered by the workaday concerns of less privileged people.

But without the fortune and privilege, what sort of man might Nelson Rockefeller have been? Assuming an average start in life, the man began with considerable genetic gifts. He was physically robust, handsome, blessed with high energy and ample intelligence. To these assets, add soaring confidence, a hardness of character, and a will, or, better still, a willfulness. Nelson Rockefeller, born either rich or poor, would probably have been a tough customer.

Would he, therefore, have scaled great heights, become the governor of a major state, been considered for the Presidency? We cannot know. But one can imagine Nelson, even given the most modest birth, succeeding in any number of roles, a union boss, a Marine Corps general, a night-school lawyer, a police chief, the biggest Chevy dealer in Houston. One sees him easily as a handsomer version of the scrap-iron king whom Broderick Crawford portrayed in *Born Yesterday*.

But he was not born poor or even middle or upper class. He was born into a web of power and privilege that, quite literally, exceeded anything that money can buy. And it is against this background that his life's work must be judged and against which he set his own standards of expectation. By that standard, his life may be judged wanting. If he had expected less of himself, the judgment would be kinder, for his career was extraordinarily useful. But the investment of $17 million and a lifetime of effort producing a governorship, however superior, of one state, and a lame Vice-Presidency was, by *his* measure, not enough. His failure to achieve all that he set for himself raised the hardest question he had to face within the secret recesses of his heart: Did Nelson Rockefeller the man, as contrasted to Nelson Rockefeller the heir, have what it took to gain the mountaintop? He could never know.

In his personal life, the blessings of being a Rockefeller came at high cost. Outside the family, he could not trust fully, and consequently he could not love easily. He could embrace few other human beings in unrestrained, unquestioning friendship. He liked many people, but a wall, felt though unseen, forever shielded him from their unpredictable designs. "Never get too close to the line," his father had preached. "Never show more surface than necessary." He neither bared his soul nor invited others to bare theirs.

He clung to a vision of himself as a simple man. "I'm not that complicated," he liked to say. He was indeed often simplistic, but rarely simple. The plainness of speech and manner was a relic of the family's Baptist origins, but Nelson had become a Byzantine Baptist, whose seeming ingenuousness cloaked a complex and restless inner man. He was fascinating, not for any native genius or originality of thought. Indeed, the mind was often prosaic, though the spirit animating it was vibrant and irrepressible. But the behavior of those who possess unimaginable wealth and power is automatically interesting to those who do not. Even as they do boring or silly things, we are curious to know why.

After his death, while I was appearing on a television talk show promoting a book I had written, the host drew me into a discussion of my years with Nelson Rockefeller. The conversation was going well until he suddenly fixed me with a sympathetic gaze and said, "You loved him, didn't you?" The all-seeing camera's eye must have caught my confusion. Love was not the word. Admiration, respect, amusement, exasperation—all these, yes. But beyond the bosom of the family, people who "loved" Nelson Rockefeller were usually those whose contact with him was irregular, those occasionally exposed to his impressive bursts of energy, optimism, and enthusiasm, his talent for getting things done and his resources to do so.

Among those associates who were in close contact with him over periods ranging up to twenty years, a curious ambivalence prevailed. To the question, "Did you like Nelson Rockefeller?" not many answered without a hesitation. One man who had worked with him long and as closely as any associate in his lifetime, said, after pacing his office, hands jammed into rear pockets, "Tough question." He then held up two fingers in the form of a V. "If there's something, a feeling somewhere between like and dislike"—he moved a finger in the space of the V—"that's about where I'd be."

To his personal staff during those last two years of private life, Nelson had become irascible and imperious. With so much time on his hands, his habit of magnifying the inconsequential to fill his day had reached exasperating peaks. He was not looking after himself physically as well as he should. Still, he was attacking life with an almost bellicose zeal to the very end, his departure as flamboyant and controversial as his days on earth had been. His life ended in his seventieth year in a house where he had lived as a child, a life of princely scale with common touches; of dreams pursued and fled; of some nobility and some farce; of public service and self-serving ambition; of passions disciplined and others indulged. It was a life lived at an extraordinary and extravagant altitude, lavish, and tinged with some sadness. It ended as it had begun, on the front page of *The New York Times*.

"After his death, my children and I were startled at how small his body looked," his daughter Ann said. Hers were the most moving words uttered at the memorial service held a week after Nelson Rockefeller's death. The service was held in the Riverside Church, Gothic, majestic, a gift of Nelson's father, given in the 1920s to celebrate the spirit of interdenominationalism and the harmony of religion and science. Two American Presidents attended, Gerald R. Ford and the incumbent, Jimmy Carter. Dr. William Sloane Coffin, Jr., Riverside's Senior Minister, delivered the invocation, and the Reverend Martin Luther King, Sr., offered a prayer. Roberta Peters of the Metropolitan Opera sang "Dear Lord and Father of Mankind." Nelson's firstborn, his son Rodman, and his brother David delivered eulogies, flat, dry, staff-prepared prose exposing little of the human heart. "In reviewing Nelson's accomplishments," said David, "one sees the fulfillment of his heritage—the establishment of the New York Arts Council, the creation of the Adirondack State Park and the dramatic expansion of the State University, to mention just a few." Henry Kissinger, voice quavering, caught the humanizing contradictions in the man. "At once outgoing and remote . . . both naïve and profound . . . ebullient yet withdrawn, gregarious and lonely . . ."

At the close, the family led the way out, Happy Rockefeller, bearing an expression of resolute resignation, sons, daughters, grandchildren, Tod, the first Mrs. Nelson Rockefeller, looking like a composed, distant relative, and the surviving Rockefeller brothers, Laurance and David. The guests marched out to Nelson's favorite song, "Sweet Georgia Brown," performed by the vibraphonist Lionel Hampton. The music was unexpected and utterly appropriate. Nelson would have enjoyed the up-tempo farewell.

Afterward, down in the vaulted, medieval basement of the Riverside Church, I watched a scene that I had witnessed countless times in hotel ballrooms, auditoriums, and convention centers in a hundred American cities—long tables where reporters bent over typewriters, banks of telephones, coffee urns and trays of sandwiches, fresh stacks of press releases spilling to the floor. All about were the familiar faces of the advance men who had again made it all come off without a hitch. But, for once, they were uncharacteristically still, not rushing off to arrange Nelson's next stop.

Back at Room 5600, a painting that Nelson had hung personally looked down on his now silent office, Rouault's masterpiece, *The Old King*, the face calcified by the years, the eyes bare slits, as remote as a lost planet, the chin firmly set in an ancient defiance. For Nelson, the painting may have had an unintended symbolism, reflecting a prince, in his case, who had grown old and who had never inherited the kingdom.

INDEX